Chiang Kai-shek

MARSHAL OF CHINA

A DA CAPO PRESS REPRINT SERIES

China

in the 20th century

Chiang Kai-shek
MARSHAL OF CHINA

by

SVEN HEDIN

Translated from the Swedish by

BERNARD NORBELIE

DA CAPO PRESS · NEW YORK · 1975

Library of Congress Cataloging in Publication Data

Hedin, Sven Anders, 1865-1952.
Chiang Kai-shek, marshal of China.

(China in the 20th century)
Reprint of the ed. published by John Day Co., New York.
Includes index.
1. Chiang, Kai-shek, 1886-   2. China—History—Republic, 1912-1949.
DS778.C55H42   1975   951.04′2′0924 [B]   74-31277
ISBN 0-306-70690-3

This Da Capo Press edition of *Chiang Kai-shek Marshal of China* is an unabridged republication of the first edition published in New York in 1940.

Published by Da Capo Press, Inc.
A Subsidiary of Plenum Publishing Corporation
227 West 17th Street, New York, N.Y. 10011

CHIANG KAI-SHEK

Chiang Kai-shek

MARSHAL OF CHINA

by SVEN HEDIN

Translated from the Swedish by
BERNARD NORBELIE

ILLUSTRATED

THE JOHN DAY COMPANY

NEW YORK

TO
MADAME CHIANG KAI-SHEK
AS A TOKEN
OF ADMIRATION

Acknowledgments

Quotations from the following books are used with the kind permission of the authors or publishers: *Sian: A Coup d'État*, by Mayling Soong Chiang (including in the same volume *A Fortnight in Sian: Extracts from a Diary by Chiang Kai-shek*), published by Doubleday, Doran & Company, New York; *Red Star over China*, by Edgar Snow, published by Random House, New York; and *Japan's Gamble in China*, by Freda Utley, published by Secker and Warburg, London.

Passages from *Chiang Kai-shek: Soldier and Statesman*, by Hollington K. Tong, published by The China Publishing Company, Shanghai, are quoted with the kind permission of the author, through the courtesy of the Consulate General of the Republic of China, New York.

Contents

Contents

PART II

Illustrations

Preface

FOR NO LESS THAN FIFTY YEARS I HAVE FELT STRONGLY attached to the Middle Kingdom and I have spent the happiest and most successful years of my life in that vast country. The first time I set foot on Chinese ground was in 1890 and I was last there in 1935. And now—in 1940—when the whole world is being rent asunder by new bloody wars, I can see an endless row of never-to-be-forgotten memories, all emanating from the Yellow Earth and in some way or other connected with the pleasant and patient people of China.

I entered into very intimate and confidential relations with the Central Government at Nanking when late in the summer of 1933 I was offered and accepted the task of staking out, and, with the assistance of Chinese experts, of mapping and describing two automobile highways for that Government, which roads were to be built between China proper and the province of Sinkiang. Earlier, in the spring of 1929, I had had the honor of meeting the great Marshal, General Chiang Kai-shek, in Nanking, and after my return from the automobile journey in February, 1935, I had the pleasure of going to Hankow and rendering an account to him and his charming wife of the results obtained by the expedition. On both these occasions the Marshal's splendid personality made a deep and indelible impression upon me.

Like all true friends and admirers of China, I was profoundly grieved by Japan's attack on her great neighbor, and by the extensive invasion which commenced on the seventh of July, 1937. Undoubtedly Japan was driven to this step by forces as natural as they were strong. Her rapidly growing population required living space and her flourishing trade and industry needed raw materials. I had always admired Japan and her diligent, intelligent, and patriotic people whose love of liberty and loyalty to the Emperor became world-famous when the Russian advance into Manchuria threatened Nippon's position in East Asia and in the Pacific. It had long been realized that the problem would have to be solved in one way or another. Unfortunately the hopes that this might be achieved by amicable agreements between the two great peoples of East Asia were disappointed, and now the people of China have already endured three years of inexpressible suffering without the attackers having made any very great progress.

The series of about forty volumes that is to contain the results of the scientific work of my fellow workers and myself in Central Asia and Tibet during the years 1927-1935, twelve volumes of which have so far been published, has occupied most of my time since my return home in 1935. But I have carefully followed the course of the Sino-Japanese war, and was so captivated by the Marshal's great qualities as a statesman, strategist, and patriot that I could not refrain from writing a book on him and his historical achievements.

This book was practically ready for print when the revolutionizing events between August 21 and September 3, 1939, occurred in close succession and filled my spare moments with studies and thoughts of an entirely different kind. When Soviet Russia on November 30, 1939, made the unjustified attack on the peace-loving Finnish people, the hot winds of war came closer and closer to the boundaries and coasts of my own country, and the Swedish people gathered in greater determination than ever around Finland and the defense of our own glorious country, which has never been conquered by a foreign power.

When these events took place, my book on Chiang Kai-

shek was already complete in its Swedish edition. In this connection I must relate the story of the American edition. The
Nobel Prize in Literature for 1938 was awarded one of the
most famous and widely read writers of our day, Pearl Buck.
Being one of the eighteen members of the Swedish Academy
which awards the prize—Selma Lagerlöf, another famous
woman author also having been a member—I had the pleasure of receiving and meeting the charming and immensely
popular Pearl Buck on several occasions during her stay in
Stockholm at the beginning of December that year. To me, as
a friend of China, it was a pleasure and an honor to talk
to one of the most remarkable women of today, the woman
who knows China and its wonderful people better than anyone else.

At the time of her visit to Stockholm, Pearl Buck was accompanied by her husband, Mr. Richard J. Walsh, President
of the John Day Company, publishers, and by his young
daughter. While walking about in my Asiatic library, we did
not lack for topics, and they all circled round China. We
spoke not least of Chiang Kai-shek, his heroic defense of his
country, and his admirable ability to gather, educate, and
inspire his people. But it was not until about a year later that
I sent a copy of the Swedish edition of this book to my
friend, Mr. Richard J. Walsh, inquiring whether he was willing to publish it in America. The result was that Mr. Walsh
cabled me an offer which I gladly accepted.

The Swedish text was translated in Stockholm by Mr. Bernard Norbelie, who carried out his work most conscientiously.
The English text was read and approved by me and Mr.
Folke Bergman, who, being a member of my Asiatic staff,
is thoroughly familiar with Chinese conditions. In selecting
the illustrations I received valuable assistance from Dr. Gösta
Montell, also one of my Asiatic companions.

The Swedish preface is dated October 3, 1939. The progress
of the war between Japan and China since that date is thus

not commented on in this book. But the world press has kept us up to date regarding the course of the war, and we know that after three years the Japanese have not yet succeeded in accomplishing their aim—the conquest of China. I feel convinced that the sons of Nippon will never reach that goal. Each month carries them farther away from it, for the Chinese resistance is growing and the Marshal's armies are improving in strength, training, and size. Lately the Chinese have also in several places changed their tactics from the defensive to the offensive and have driven the intruders out of the positions they had gained. According to the last telegrams, the Marshal has declared that he will not make peace until the last Japanese soldier has left Chinese ground.

I have dedicated this book to Madame Chiang Kai-shek as an expression of my admiration for the excellent work and glorious bravery she has displayed in this war.

In order to give the description a more personal touch I have here and there related my own reminiscences from Japan and China. It would lead too far were I to name all the sources I have used—I mention only my countrymen, Professors J. G. Andersson, Bernhard Karlgren, and Erik Nyström, and Colonel Carl Taube, all of whom are thoroughly familiar with East Asiatic conditions. I wrote the Epilogue with my thoughts centered on the dangers that formerly swept over Europe from Asia and the danger I considered to be threatening our continent from the endless Bolshevik hordes.

With cordial greetings to Madame Chiang Kai-shek, Miss Pearl Buck, my old friend Dr. Hu Shih, Chinese Ambassador in Washington, and my publisher, Richard J. Walsh, I have the pleasure of submitting to my friends in the United States this book on the great Marshal of China.

Sven Hedin

Stockholm, June 17, 1940.

PART I

I

Visiting the Emperor of Japan

IN NOVEMBER, 1908, the mighty Japanese war machine carried out extensive combined maneuvers by land and sea. So important were these maneuvers to the development and greatness of the country that they were attended by the Emperor himself, the great Mutsuhito.

In response to an official invitation, I was at that time spending five weeks in the Land of the Rising Sun, where I was to lecture at the Geographic Society and before the students of the Tokyo and Kyoto universities. Only a few months earlier, after my discovery of the huge mountain system of the Tibetan Trans-Himalyas, I had returned to India and spent some time as the guest of the Viceroy and Lord Kitchener. The latter advised me to accept the Japanese invitation without hesitation, and I have never had reason to regret that I followed his advice. For the hospitality, the marks of honor, and the enthusiasm with which I was greeted everywhere in Japan, Korea, and Port Arthur, surpassing anything that I had experienced, remain among my happiest and most precious memories of Asia.

On the twenty-fifth of November, Mr. Gustaf Wallenberg, the Swedish envoy at Tokyo, in whose hospitable home I was staying, was informed by the Court that the Emperor, who had just returned to the capital from the maneuvers, desired to receive me the following morning at ten o'clock.

We were at the Palace in ample time and were received by a Master of the Imperial Household. After a little while, I was requested to accompany that gentleman to a room decorated in true Japanese style. There was nothing of the splendor and magnificent luxury, the plafonds, the gleaming chandeliers with their flashing facets, or the height and loftiness characteristic of halls and drawing rooms in the palaces of European capitals. The ceiling was low, and no expensive furniture was to be seen. And yet in this room I met one of the greatest and most remarkable men of those days, the Emperor of Japan, Mutsuhito, Equal with Gods, Meiji, Mikado.

Approaching with slow steps, with a distinguished, yet unpretentious demeanor, he met me in the middle of the audience chamber. The Master of the Imperial Household withdrew. There was but one more person in the room, the interpreter, who spoke only Russian besides his own language and who remained humbly at a few steps' distance.

If just before the audience I had to a certain extent been a prey to the feeling of solemn excitement that seizes a person with or without his own will when suddenly facing the man who more than anyone else in our time influenced the eastern half of Asia, all such feelings vanished almost completely when the Emperor with a kind smile extended his hand to me. That time was just forty years past when the mortals granted the favor of entering the presence of the divine Mikado had had to lie prone during the whole audience, their foreheads touching the floor, upon penalty of death if they dared let a glance from their wretched mortal eyes fall upon the divine sovereign. In his movements, his gestures, and his whole behavior, the Emperor was nothing but a human, and everything indicated that he personally did not demand that he be looked upon as a divine being.

Physically and mentally the Emperor Mutsuhito was head and shoulders above all his subjects, a tall man with a slight stoop. At the time he was fifty-six years of age, but in spite of his raven-black hair and his black mustache and imperial, he appeared old. His features were coarse and lacked the refinement that might have been expected in a man of such noble lineage. But his eyes and his smile betrayed a goodness of heart and a nobility that made him very winning and sympathetic.

The uniform he wore was bluish-black and of European cut and he wore but one decoration, the Swedish Order of the Seraphim—a charming display of courtesy.

After inquiring about my route from India to Japan, the Emperor dwelt particularly on my travels in Tibet and asked about the character of the country, its mountains, rivers, and lakes, its climate, inhabitants, temples, Lamaism, and especially about the ecclesiarch, the noble Tashi Lama. A brief account of the audience could be read in the official newspaper the following day. Among other things it said:

"His Majesty made careful enquiries about the places visited by Dr. Hedin as well as regarding his plans for future explorations. His Majesty was informed that it was Dr. Hedin's intention once again to return to Tibet in order to supplement his studies, and the Emperor expressed his admiration of such perseverance, but also urged Dr. Hedin to take all precautions for his own personal safety. . . . The interest displayed by the Emperor was very remarkable."

I shall never forget one thing the Emperor said. That was: "You have been successful in crossing Tibet in several directions with three expeditions. But do not forget that one must be the last and that you cannot expect your projected journey to be as successful as the previous ones. You have accomplished enough already; be satisfied, settle down, and do not expose yourself to new dangers."

On account of his almost fatherly solicitude for my well-being, the Emperor made an indelible impression upon me, and I cherish his picture and his person in grateful remembrance.

II

Chiang Kai-shek's Years of Study in Japan

WHILE THE RULER OF DAI NIPPON WAS KINDLY TALKING TO me about the distant Land of Snow a young Chinese was staying in his country, perhaps even in the capital itself, who thirty years later was to appear as Japan's strongest and most formidable foe and who against his will was to force the Japanese to engage great parts of their military forces by land, by sea, and in the air, in one of the bloodiest wars ever fought on Asiatic ground.

While in Tokyo, I may some time have passed in the street the man who was destined to play a great historical part, to rise to the highest post in the world's greatest republic, to educate, reform, and remold to righteousness, discipline, and unity a population of 450 million humans, living without a goal and without hope, and who, thanks to his foresight, his statesmanship, his unflinching faith, his adamant energy, and his endless patience was able to arouse this throng of humans to glowing patriotic enthusiasm and to willingness to sacrifice their lives, homes, and fields for the defense of the Middle Kingdom, the country where their forefathers lived from time immemorial and whose history goes four thousand years back in time.

Chiang Kai-shek was reared in honesty and chastity at his home in Fenghua in the province of Chekiang, where old-world Chinese honor was held high, and he grew up as a youth with far-reaching thoughts and a deep feeling for the seriousness and responsibility of life. His peasant origin left him a rich and harmonic heritage of the very best qualities of the Chinese race. In his memoirs written a few years ago he speaks with pathos and filial gratitude of his childhood and youth and of the strong family bonds which in China have been the firm foundation of the state. He still speaks of his mother with reverence and admiration. "She was greater than anyone." He tells of how she made him go to school and forced him to become a soldier.

In 1906 he studied for a short time at the Paoting Military Academy, founded by the Chancellor Yüan Shih-k'ai. But there Chiang Kai-shek felt too much of the antiquated, egoistic atmosphere around Yüan Shih-k'ai. Filled with repulsion for the old Manchu regime which long enough had been in a fair way to bring China to dissolution and corruption, his national pride wounded by the bullying of foreigners, and fully realizing that only a revolution with expurgation, restoration, and a firm unifying and enlightenment of the whole people could save China from certain destruction, he went to Japan at the beginning of 1907, where he spent almost three years completing his military studies. There he delightedly joined the group of Chinese revolutionists whose ideals were the same as his own and among whom he found Sun Yat-sen, the "Father of the Revolution," Wang Ching-wei, and Chang Chi, who in 1930 was the highest leader of the Kuomintang in Northern China.

No imagination is required to understand that the years in Japan greatly influenced Chiang Kai-shek's development. Wherever he turned he saw a people of heroes, a political constitution of imperturbable strength and authority, an administration working for high ideals, a military power equal to that of the Great Powers of Europe, an Empire making progress in all directions. His humiliation was great upon comparing his native country, rendered torpid under the last lethargic Emperor of the Ch'ing dynasty, with the Land of the Rising Sun, which through its own efforts was on the way to creating a glorious future.

While he and his comrades with glowing enthusiasm were deliberating and planning the annihilation of the Manchu regime and the wretched Peking government and the deliverance of their native country, he studied the history of Japan, particularly that of the last forty years. The man who one day was to become the equal of Mutsuhito in power and greatness, made a careful study of the events that under the leadership of Ito, Inouye, Yamagata, Saionji, and the other palatines had led to the Imperial Oath in March, 1868, when the new era, Meiji, the period of "the enlightened administration" began, when the antiquated traditions were effaced, the restoration, the reformation, the social reconstruction were inaugurated, and no obstacles were allowed to impede the work of the energetic leaders.

As an eight-year-old in Fenghua he had perhaps some time or other in 1894 heard of the war between Japan and China, which, however, was incomprehensible to him. To the mature Chiang Kai-shek, who in Tokyo had studied the events from 1894, the reason for the outcome of the war—so unfortunate for China—was perfectly clear. It was natural that in spite of its ancient, wonderful history, its wealth of people, and its vast domains across half of Asia, China would be conquered by "the small nation on the islands in the sea." And why? Because twenty-six years earlier the nation on the islands had carried out its revolution toward reconstruction and reformation.

That was what the Middle Kingdom needed! China must undergo the same transformation as Japan. During his years in Japan, Chiang Kai-shek accumulated a world of useful knowledge, a wealth of practical wisdom. Not only did he in Japanese military schools become a modern soldier according to German pattern, but he also studied and mastered the requirements for the making of a great power, and he acquired intimate knowledge of Japanese as well as Occidental politics; in other words, of the great gamble for power over land and people. He must have been horrified to see that the defeat cost China Formosa, Southern Manchuria, Port Arthur, and other possessions, as well as a war debt of 200 million taels.

But the game was complicated. In the north, China had a neighbor, maybe stronger than Japan. In 1894 Russia grudged Japan the profits of her victory over China. Japan was forced to surrender Southern Manchuria and Port Arthur to Russia. At the same time Russia forced China to grant her a concession for the construction of the Chinese Eastern Railway through Northern Manchuria to Vladivostok and also the line from Harbin to Dairen. If Chinese patriots already at that time suspected that Japan might become a dangerous foe in the future, they may also have looked upon Russia as an ally in case of new aggressive steps on the part of Japan.

It was not difficult for the statesmen and military forces of Japan to divine Russia's intentions. Russia established her position on the coast of the Pacific and turned Port Arthur into a modern fortress. It was a matter of life or death for Japan. Her whole existence in Eastern Asia and on the Pacific Ocean was directly threatened by Port Arthur on the Yellow Sea, as it already was on the Sea of Japan by Vladivostok. The Russo-Japanese War in 1904-05 was inevitable and disclosed to the whole world the position Japan already had attained as a great power. Oku defeated the Russians on the Yalu, Nogi took Port Arthur after Togo literally obliterated the fleets under the command of Makarov, Roshestvensky, and Nebogatov; and Kuroki and Oyama forced Kuropatkin's armies to retreat at Mukden. For the first time in history, Asia was victorious in a battle between an Asiatic and a European great power. A new factor had entered the great gamble for the distribution of power in the world, and in the Far East no one was stronger than Japan.

During 1907-09 Japan without knowing it harbored the man who thirty years later was to appear as an antagonist more dangerous than the Czar. Certainly the Russian military forces were not up to the demands of the times. The organization was imperfect; the long line of communication was insufficient; the officers lacked the efficiency and strategic qualities that are a *conditio sine qua non* for victory; battleships and cruisers were old and inferior, owing to fraudulent practices; and the troops lacked the martial spirit without which a war never can be brought to a successful end. When visiting Moscow during the war, I talked to some soldiers who were going out to the Far East front, and asked them why and whom they were going to fight, and I then found them generally to have very vague ideas on the subject and to show no enthusiasm. And when Kuropatkin rode around on horseback and distributed icons to his regiment he did not succeed in inspiring the soldiers with fighting spirit.

In September, 1908, I often spoke to Lord Kitchener about the Russo-Japanese War, and once expressed the opinion that the outcome of the war was clear evidence of the high military qualities of the Japanese. Kitchener very wisely replied:

"The fact that the Japanese defeated the Russians is no proof of their ability, but rather of the insufficient training of the Russians."

Chiang Kai-shek understood more than well that if he was ever to partake in the struggle for the welfare and future of China, he must thoroughly study and learn the methods adopted by the Japanese throughout their restoration work in the Meiji period. And he is no doubt greatly indebted to the knowledge he gained in Japan for the manner in which he has been able to unite his people to a resistance that is filling the whole world with astonishment and admiration.

III

The Fall of the Manchu Dynasty

BUT LET US RETURN TO THE TIME WHEN WE LEFT CHIANG Kai-shek in Tokyo. It will be sufficient in this connection to bring to mind a few important dates, and I shall insert the episodes where I myself came into contact with the events and leading personages of the time. The fact that I have occasionally had a chance to cast a glance between the spokes of the wheels of time, and that so many years of my own life have been spent in the wilderness and human deserts of Asia, are good reasons for my feeling intimately connected with the gigantic drama now being enacted in East Asia.

One day in November, 1908, I was on my way to a reception in the company of the Swedish Minister in Tokyo. We passed the Chinese Legation, where the yellow dragon flag was flying at the top of the staff. When we returned the same way an hour later, the symbol of the Middle Kingdom was half-mast high. We stopped and entered. In reply to our inquiry, a subordinate official of the Legation told us that a telegram had just been received announcing the death of the Emperor Kwang Hsü and the Empress Dowager of China.

So the second last Manchu emperor had ended his days under mysterious circumstances, and the Dalai Lama, who was just then in Peking, read the requiem for him and the Empress Dowager. But the wavering flame was not quite extinguished. It fluttered a few years longer, the Boy Emperor, Hsüan T'ung (Pu Yi), holding the dragon throne. In 1912 he was definitely dethroned and this was the end of the once so brilliant saga of the Manchu dynasty, Ta Ch'ing, in China. Pu Yi is now a puppet emperor in Hsinking, the capital of Manchuria, where he is vegetating by the grace of Japan.

Then followed Yüan Shih-k'ai's ascent to power in China, the first revolution, and the second in 1913 when Yüan Shih-k'ai was victorious. On January 1, 1912, a new government was set up in Nanking with Sun Yat-sen as President. China then had two governments, one in Nanking and one in Peking. Yüan Shih-k'ai had one foot on the steps of the dragon throne when he ended his days in June, 1916.

In 1917, Sun Yat-sen formed a new government in Canton, appointing his friend from Tokyo days, Chiang Kai-shek, secretary and chief of the army's department of education. At the same time Chiang carried out several important military commissions. Already in 1910 he had become a member of the "Restoration Movement" which was to be the root of the Kuomintang, or the national democratic party. The revolution was in full swing, and one event succeeded another under the leadership of Sun Yat-sen and Chiang Kai-shek. In June, 1922, they had to subdue the dangerous conspiracy against the life of Sun Yat-sen, staged by Chen Chiungming. At the last minute and thanks to Chiang's presence of mind and initiative, the great revolutionary leader escaped in disguise. They boarded a cruiser which took them to Hong Kong and Shanghai. The following year Canton was once more in the hands of the revolutionaries and became the base of the Kuomintang's renewed operations.

During a short visit to Moscow in 1923, Chiang got a glimpse of Russian military conditions. His experience of the world outside of China was increased during that trip. After his return home he served as governor of Canton while Sun Yat-sen went to Peking. In Canton, Sun founded the Whampoa Military Academy of which Chiang Kai-shek was made principal. It was in Moscow that he had learned how to organize such an institute. Already in 1922 Karakhan had come to Canton as adviser to Sun Yat-sen. He was soon joined by

Borodin and Galen, the latter famous under the name of Marshal Bluecher. With their help an intimate co-operation was established with Moscow, and in January, 1924, the communists were received into the Kuomintang party, whose organization then had to undergo a number of changes.

Karakhan, the "Black Prince," the tall, handsome Armenian, Sun Yat-sen's once so influential adviser, and the friend of the Kuomintang, met a tragic end. His star set in blood. A few years ago he was one of those who fell in Stalin's great purge.

After the death of Yüan Shih-k'ai, Peking's power rapidly dwindled. In 1918 only three provinces paid taxes to the government there and a few years later taxes could be collected in the city only.

Sun Yat-sen's trip to Peking had a sad end. On the twelfth of March, 1925, the "Father of the Revolution" died there and was embalmed by Paul Stevenson, the American professor of the Peking Union Medical College. Two years later, in the spring of 1927, the corpse was still in its sarcophagus in the Pi-yün-sse temple in the Western Hills, where I had a chance to see it. Toward the summer of the same year it was removed to the magnificent mausoleum on the Purple Hill at Nanking, now one of the most important places of pilgrimage for the Chinese, second only to the grave of Confucius and the Sacred Mountains of China.

IV

The Northern Campaign

IT IS UNFATHOMABLE TO A WESTERN MIND THAT A COUNTRY can exist at all for twenty years of uninterrupted revolutionary war. It is only in a country of China's size and population that such a thing is possible. About fifty generals, many of whom might better be termed bandit leaders, fought each other in warring expeditions between different provinces and in battles that often were less blood-drenched than settled by treachery and bribes. The most fantastic conditions prevailed; governmental order and the existence of the whole people became an inextricable chaos. The national finances were in a hopeless state of disorder. The unscrupulous quasi-heroes who brought destruction over their own country and for paltry gold waged war on their own people, raised loans with strangers, and consequently these latter were also exposed to the hatred of the honest Chinese. Outraged by the unchecked violence and the foreign intervention in China's domestic affairs, for which the rival generals themselves were directly responsible, Chiang Kai-shek together with the leading men of the Kuomintang party decided to assault the domestic militarism and the demoralizing oppression of foreign profiteering. At the Whampoa Military Academy Chiang educated and trained three thousand young Chinese into a *corps d'élite* of able officers, all inspired with the same energy and spirit as he himself.

Thus, in 1926, the plan for the "Northern Campaign" was born, the campaign that in two years swept through the whole of China from Canton to Peking, and that was to

purify the huge country from the crude and barbarized soldiery and its unworthy bandit generals.

On July 9, 1926, Chiang Kai-shek became commander-
in-chief or Generalissimo of the national revolutionary army
and on the same day began the Northern Campaign which
proved Chiang to be as ingenious a general, tactician, and
strategist as he was a politician and statesman, and able to
cope with the most difficult situations. In the manifesto,
glowing with patriotism and exaltation, that he distributed
to his troops, he said that death was worth more than life
without honor. "Your own life means nothing, you must sacrifice everything for your country and its people."

The army marched northward. Changsha was stormed,
Wu P'ei-fu, the old Spartan, was put to flight. Hankow and
Hanyang fell; Nanchang, Kiukiang, and Fukien were taken.
In February, 1927, Chekiang, Chiang Kai-shek's own home
province, was conquered and cleaned up, and in the same
month Hangchow fell, that beautiful town which Marco
Polo loved more than any in China and which he so vividly
painted in his immortal descriptions. On March 22, Shanghai
was taken and Nanking the following day.

The communists who had been expelled by Chiang Kai-
shek not only from the Kuomintang but also from Canton,
now started the so-called "Nanking Affair" in order to in-
criminate Chiang, firing on the foreign consulates, murdering, and looting. That was on March 24, 1927. These events
aroused a storm of indignation, and the foreign newspapers
raged. Chiang Kai-shek shouldered the whole responsibility
and guaranteed the safety and property of the foreigners.
Thus he straightened out the complicated Nanking Affair
with tact and cleverness in a manner satisfactory both to him
and the foreigners. And above all, the communist attempt to
overthrow Chiang was a complete failure.

Difficulties were towering up everywhere around Chiang
Kai-shek and seemed unsurmountable to the solitary leader.

How would it ever be possible to unite under one single, strong will a country so severed by civil wars, so torn by egotism and corruption? How could this so heterogeneous people become united and agree around one common aim? But Chiang never lost courage. Self-possessed and with head erect he continued on his *via dolorosa*, firmly determined in time to change it into a *via triumphalis*.

His tasks already shouldered—to bring to a successful issue the Northern Campaign, to subdue the rival generals, and to frustrate the communist plans—were not to suffice; he was now also threatened by a new danger within the Kuomintang itself, as it was split into one left- and one right-wing group. The former, together with the communist party, was led by Wang Ching-wei and Eugene Chen, and at the beginning of 1927 formed a government of its own in Hankow. They called themselves the Wuhan group after the three towns of Wuchang, Hankow, and Hanyang. Their aim was to oust Chiang Kai-shek. But their leaders lacked his capacity, and by intrigues and outrages they made themselves obnoxious. Finally the more balanced elements of the Wuhan group had had enough of the communists and expelled them.

The removal of Chiang Kai-shek was demanded by the Wuhan wing before they would consider any reconciliation with the right-wing group and Nanking. He declared himself willing to resign, duly did so on the thirteenth of August, 1927, and returned to his childhood home at Fenghua in Chekiang. He could not co-operate with a group that still tolerated Borodin and the communists. For co-operation he demanded that Nanking and Wuhan come to an agreement and form a national government at Nanking, that all military resources be mobilized for the effectuation of the national revolution, and that communism be extirpated throughout China. Then he went to Japan.

Things did not look promising for the man in whose hands

Chiang Kai-shek—in response to express demands—had placed the power and responsibility. Feng Yü-hsiang, the "Christian General," who did belong to the Kuomintang, but of whom nobody knew anything, and who always went his own way, had taken Sian and Tungkwan, and his power extended along the Lunghai railway. In his attempts to advance southward, the villainous general Chang Tsung-chang had been defeated, but still existed; and when finally the warlord, the great Chang Tso-lin, also started moving against the Nanking government, it was too much for the new masters, and Wang Ching-wei was clear-sighted enough to send for Chiang Kai-shek in Japan. Presumably that was what Chiang had been waiting for. He came, saw, and conquered, and the first to succumb to his superior warfare was Chang Tso-lin, who in August, together with his allies, had advanced as far as Pukow, quite near Nanking.

Anyone who spent the winter of 1926-27 and the following spring in Peking will have had the opportunity of studying at close range the great change which at that time took place in China. From the end of November until the beginning of March, life went on as usual, and when I wanted to start an expedition, partly with a view to investigating for Deutsche Lufthansa the prospects of opening an air line from Berlin to Peking right across Inner Asia, and partly to carry out geological and archaeological research work, this was certainly met with a natural suspicion with regard to the air line, but on the other hand with complete understanding for the scientific projects. The old bandit general Chang Tso-lin was the ruler of Manchuria and Northern China. Wellington Koo was the Minister for Foreign Affairs, and I negotiated with Wang Yin-t'ao, the vice Minister for Foreign Affairs, who, incidentally, had received his education in Germany and who was married to a German lady, about permits, passports, and recommendations for the projected expedition. For the scientific work and our relation to Chinese scholarship we had to consult Dr. Wong Wen-hao, the head of the Geological Survey of China. We were met with kindness and understanding everywhere and on January 1, 1927, the desired permit was granted.

But other winds blew across Northern China at the beginning of March. The heralds of the new time were advancing from the south with nationalism and hatred of foreigners on their banner, the white sun shining from a field as blue as the heavens. China was awakening from her coma. China for the Chinese! The Sun Yat-sen revolution was to be victorious everywhere. Chiang Kai-shek, the standard bearer of the new era, had already begun his advance northward, the campaign that was to end the civil wars and to crush the Chang Tso-lin rule. The new ideas appealed to students and university teachers, and some of them decided to put a stop to foreign exploitation and exploration of China and her possessions. China's own scientists were fully capable of looking after the scientific work. At first the learned Chinese opposition to our plans seemed to take the form of obstruction. After long negotiations, however, they agreed to an amicable settlement but on conditions that apparently were very disadvantageous for us. But the relationship between our Chinese companions and ourselves in our work in the field during the following years was most cordial and friendly, and all wishes expressed by us were obligingly and generously fulfilled.

Even after the beginning of our peaceful campaign in the summer of 1927, its first months were characterized by a feeling of uncertainty. Nobody knew what would happen and whether the effects of the civil war would extend as far as Suiyuan and Inner Mongolia. We bought 300 camels at our headquarters in the latter country and from time to time there were rumors that they would be confiscated by this or that general or by the great robber bands north of Paotou, through whose territories we had to pass and through which we were escorted by Chinese brigand-soldiers on horseback. But we were ready to start in time and when we had penetrated far enough into the deserts in the west, we could no longer be threatened by dangers of war. It was during our absence in Gobi and in the province of Sinkiang that the great change took place.

On January 9, 1928, Chiang Kai-shek once more took over the command in Nanking of the national revolutionary army which was reorganized, whereupon the Northern Campaign was resumed after a brief interruption. The Minister of War, General Ho Ying-ch'in, was in command at the front. Pukow, Hsüchow, and Shanghai were recovered. The great warlords Yen Hsi-shan in Shansi and Feng Yü-hsiang, the "Christian," sided with Chiang Kai-shek and met him at Kaifeng. There they decided to make a joint attack on Chang Tso-lin. Feng had been defeated by his Mukden troops and had retreated to Kansu, from where he had advanced into Shensi, defeated the Mukden troops, and continued to Honan.

And now Chang Tso-lin was attacked from all sides. But once more Chiang Kai-shek was interrupted by an intermezzo. On April 19 the Japanese landed an army corps at Tsingtao in the Kiaochow area on the southern coast of the Shantung peninsula, which area was leased by Germany in 1898 for 99 years. The Chinese government protested. Japan declared that it was done merely to protect her subjects on the Kia-Tsi railway. China claimed that the Japanese had broken international treaties and that by violating Chinese territory during a civil war whose aim it was to unite China, they were assuming a great responsibility and disturbing the good relationship between the two countries.

When Chang Tso-lin and Chang Tsung-chang had withdrawn their troops, Chiang Kai-shek took possession of Tsinan, the capital of Shantung, on May 1, 1928, and when he had made himself responsible for the safety of the Japanese subjects, the Japanese troops withdrew. But only for a few days, Tsinan then being occupied again. Chiang Kai-shek did not resort to violence against them, which might have led to dangerous consequences.

One need not search long for the reason for these repeated thrusts on the part of Japan. Already in May, 1927, troops had landed in Shantung and new troops were now arriving from time to time. The pretext that this was done to protect the Japanese subjects is not acceptable. The real reason must have been to worry and irritate Chiang Kai-shek and to disturb his energetic struggle to unite China. The Japanese may also have feared that if Chiang Kai-shek conquered Chang Tso-lin and occupied Peking and Tientsin, disturbances might break out in Manchuria against Japan. At any rate a state of irritation was successfully created. A growing hatred toward Japan was the result. Effective and thorough anti-Japanese action was started against all Japanese wares, banks, and enterprises. Later, this action against Japan was to be used as a pretext for new insults. The Japanese realized that Chiang Kai-shek was a dangerous foe, a man who would succeed in his endeavors if he were left alone.

When Chang Tso-lin had been defeated on all fronts, he understood that the northern provinces with Peking and Tientsin, with its large customs revenues, were lost to him. Peking had been his headquarters for three years, when in the beginning of June, 1928, he left the old imperial city forever and retired north of the Great Wall. On June 4, just as his train was entering Mukden railway station, his carriage was blown up when crossing a bridge and he was killed.

Chang Tso-lin, short, stooped, pale, and thin though he was, still gives us an excellent picture of a great Chinese warlord, thanks to his adventurous career.

The white and blue national flag was hoisted in Peking on all official buildings. Chiang Kai-shek had accomplished his

Marshal Chiang Kai-shek.

Chang Tso-lin and His Sons. Chang, the Ruler of Manchuria and Northern China, Was Assassinated on June 4, 1928.

aim and completed his great mission, an undertaking started by Sun Yat-sen in his dreams and plans, but carried out by Chiang Kai-shek. By the sarcophagus of the great revolutionist he announced the significance of the victory as if he were speaking directly to the dead and as if he were listening to his words. He said that the time of martial exploits was past and that the peaceful work of reconstruction would now begin. In two years the national army had united China—only Manchuria was yet missing.

V

Chiang Kai-shek's Mission

EVER SINCE 1927 CHIANG KAI-SHEK HAD SERVED HIS COUNtry as President of the National Government at Nanking and in the field as Generalissimo of the army, the navy, and the air forces. He was without comparison the mightiest man in China, the country with more inhabitants than any other in the world, as populous as the United States, Russia, Germany, France, and Italy together. His authority was unlimited. In reality he was China's dictator, but on no condition did he want to be looked upon as such. His career had been dazzling. He had shot like a meteor through the heavens of China. Considering the high claims he always had placed on himself and recalling the following ten years of his life, one can be certain that he was not by far satisfied with the progress already made.

Like all great people he was surrounded by antagonists, grudgers, and adversaries, who begrudged him his successes and were lying in wait for a chance to put a spoke in his wheel. Certainly Chang Hsüeh-liang, the son of the murdered Chang Tso-lin and his successor as Marshal in Manchuria, did go over to the National Government at the end of 1928, but Yen Hsi-shan in Shansi, Feng Yü-hsiang in Honan, Li Chi-shen in Kwantung, and Li Tsung-jen in Hupei, all four had their own political councils or governments and were in opposition to Chiang Kai-shek. Otherwise China could be considered to be under the rule of the National Government at Nanking. Naturally he had to subdue his enemies and compel them to obey him, but in such matters he has often displayed a great reluctance to use violence.

He has shown himself to be conciliatory and reasonable, slow in using harsh words and violent actions, quick to make peace and friends, and never has he lost the superhuman patience without which he could not have accomplished his aims. Once, a few years ago—I do not remember exactly when or where —one of my Chinese friends told me, "Accompanied only by a secretary and a couple of adjutants the Marshal has flown to different places in twelve provinces where disturbances or revolts have been attempted. He has descended straight from the sky and gone right into the lion's den. Calm and unafraid and with suppressed eloquence he has spoken of the needs of our country and of the threatening dangers. Having tamed the wild animals and transformed them into his willing confederates, he bids them a kind farewell a couple of hours later and flies back home."

And what a country destiny had selected for him to rule! No, not only to rule, but to unite! Fancy uniting vast seas of people! And these people are anything but a homogeneous race. China is not a land, a country; it is a continent, bounded on the east by an ocean, in the west by the highest and mightiest mountain region and the greatest deserts in the world, and its people is made up of heterogeneous elements who under the influence of different climates and conditions have developed into tribes as different as the peoples of Europe. The only bond between these groups, who do not understand each other's language, is the writing, which is the same everywhere. When a Chinese from the North meets one from the South he has no other way of communicating with him except by writing. It is amusing to observe two such men. One draws with the index finger of his right hand the different ideograms in his left palm while the other nods and portrays his feelings by his facial expression.

It really did seem to be beyond human power to change into disciplined individuals of modern thought these tribes with their ancient inveterate prejudices, their conceptions, so bizarre in our eyes, their picturesque superstition, their gods, dragons, and mystic spirits, their fears of losing face and their reluctance even to seeing their enemies lose face—to change and remodel into a consummate whole this vast and surging sea of 450 million humans. Centuries and armies of powerful and confident reformers would seem to be needed to carry out a task of such gigantic measures.

From father to son, from one generation to the other, China's unique culture, her tales, legends, and traditions, had been handed down for four milleniums, in many cases originating thousands of years before the dawn of historic times.

From the midst of this mystical, mist-enshrouded seething sea of humans there had now emerged one single man from a modest home in Chekiang, a man who had unfailing confidence in his own power, who believed implicitly that the Christian God would help him, and who firmly relied on the faithfulness of the Chinese and their ability to endure purgatory and undergo regeneration. Had he doubted his God, himself, or his people he would have given up the struggle long since. He saw before him the united country, the firm, unifying organization, the strong resistance to foreign intrusion, a people who, after poverty, misery, and oppression at the hands of wretched, corrupted leaders, should be lifted to a worthy standard of living, a country rich in all products of the earth, utilizing its resources and thanks to the fidelity, patience, and industry of its inhabitants, rising to the rank of a new great power in the Far East.

This man was indeed well equipped for his enormous mission. His rigid upbringing to honesty, discipline, and work, his training at the Paoting Military Academy, the broad-minded and extensive view he had acquired of the world and world conditions when he lived in Japan with Sun Yat-sen, his military studies at Moscow, his directorship of the Military Academy at Whampoa, the brilliantly clever Northern Campaign, the diplomatically tactful affair with the Japanese at

Shantung, his judicious treatment of the warlords in Southern and Northern China, the expulsion of Chang Tso-lin—all these burdensome and exacting steps on a thorny road had developed and steeled him into a man of unusual capacity, with an iron will, a character of steel, a discrimination clear as crystal, and a versatility and knowledge of human nature that made him fit to cope with tasks of even much greater importance.

He knew more than well that he was the only one in China who could liberate his people from the constraint of thousands of years, from darkness, abasement, and slavery, and with a steady hand lead them to meet the new era with spiritual and material freedom, self-respect and discipline, patriotism and national strength, honor and greatness. With glowing eloquence he appealed to the vast multitudes. He was a superior orator and appeared like an apostle who wished to save a whole nation from destruction, to deliver it from its great distress.

And yet, when the Northern Campaign had been brought to a close and, as he said, the years of war were to be succeeded by a period of peaceful work and consolidation—how endless was the distance that remained for him to go in order to reach the goal of his desires!

VI

My First Meeting with the Marshal

ON JULY 7, 1928, MARSHAL YANG, THE COMPETENT OLD governor general of Sinkiang, or to use the more modern title, president of the Provincial Council, was murdered at a banquet at Urumchi, and one of the conspirators, Chin Shu-jen, the head of Yang's own chancellery, usurped the highest power and its insignia. He regarded our Sino-Swedish expedition—and not least its Chinese members—with suspicion, and as often as he could he put obstructions in our way. Late in the autumn of the same year he also refused to grant me permission to make a trip to Lop-nor where I wanted to examine the hydrographic changes from 1921, and I then decided to protest before the Central Government at Nanking and, if possible, also before Chiang Kai-shek himself.

Accompanied by two members of the expedition, Professor Hsü Ping-ch'ang and Dr. David Hummel, I started from Urumchi in the middle of December and traveled via Semipalatinsk and Novo Sibirsk to Mukden and Peking, which city we reached on the tenth of January, 1929.

I spent the month of March in Nanking, looking for the ministers who might help us to get the better of Chin Shu-jen, the almighty chief of Sinkiang. As usual in China, times were troubled. The Wuhan generals had opposed Chiang Kai-shek and the Central Government, and the Marshal had decided to quell them. His headquarters were in Nanking, and he was busy with preparations for a new campaign. At the same time, hundreds of representatives of the Kuomintang in different provinces had gathered in the capital for one of their annual councils. Different political views and aspirations were seething among them and did not contribute to the quiet before the storm.

The Central Government consisted of five Yuans. The prime minister and president of the Executive Yuan was Tan Yuan-kai; president of the Legislative Yuan, Hwang Chung-hüeh; and of the Supervisory Yuan, old Ts'ai Yuan-p'ei, who is now president of Academia Sinica and whom we already had learned to know as an extremely charming, pleasant, and cultivated gentleman, who also spoke German.

Ts'ai Yuan-p'ei accompanied me and my two companions to the council house. It was carefully guarded; we had to cross three courts and pass the same number of doors before we reached the main entrance, and at each door there were two rows of soldiers, who presented arms as we passed. We entered the tremendous council chamber, in the middle of which there stood a long council board with chairs along either side, and paper, ink pots, and brushes on top. In the corner to the right of the entrance was a round table surrounded by a corner sofa and comfortable armchairs, all in Western style.

We were received there by Tan Yuan-kai and Hwang Chung-hüeh and had a short talk with them. They told us that an important cabinet council was to be held on the war against Wuhan. However, the Marshal would receive us; he had personally fixed the time, ten o'clock, and now only a few minutes remained.

Suddenly the door opened. Everyone arose and stood bolt upright. The Marshal approached us with firm, quick steps, pressed my hand, and greeted the others one by one. Then he motioned to us to sit down and took a seat himself.

Chiang Kai-shek was above middle height, thin, but powerfully built and well proportioned. His features were very serious and his expression never changed. A very small, short mustache shaded his upper lip. His appearance was pleasant, and he created the immediate impression of a person of high authority, determination, and character. The uniform he wore was of European cut, field gray with a touch of yellow. There was nothing to indicate his rank, the highest in China. In response to an almost imperceptible gesture, a short man with a distinguished, almost jovial face came to the Marshal's side. He was the interpreter and certainly the most eminent interpreter I ever had to translate my words and wishes. His name was Sun Fo, Minister of Railways, the son of Sun Yat-sen, the father of the Revolution.

When a minor civil war is threatening and three Yuan presidents are in readiness for a cabinet council, to begin with military punctuality, the Marshal has no time for unnecessary polite questions. He asked point blank:

"What do you want, and how can I be of service to you?"

Sun Fo translated his words, adding that I must express myself briefly and concisely as the Marshal was very pressed for time.

With a few short, clear sentences I gave an account of the Sino-Swedish expedition and its scientific aims, and expressed my regrets that our work and studies in Sinkiang were being obstructed by Chin Shu-jen, the new governor-general. I emphasized that our activities were of importance for international science and especially for China, and I requested the Marshal to afford us and our Chinese fellow-workers his powerful protection and to issue an order to Chin Shu-jen to put an end to the difficulties raised by him.

The Marshal, already informed on the matter by Ts'ai Yuan-p'ei, replied that he would issue an order to the governor-general of Sinkiang to do all in his power to facilitate our work, and would inform him that the expedition was under the direct patronage of the Central Government. He then turned to Professor Hsü Ping-ch'ang with a few questions on details, nodded his comprehension, and gave him the same assurance. Finally he rose, extended his hand in parting, and moved to his seat at the long table while we bade the other ministers farewell. We departed. Ts'ai Yuan-p'ei advised us to remain in Nanking until the telegram had been dispatched and a reply received. Being aware of the long time such matters usually take in China, we could prepare for a long time of waiting and spent a few days visiting Soochow, the Venice of China, one of the most picturesque towns in the world, but now partly destroyed by the Japanese, and Hangchow, Marco Polo's town. Upon our return to Nanking there was still no reply from Urumchi to the government's telegram, but now we were besieged with invitations to give lectures at academies, institutes, and universities, yes, even at colleges for young girls, an occupation that completely filled our time.

One of these invitations resulted in a unique lecture. As mentioned above, the Kuomintang party assembled at that time for its annual meeting in Nanking, and as the government was fully occupied with the Wuhan business, the ministers did not wish to be disturbed by the political discussions of the Kuomintang representatives, but tried to divert their attention in various ways.

I had therefore been asked to take care of the politicians one evening and had promised a lecture on travels and adventures in innermost Asia. The lecture was to begin at eight o'clock. Professor Hsü, Dr. Hummel, and I presented ourselves in ample time in the large hall which was brightly illuminated—but quite empty. Eight o'clock struck, and a quarter past, but not a soul turned up. Silence reigned. Finally I ascended the platform and started speaking at the top of my voice, causing an echo throughout the empty hall: "Ladies and gentlemen! The trip I shall have the pleasure of describing tonight . . ." I got no further, for I was silenced by Hsü's and Hummel's roars of laughter. We never learned what had happened. Some said that the tension between Wuhan and Nanking had become acute that very evening and occasioned sudden political meetings and discussions; others said that we simply had been given the wrong date.

As an illustration of the power and influence of the Central Government over Sinkiang in 1929, it may be of interest to mention the telegram which the government sent on March 13, at the command of Marshal Chiang Kai-shek, to Governor General Chin Shu-jen, signed by the Executive Yuan. Its tone was courteous and considerate, and in conformity with ancient custom it carefully avoided the use of words and expressions that might possibly cause Chin to "lose face." I had asked permission for three new members of the expedition to go to Urumchi via Chuguchak, and also for us to continue our archaeological excavations and our sending up of pilot balloons. After an explanatory introduction regarding the composition and purpose of the expedition, the telegram goes on:

"For this reason we ask you to issue orders to the authorities in your province to verify the passports on the journeys of the expedition and to afford its members your protection, and also, within the boundaries of the scientific work of the expedition, for instance excavations and the ascent of pilot balloons, in all respects to assist them in their work and in no manner to raise obstacles in their way.

"Scientific progress and still more important ideas of the new time as well as the responsibility attached to it, make it a duty of the Government to accord them (the members of the expedition) all possible assistance. So we send you this telegram and it is your duty to act according to what has been said above."

Some of the ministers advised me not to wait for a telegraphic reply from Chin, as a telegraphic order from the Central Government to the governor of a province required no answer other than absolute obedience. Others, however, for instance the Minister of Education, advised us to wait for the reply, which we did, as related above. As we had heard no word from Urumchi by the beginning of April, we could wait no longer, but returned to Peking.

In the summer, I learned from our friends, Dr. Ambolt and Dr. P. L. Yuan, that in June, three months after the dispatch of the telegram from Nanking, Chin still denied that he had received it. It was a known fact that it had been delivered, but Chin completely ignored it, and the members of our expedition whom I had ordered from Sweden to Sinkiang, were stopped on the border at Chin's command; and after months of idle waiting they had to make a nice little round-about trip through Vladivostok, Peking, and Inner Mongolia to reach Central Asia. Our loss of time and money could gladden no one but Chin. The power of the Nanking Government thus did not yet extend so far as to Sinkiang, and during my stay in the capital I had gained a wrong conception of the value of its protection and the extent of its influence.

But Chiang Kai-shek was at that time absorbed by his task to unite China, and his spirit was already hovering over eighteen provinces. He had still far to go to reach his goal. The small episode related above, very unimportant in the big game, but of great importance to us, also gave me insight into one of the weaknesses of the organization of the Chinese administration, the decentralization, the arbitrary rule and corruption of the magisterial, despotic satraps, and their habit of turning a deaf ear when they received orders from the central authority. "God is in his heaven and it is far to the court of the Great Khan!" The longer the distance from Nanking, the greater the liberties. A few years later, the last hour was to come for the conceited and greedy satraps, the vices of the old system then being extirpated by Marshal Chiang.

In January and February, 1935, I traveled from west to east through the whole of Kansu and could witness with my own eyes—and also hear from one or two honest mayors—how terrible were the sufferings that the peasants and townspeople had to endure under the lash of the Tungan generals of the Ma family. The unfortunates were completely impoverished by inhuman taxation, were thrown into hopeless debt, and were beaten within an inch of their lives when they could not pay. But such beastly brutality and cruelty were part of the weeds Chiang Kai-shek had decided to pull up by the roots and throw on the fire. It is easy to understand that the bloodsuckers who were to lose their incomes and who were to be swept away by the reconstruction work of the Marshal hated him. Their time was up, but their resistance made his task and his work of reformation doubly hard and his high ideals so much the more admirable.

VII

The Communist Revolt

IN MARCH, 1929, CHIANG KAI-SHEK SUBDUED THE WUHAN
generals, took Hankow and the southern provinces, and continued on his way toward uniting the country. Already he
had forced twenty-two provinces to pay taxes to Nanking.
But calm and order were still lacking. New revolt movements
cropped up here and there. Feng Yü-hsiang and Yen Hsi-
shan, who joined forces in 1930, were the greatest danger.
They were beaten, the victory being facilitated by the fact
that Chang Hsüeh-liang sided with Chiang Kai-shek. I spent
1930 in Peking and could follow the effect of the civil wars
on public feeling in the old city. The adventurous fortunes
of Feng Yü-hsiang, the "Christian general," led him via the
post of Minister of War at Nanking to the contemplative
passivity of a hermitage, and finally he disappeared from the
stage. Ch'en Chi-t'ang, who had the power in Kwantung, was
crushed and fled the country. The resistance was also broken
in Kwangsi and the province placed itself under Nanking.
Thanks to Chiang Kai-shek's ability, vigilance, and energy,
the great task of uniting China approached its completion
step by step. It had already taken nearly ten years.

It will thus be seen that Chiang Kai-shek was faced with
numerous minor troubles—every one of which, however, was
quite considerable according to ordinary European standards.
But his great preoccupation was provided by the goal toward
which he was striving, the absolute unity and national homogeneity of China based on the revolutionary ideas and Three

Principles (*San min chu i*) [1] of Sun Yat-sen, the New Life Movement which was to raise the people to a more worthy standard of living, and the economic construction work which was to increase the wealth of the country and promote its prosperity. All the internal struggles he had to fight with recalcitrant generals and rebellious provinces as well as all his peaceable and educational efforts for the regeneration of his country were overshadowed by the great threat he saw in communism. But the greatest menace of all to the peaceful development and future of China was certainly Japan's offensive and aggressive policy, and for many years Chiang Kai-shek lived in the belief, subsequently proved to be wrong, that no effective resistance could be offered Japan until communism was effaced from China.

The part played by communism was indeed strange and surprising. In 1920 bolshevik ideas were embraced by several professors and students in Peking, and Sun Yat-sen himself consulted Joffe in Shanghai in 1922. It was not long, however,

---

[1] In his book *Maktkampen i Fjärran Östern* ("The Struggle for Power in the Far East"), Professor Bernhard Karlgren writes as follows regarding Sun Yat-sen's doctrine: "The main points in his paper '*San min chu i*,' 'The Three Principles,' which every Chinese schoolboy nowadays must know practically by heart, were in reality very simple and elementary, but in a country such as China with the social and political structure it had had so far, they were nevertheless a revolutionizing novelty, a revelation. They were, briefly expressed: The principle of the 'People's Nationalism,' i.e. the assertion of China's absolute freedom from foreign oppression and tutelage, what was called 'Imperialism' in various forms; the principle of the 'Sovereignty of the People' in full measure, and the principle of the 'People's Livelihood,' i.e. a really democratic, parliamentary rule, that is social and economic reforms; economic equality and justice, reformation of the tyrannical landownership conditions, limitation of private capital, and a gradual introduction of state capitalism. Sun thought that this program could best be realized in 'three stages.' First a period of military dictatorship exercised by the Kuo-min-tang leaders, during which all 'warlords' were to be annihilated and the whole of China united in the hand of the new national government; then a period of 'political tutelage' during which China, as yet unprepared for real parliamentarism, was to be completely led by a small, powerful, and capable political unit, the Kuo-min-tang party, which was to rule in very much the same way as the Bolshevik 'party' in Russia, first educating the Chinese in democratic administration in communities and districts and then in larger and larger units; finally a third period of absolute parliamentarism."

before he realized that the Russian Soviet ideas were not suitable for the trend of the Chinese revolution, and we have already seen how Karakhan, Borodin, and Galen (Bluecher), together with their Chinese converts were removed by Chiang Kai-shek. But after the death of Sun Yat-sen, communism nevertheless reappeared here and there, and large numbers of Chinese were still convinced that the revolution could not be accomplished without the co-operation of the Soviet Union, that country to support and assist the Kuomintang.

In 1926 and 1927 the clamor for communism grew louder and louder. Chiang Kai-shek's campaign in 1930 and 1931 against communism met with no success. The movement was already spreading like an epidemic, it was embraced by ten provinces, and on the seventh of November, 1931, these provinces established their own government in Kiangsi. The Marshal had 900,000 men in the field against the communist armies in Kiangsi, Hunan, Anhwei, Honan, and Hopei. In April, 1933, the Marshal had not yet succeeded in getting the better of the communists, whose army then consisted of 180,000 men. It was only after the fifth campaign, when Chiang Kai-shek followed the advice of General von Seeckt and surrounded the communist forces by a system of blockhouses, that he won a decisive victory, costing the lives of 60,000 soldiers and innumerable civilians.

Then the communist struggle for existence entered a highly dramatic, almost fantastic phase. Their leaders, such as Mao Tse-tung and Chou En-lai, inspired by Soviet Russian ideas, were unusually able, determined, and dauntless men. Numbering but 90,000, the communist army at the end of 1934 began its migration all the way through Hunan, Kweichow, Yünnan, and the borderlands of Hsikang to Szechwan and Shensi, through the most rugged country, over steep mountains, through deep valleys and across roaring rivers, like the lemming shunning no obstacles. Some troops were lost on the way, others stayed in Szechwan, and still others threatened

Chengtu, the capital of the province. It was only the remainder, about 20,000 men, that endured as far as northern Shensi, some bandit leaders joining them there.

Such a feat is expressive of the endurance and will power of the otherwise peace-loving and indolent Chinese when something is at stake. Their march through vast areas of China proper brings to mind Xenophon's Anabasis and the retreat of the ten thousand men, and the tragic but heroic march of the Torguts from the Volga back to Central Asia. An army able to stand such a strain and to survive a whole year of uninterrupted hardships is not composed of poor material. It had performed a feat which is bearing fruits in the present war and nobody knows whether a Japanese army under similar unfavorable circumstances could endure hardships of a similar character.

It was certainly not pleasant for the country, towns, and villages that lay in the way of these wild and plundering hordes. But there is no doubt that the poor peasants who were being impoverished by landlords, officials, and militarists, welcomed them, and that they were treated well at the hands of the communists. At the end of January, 1935, when I was returning with my string of cars along the old "Imperial Highway" from Sinkiang via Liangchow and Lanchow to Sian, I sensed a hurricane approaching from the south. There was already talk of a stream of communists which was known to be on its way northward, and people were apprehensive as to the fate of their towns and communities. Certain contingents of heralds had already reached our road, and more than once the magistrate of a locality said: "Be careful when you come to the second or third village from here, for according to reports it was occupied yesterday by red fugitives." Hordes of bandits were roving around everywhere and the risks to which we exposed ourselves became greater and greater the farther east we went. But we were guided by a lucky star and managed to steer clear of all dangers.

At the end of 1934, the communists were thus defeated and ousted from Kiangsi. Let us leave them for a while in their new headquarters in northern Shensi and Kansu, where they probably had a feeling of closer proximity to their old friends and masters, the Russians, via Mongolia.

The province of Kiangsi, pillaged and ravaged during the communist period, was rebuilt and reorganized when it had been liberated from the rebellious hordes, and this stimulated other parts of the country to follow suit, to the good of the farming population.

VIII

Manchuria

IN 1927 WHEN CHIANG KAI-SHEK WAS BUSY PURGING THE Kuomintang of the Soviet Russians imported by Sun Yat-sen, and when Marshal Chang Tso-lin, the ruler of Manchuria, moved his residence from Mukden to Peking, the Japanese found the time suitable for all kinds of intrigues in Manchuria. The increasing uneasiness that this caused among the Chinese in Peking was allayed by Yoshizawa, the Japanese minister, who assured the newspapers of the capital that Japan had no thought of invading Manchuria. In Tokyo, on the other hand, it was stated in leading quarters that the Japanese had no reason to give Chang Tso-lin their support, as he openly denounced Japan's politics in China, while Yang Yü-ting, the chief of his General Staff, defended the rights of the Chinese.

During a visit that I paid Marshal Chang Tso-lin in the spring of 1927, at his headquarters in the western part of Peking, he said to me, "The Japanese never miss a chance of stabbing me in the back. They try to upset all my endeavors to build up Manchuria and improve conditions."

I was just on the point of starting for Sinkiang with my large Sino-Swedish expedition and so asked Chang Tso-lin for a letter of introduction to the governor general, the powerful and capable Marshal Yang Tseng-hsin. I got it and upon my arrival at Urumchi in February, 1928, I handed it to Marshal Yang. He read it with an expression of contempt and said:

"The generals in the provinces at home are traitors to China. There will be no peace and order in the country until they have disappeared."

On June 4, 1928, Chang Tso-lin was murdered at Mukden, where the Japanese had advised him to return from Peking. His son, Chang Hsüeh-liang, the "Young Marshal," became his successor. He acknowledged the Kuomintang, Nanking, and the national flag, which was a disappointment to the Japanese as it made it more difficult for them to realize their plans with regard to Manchuria. In Japanese opinion, however, it was General Yang Yü-ting, the chief of the General Staff, who was the real ruler at Mukden.

Upon my return to Peking on the tenth of January, 1929, the first news I heard was that General Yang Yü-ting had been murdered the same day. He had been shot by Chang Hsüeh-liang's bodyguard in the latter's palace. The family received $100,000 as consolation and the funeral was magnificent. The rumor circulated in China that Yang Yü-ting had been in collusion with the Japanese with a view to severing Manchuria from China proper and making it into a separate state with Yang Yü-ting himself as its head. The murder was consequently considered just as unwelcome to the Japanese as the Young Marshal's acknowledgment of the Nanking government. Among permanent European residents in Peking, General Yang Yü-ting was considered to possess the clearest head and the best character, and to be the ablest officer in Northern China. He also had the great and rare merit of dying poor. His death was looked upon as an enormous loss to China in a very troublesome time.

The Japanese prime minister, General Tanaka, dreamed of enlarging the Japanese dominion on the mainland of Asia and of conquering China. Twice already he had sent war expeditions to the coast of China, but had not succeeded in subjugating Chiang Kai-shek. It seemed as if Japan had no choice but to acknowledge the Nanking government, which could be done if China waived her claims to Manchuria. On July 1, 1929, General Tanaka retired and three months later he died under mysterious circumstances. What will more than anything else keep his memory alive in China is that, thanks to his hatred of the Kuomintang, Nanking, and Chiang Kaishek, he involuntarily assisted in molding together China and her people.

The most prominent figure in Japanese politics was now General Minami, the commander-in-chief in Korea, the man whose ruthless determination involved Japan in the great adventure on the continent. He was the head of the military, the standard bearer of bloody, medieval tyranny, which always spoke grandiloquently of patriotism, but in reality only thought of conquests and soon succeeded in supplanting every trace of moderation and sane judgment.

Those in power now declared that Manchuria was not part of China and that in the hands of a foreign power it might become a direct threat against Japan. No one had a greater right than Japan to claim this country, where she had made such large investments and built so many railways. In the Russo-Japanese war, Japan had forced Russia out of Manchuria and had since protected its peaceful development. Due to the outcome of the Great War, Russia had become paralyzed and Japan could make her attack on the mainland without having to fear anything from that direction. One of the great highways round the world ran through Manchuria, and the possession of the country would also improve Japan's unsound finances. Chiang Kai-shek had his hands full trying to unite China and expel the communists. It was the right moment. In case of delay, the Chinese might strengthen their position in Manchuria.

Baron Shidehara, the Japanese prime minister, did not share the opinion of the military. As late as January, 1931, he fought in parliament for a peaceful settlement. He praised Chiang Kai-shek's efforts to restore China. It was that looming improvement that the military party regarded so unfavorably. The Nanking government was on its way to abolish the extraterritorial rights and the foreign control of the settlements in the treaty ports, and would in due time also introduce customs autonomy. As time went on the new nationalism would grow stronger and the self-consciousness of the Chinese people would develop under the guidance of the Marshal. In addition, England had left the gold standard, the United States had millions of unemployed, China's main artery, the Yangtse River, was overflowing, putting densely populated and valuable districts under water. Everything thus contributed to making the time appropriate for action. Minami, the Minister of War, expounded the situation in Manchuria and Mongolia to the divisional generals. He scoffed at the pacifists in the Disarmament Conference at Geneva and demanded a reward and encouragement for the army for its loyalty. It was the same spirit as in the "Twenty-one Demands" presented by Japan in 1915, which, had they been accepted, would have made China a tributary state under Japan.

The murder of a Japanese officer in Manchuria was the spark that started the fire. The night of September 18, 1931, Japanese troops entered Mukden. They met no resistance. Chang Hsüeh-liang, the ruler of Manchuria, was at that critical period ill in Peking. No one could be less suited than he to make a stand against the Japanese troops. Without lifting a finger he witnessed the loss of his three provinces and his thirty-five million subjects. The European great powers and the United States were powerless when confronted with the occupation and confined themselves to protests, as they did a few years later when Abyssinia was occupied. Japan consistently continued her action without letting herself be disturbed, convinced that none of the great powers would risk a war in East Asia for the sake of Manchuria. Strangely enough Russia also kept her peace, although the Japanese advanced northward as far as the neighborhood of Amur.

Without firing a shot, Russia in April, 1933, even made over
to Japan the precious Chinese Eastern Railway from Manchuli over Harbin to Vladivostok, and as a result of their
unexpected passivity, they annulled their grand Pacific Ocean
policy, which was so prominent at the beginning of the century. The occupation of Manchuria greatly impaired Soviet
Russia's strategic position in case of a war against Japan.

Thus here, too, the Japanese took all the tricks. The Chinese generals who attempted a defense against the invaders
were defeated, and gradually the Chinese troops were driven
northward and forced to cross the frontier and seek refuge
in Russian-Siberian territory. On the Russian side they were
disarmed and transported through Siberia to Chuguchak and
Urumchi in Sinkiang. There these disarmed and rather poor
troops were incorporated with the provincial army and took
part in the revolts and battles which in April, 1933, ended
with the defeat and flight of the incompetent Governor General Chin Shu-jen. During my stay in Urumchi from June
to October, 1934, it was rumored that about twenty of the
leaders of the Manchurian troops had been executed one summer night at the order of the new military governor general,
Shen Shih-ts'ai, who, by the way, also received his military
training in Manchuria.

America's minister of foreign affairs, Stimson, was all in
sympathy with China, wanted to declare war on Japan, and
suggested to England a common action and sanctions. Stimson protested against the new order in Manchuria for the
reason that the three northeastern provinces, through the
Nine-Power Treaty in Washington, of 1922, were guaranteed integrity with China and were thus open to trade for
all nations. England was just as reluctant as the American
navy to adopt violent measures. The Dominions, Canada,
Australia, New Zealand, and South Africa were on the side
of China. Actually England also sympathized with China,

but British interests in East Asia were too great to be hazarded by hostile actions against Japan. As a consequence of England's refusal to support the American plan, China lost the game and Japan won.

Another losing game for China was the silver question. When Roosevelt put silver under government control and entirely forbade its export, and when the price of silver went up, China's finances were severely affected. Her protests in the United States were of little avail.

In accordance with instructions received from Chiang Kaishek, Chang Hsüe-liang had given orders for his troops to withdraw, thus demonstrating to the whole world that the Japanese were responsible for what had happened.

Minami declared that the attack was a military necessity, a statement which Shidehara contested. But civil authorities were dethroned and the power lay in the hands of the military. Airplanes were sent out over the city of Chinchow. They were shot at and answered with bombs—in self-defense! The government at Tokyo reassured foreign powers with the statement that "there was no war in Manchuria." But the troops marched on, and in reality the war was in full sway.

Already, at the outbreak, the Nanking government had applied to the League of Nations for help. And the League of Nations, the guardian angel of all wronged peoples, announced from the heights of its temple "that both parties ought to withdraw their troops." In other words, the *Chinese* should withdraw their troops from their own country! The League of Nations also advised China to settle the dispute "by negotiation." Japan as well as the rest of the world laughed outright at the ridiculous part played by the League of Nations. The League had never shown its inability better. In response to a renewed request, Japan replied that she would withdraw her troops as soon as all was in order.

In order not to remain an absolutely inactive spectator of these revolutionary events, which also concerned other great powers, the League of Nations in the summer of 1932 sent the so-called Lytton Commission to Manchuria, the whole problem to be subjected to a thorough investigation on the spot. Lord Lytton is a son of the viceroy of India who in 1877 proclaimed Queen Victoria Empress of India. The result of the investigation was an immense report, signed on the fourth of September, 1932, and which no doubt is a masterpiece of thoroughness and expertness, a monograph of very great value, in which Lord Lytton and his staff declared that they could not look upon the Japanese action in Manchuria as an act of self-defense. The tributary state, Manchukuo, was a creation irreconcilable with international justice and in opposition to the autonomy of the people. Lord Lytton advanced the well-meant and hopeless proposal that Manchuria should be granted autonomy under the supervision of China, and that Japanese interests in the country should be specially looked after. The assembly at Geneva, including Japan, approved the proposal. The sincerity of Japan's attitude soon became evident when Japan withdrew from the League of Nations and prepared for new and very much greater conquests in China proper.

The Chinese could not meet the attack on Manchuria in any other way but by a general boycott of Japanese goods, thus inflicting great losses on the enemy. Chiang Kai-shek took all violence very calmly. He regarded it as a means of helping him to unite China—and he was not mistaken. The non-resistance of the Chinese stimulated the appetite of the Japanese. They had learned at Chinchow that air raids on open cities were a safe sport for the attackers, a sport that a few years later was to develop on a large scale farther south.

The Japanese delegate at Geneva informed the League of Nations that Nippon's subjects in Manchuria could not be left without the protection of troops and that they also were necessary since a quarter of a million Chinese soldiers had been released and had become bandits. These hordes looted villages and farms and were hunted down by the new lords of the country. Even to this day there remain large contingents of them; a couple of years ago they were estimated at 120,000.

As late as 1937, between two and three hundred Japanese soldiers were killed by Chinese bandits and guerilla bands. When troops crossed the Chinese Eastern Railway, the Russians became uneasy, but did nothing.

In spite of subsequent assurances from the Japanese that the bandits were exterminated in Manchuria, it was learned from other sources that the South Manchurian Railway area was full of bandits, and the telegrams told of repeated armed attacks on the trains on the Manchuli-Harbin-Mukden line.

On March 28, 1935, I left Peking for home, traveling via Manchuria and Siberia. There was then an armored carriage immediately behind the baggage car and the tender, and an ordinary military carriage in the middle of the train. When we passed Fu-la-erh-ti beyond Tsitsihar at one o'clock in the afternoon of March 30, we were informed that the most dangerous zone began there. The usual trick of the bandits was to unfasten the rails, but leave them on the sleepers. When a train came along, it was derailed and was immediately attacked by strong bands of robbers. A gentleman on the train had been present on one such occasion, and the train had then run 1200 meters on smooth, hard ground beside the track. The staff on the train had consequently had time to take up their positions, and the bandits had not dared to approach. The district of the Barga Mongols commenced beyond Fu-la-erh-ti. As they tolerated no bandits, it was safe for trains to pass there even at night.

Through all the hard struggles Chiang Kai-shek already had had with rival generals, communists, and rebellious provinces, his character had become hardened and steeled, and, confronted with the ever-increasing tasks, he became increasingly able to cope with them. His attitude was that as long as the communists were plotting and planning and China was not united and disciplined, there was no chance of offering any resistance to the Japanese. First internal order and homogeneity—then resistance to the Japanese attacks.

The Chinese hope that the Manchurian troops would be able to meet and prevent the Japanese invasion in the three northeastern provinces was not at all realized, the invaders already in February, 1933, being able to continue their advance. The province of Jehol was the next step. In the summer of 1930 I had met the military governor, General T'ang Yü-lin, in the city of Jehol. A Belgian Father, the learned and charming père Joseph Mullie, my two countrymen, Dr. Montell and Mr. Söderbom, and I had been invited to a banquet at his *yamen.* In spite of the hospitality shown us by this General T'ang Yü-lin, with guards of honor and bands, and in spite of the freedom he allowed us, we could not help seeing what a misfortune it was for Northern China to have to place its defense in the hands of such an incapable and unscrupulous person at such a fateful time and in such an exposed area.

He was of medium stature, powerfully built and had coarse features. His behavior lacked all culture. The temples of Jehol from the time of the great Manchu Emperors had probably been robbed of most of their treasures of ecclesiastical art by his predecessors, but a few things had not yet been stolen and sold to Japanese agents or curio dealers from Peking. During our stay at Jehol we daily saw loaded lorries which at the command of T'ang Yü-lin, it was said, removed idols and other objects from the temples, to Mukden.

On the eve of the Japanese invasion of Jehol it happened one day in Peking that every single ricksha disappeared. It was said that they had been ordered to Jehol for certain transports of people and goods, as the lorries available had in ample time been requisitioned by the Governor for the removal of his personal belongings and stolen goods to the safety of Tientsin. It is easy to understand that Chiang Kai-shek wished to weed out those of his countrymen in a responsibile position who had no more sense of duty than T'ang Yü-lin!

IX

The Attack on Shanghai, 1932;
Armistice

THE JAPANESE NAVY COULD NOT GET OVER THE ARMY'S victories and easy conquest of the "Three Northeastern Provinces," as Manchuria is called by the Chinese, and the fact that they thus actually had incorporated 35,000,000 people with the Land of the Rising Sun. The admirals also wanted to reap laurels and sought an outlet for their patriotism.

On January 18, 1932, five Japanese priests in Shanghai were attacked by a group of Chinese laborers. This resulted in riots with the police. So the war was let loose in Shanghai and it was necessary for the navy to interfere. It was not hard to find excuses for violence. In reality the plan of campaign was ready and was not influenced by small episodes which could easily be adjusted. The Chinese troops defending Shanghai offered strong resistance. On February 21, the Nineteenth Route Army advanced with such fearlessness that the Japanese had to retire. At a celebration in Shanghai on April 29, 1932, a bomb exploded, wounding and killing several prominent Japanese. Similar episodes inspired the intruders.

In the meantime the anti-Japanese boycott was going on, although already forbidden by the Nanking government. The Chinese were becoming furious. If they could not get at their sworn enemies and torturers in any other way, at least they wanted to injure their trade. The Chinese have shown themselves unsurpassed in the art of exercising boycott, and the Japanese are highly sensitive to that weapon. They also wailed loudly, at the same time declaring that the action in Shanghai had nothing to do with the operations in Manchuria. The Chinese rightly claimed that the two actions were part of the same plan.

Dark, secret powers were active in Tokyo. On the fifteenth of May a group of young officers forced their way into the office of the Prime Minister, Inukai, having first shot all who tried to stop them, and riddled the country's highest statesman with bullets. In Japan political murder is an institution, incomprehensible to Western mentality. A statesman opposing the reigning military party and disapproving the conquest of China is in constant danger of his life. He receives a package by mail and finds a dagger—the first warning; he is sentenced to death like a marked tree. Then comes the bullet. And the remarkable thing is that the murder is not looked upon as a crime but as a virtue, and the murderer not as a criminal but as a patriot. It is not the honest statesman who has shown *le courage de son opinion,* but the murderer who is the national hero. He becomes the object of general admiration; he has shown proof of the greatest and most noble patriotism.

The Chinese population in Manchuria hated the Japanese just as thoroughly as their countrymen in Formosa and Korea, but not by far so intensely as the population of China proper a few years later, whose hatred is apparent in a determination and a resistance that will be a heavy burden for the Japanese, no matter how the war ends. A couple of years after the conquest of the "Three Northeastern Provinces," the Chinese settlers and farmers in Manchuria fully realized that they preferred bandits to the invaders.

In February and March, 1932, Manchukuo was proclaimed an independent state, the last Manchu emperor, Henry Pu Yi, being made its head, with his residence at Hsinking north of Mukden. He was later given the name K'ang Teh and the title Emperor of Manchukuo. How the spirits of K'ang Hsi and Ch'ien Lung must have revolted at the sight of a Manchu descendant acting as a puppet on the throne in the tributary state which once in the glorious past was the native land of their victorious ancestors, but which the men from the islands of Nippon had now torn from the Middle Kingdom, the great conquest of the first Manchu emperor.

After the occupation of Jehol there was a period of relative quiet, and the statesmen of the West hoped that the storm had passed. However, it was only a pause in the great action, and the Japanese were awaiting a suitable opportunity for their next leap. Already in April, 1933, Shanhaikwan was occupied, that important border town, where the Great Wall reaches the coast of the Gulf of Chihli, and a station on the Peking-Mukden railway. The Japanese then held all the important passes in the Great Wall and controlled the northern Chinese provinces at their will, especially Hopei with Peking and Tientsin. On May 30, an armistice was signed at Tangku, and a neutral, demilitarized zone was drawn up south of the Great Wall. It was easy to realize that the agreement was a *pactum turpe* against China.

During 1933 there was a feeling in Peking that the old security no longer prevailed and that a storm was approaching. The Japanese hold in the north became more and more noticeable. On March 16 a state of siege was proclaimed, and those who were out after eleven o'clock in the evening were stopped by gendarmes. From time to time Japanese airplanes flew over the city and dropped circulars glorifying the blessings of Japanese sovereignty. The occupation of the town by Japanese troops was anticipated any moment, and above all it was feared that fugitive Chinese soldiers from the demilitarized area north of Peking would swarm the town and loot it. My friends, Hu Shih, V. K. Ting, and Wong Wen-hao, were called to Chiang Kai-shek for a conference. At the end of May, traffic on the Peking-Kalgan railway was stopped, and Feng Yü-hsiang and Yen Hsi-shan, who were believed to work for the Japanese, intrigued against Chiang Kai-shek. During periods of ostensible quiet and truce the Japanese were preparing their next step and became thoroughly familiar with the huge country they intended to conquer. Their excuse for the successive invasions was that their 70 million inhabitants were far too crowded on their islands and needed elbow room on the continent, as well as minerals, coal and other products, and also raw materials for their industrial development, and further that Northern China together with' Japan would form a barrier warding off the threatening bolshevism.

To this the Chinese replied that they needed all their ground for their 450 million people. To find new areas to cultivate, millions of Chinese had for years migrated to Manchuria, and in that severe climate they had extracted their livelihood from the meager earth, while the Japanese, being less hardy and more delicate, could not become rooted and live in a land such as Manchuria. In fact, there are at present about 35 million Chinese living in the country, in the southeastern parts of which only a few hundred thousand Japanese have settled. And as far as the communist danger was concerned, Chiang Kai-shek had already shown that, without the help of Japan, he was strong enough to keep it at a distance.

No, the reason for the invasion of Manchuria in 1931 was quite a different one. It was the military party in Japan who wanted war and conquest, gain and glory, and above all the clever and far-sighted islanders feared that the Chinese, under the leadership of the forceful Marshal, would awaken and rise to a greatness and power that might become a danger to Japan. The Chinese on their part realized that the first successful Japanese operations might induce them to advance further south, to Shanghai and the Yangtse River, and they were not at all desirous that the lax and backward Manchu dynasty be revived, the last rulers of which—personifying humiliation and inferiority—would then be taking orders direct from Tokyo and constitute an obstacle to China's rise to greatness, strength, and prosperity.

Leftist groups and also other political elements in China from time to time insisted on war with Japan and blamed Chiang Kai-shek for not having declared war on them two or three years before. But the Marshal has always been too prudent to allow himself to be led into folly that infallibly would end in defeat. He knew better than those inflamed with the germs of war what China still lacked, and from his own experience in the Japanese military academies he knew the strength of the Japanese army and its superior equipment. With imperturbable calm he watched the interference and with set jaws he bided his time and left no stone unturned to strengthen and increase the Chinese defense. He knew the past of his people and was aware of the traits and resources that lay hidden in the depths of their souls. He held in his hand an enormous tool of physical strength, and the reserves were inexhaustible. The alpha and omega of his plan, however, was ever to unite this large people and to ignite its pride and willingness to make sacrifices for the good of the country. The terrain, the vastness of the country, the mountains and valleys, all tended to serve him and made the operations of an invading army very difficult. He knew what he was about and that the crisis was not far off.

China was in a state of continuous revolution and could not be crushed by military operations as if it had been a modern, consolidated state. The great country was an *immensa et indigesta moles,* a doughlike mass, which had not yet reached the solidity required for proper resistance. In a war, its focus would always be the place where the leader had his headquarters. The seizure of the capital and other important towns thus means far less in China than it would in a European state. To crush a nation of 450 million humans, in other words a continent rather than a country, is a futile project. And if these hundreds of millions suddenly burst into a flame of long latent patriotism, it is impossible even for a great power of the first order to stop them.

According to Chinese opinion the two great nations must either live side by side or perish together. But the idea that one of them is to live and the other to die is absurd according to the conviction of every thinking Chinese. In conversations with highly educated Chinese friends I have often heard the statement made that Japan cannot live without China and China not without Japan. Consequently, they mean, there must be a formula making possible the continued existence of the two nations. Sun Yat-sen, the founder of the Kuomintang, was of the belief that the two countries must keep together. The Japanese are thus wrong in their statement that the Kuomintang is the root of the Chinese hatred of Japan. The entire Kuomintang party believes in good relations with Japan.

The Chinese say that if Japan does not hesitate to perish together with China, it is China's intention to see to it that her people stop in time and do not accompany Japan on the road to destruction. Japan is under the rule of the war party which pays no attention whatever to international treaties, and which within the country agitates and frightens the people with what they call an imminent danger, which actually does not threaten at all—at any rate not from China. The aim of the gluttonous war agitators is to transform China into a Japanese protectorate, a vassal state, without autonomy or sovereignty—a plaything in the hands of foreign powers, who can divide the old country among them at will.

If Chiang Kai-shek had considered China's situation hopeless in the present war, he would long ago have tried to reach a settlement with the enemy. He desires a *rapprochement* with Japan and he would look upon the fall of Japan as a misfortune also for China. A deplorable fact in this fearful business is that the Japanese do not understand the Chinese mentality, nor do they know Chiang Kai-shek and his lofty, patriotic aims. They look upon the mighty Marshal as a man of the same school as Li Hung-chang and Yuan-Shih-k'ai, and do not reflect that they belonged to the Imperial era while Chiang Kai-shek in all respects is a son of the revolutionary spirit. He knows no compromises. He will fight his battle to an honorable end. He knows that the future of East Asia requires a free and independent China, on equal footing with Japan, and that the two countries must exist on a basis of mutual confidence. But no peace and no restoration are possible until the Japanese have ceased all hostilities and take the first step toward reconciliation.

When Chiang Kai-shek in 1934 had ousted the communists from the central provinces, paid a personal visit to Northern China, accepted Yen Hsi-shan as an ally, and had rid himself of the now powerless Feng Yü-hsiang, discussions took place in the New Year of 1935 between the Marshal and prominent Japanese, which shows that at that time he had no other thought than a peaceful agreement and a settlement of the dissatisfactory situation.

In the middle of January, 1935, the Marshal received the Japanese Ambassador in China, Ariyoshi, and his military attaché, for a conference, the result of which was immediately transmitted to Tokyo by Mr. Suma, the Japanese Consul General at Nanking. Mr. Hirota, the foreign minister, spoke in the Japanese parliament of a rapprochement between China and Japan.

On February first the same year, the Marshal made an announcement to the press, in which he emphasized China's demands for sincerity, justice, and peace. "There is nothing we covet more than peace with Japan," he said. The Chinese Government issued a law, aiming at the preservation of good neighborly relations with Japan. The prime minister, Wang Ching-wei, made a speech in which he urged that friendly relations be established with Japan. Hope dawned above the two old nations, and there was reason to believe that a mutually satisfactory solution was possible along peaceful lines.

Probably on account of internal conditions, Russia wanted peace with Japan and offered her a non-aggression pact. When Japan turned down the offer, Russia had to turn her attention to East Asia, and under the threat of a new Russo-Japanese war, it also became important to Japan to make peace with China. Possible complications with Soviet Russia thus automatically brought China and Japan nearer to each other. Anti-Japanese agitation in China was forbidden. During February, Hirota, the Japanese statesman, worked hard for peace and understanding. At the same time, the legations at Tokyo and Nanking were made embassies, a demonstration of mutual respect. The good relations seemed to become more and more consolidated, and there was reason to believe that East Asia was on its way toward a period of calm and peaceful development.

X

A Visit to the Marshal's Headquarters

IT WAS AT THAT TIME, IN THE MIDDLE OF FEBRUARY, 1935, that I met Chiang Kai-shek the second time. The expedition that I had led to Sinkiang for the Chinese government and whose purpose it was to stake out one highway from Suiyuan through the desert to Urumchi, and another via Suchow and Lanchow to Sian, then reached the capital of China, its task completed.

On the eighth of February our string of motor cars drove into Sian, where everything was still peaceful and where we had to stop a few days in order to settle our affairs and arrange for the return of our servants to Peking. On the twelfth, however, certain signs indicated that the peace and quiet might not last very long. In the afternoon a military airplane left Sian and was supposed to be observing the movements of the communist troops. It was believed that the bulk of these troops were at Mienhsien, a town 270 kilometers southwest of Sian, and along a front of 500 kilometers in the direction of the road we had just traveled from Lanchow. Many troops belonging to the army of the Central Government had that day arrived in Sian from Tungkwan. They filled the streets, and in certain parts it was hardly possible to pass. The communists gathered in southern Shensi and Kansu. They came from Szechwan and their intention was believed to be to join the Reds in Sinkiang. Some Chinese in Sian presumed that the government troops just arrived would be sent to Sinkiang to conquer that province, an assumption that seemed most improbable to us.

We had seen with our own eyes how Sheng Shih-ts'ai, the

Photograph by G. Montell

General T'ang Yü-lin, Governor of Jehol, Who Was
Banished by the Japanese.

Sven Hedin with Marshal Chiang Kai-shek and
Mme. Chiang at Hankow in 1935.

military governor general of Sinkiang, in a war against the invader Ma Chung-yin, "Big Horse," had received help from Soviet Russia in the form of troops, airplanes, and motor cars. It was not very probable that the Central Government was going to throw itself into an adventure of this kind and sacrifice troops in such distant parts, when they might be needed at far closer range. The goal of the Chinese communists was considered to be Lanchow, the capital of Kansu. If they succeeded in capturing that city, they would control the whole province, and it would then be fairly simple to continue to Sinkiang.

It became evident to us in Sian that we had managed to traverse the critical area between Lanchow and Sian in the nick of time. Red propaganda was said to flourish among the government troops, who were not always dependable, and from which deserters on a few occasions had joined the communists.

It was reported that Chiang Kai-shek had been wounded by a would-be assassin a couple of weeks before and that this was not the first attempt at his life; but he was never shaken. The year after our visit to Sian, however, he was to be the victim of a conspiracy there of unusual compass, his life then being at stake.

Great preparations were said to have been made in Sian for extensive military activity in the building line in connection with Chiang Kai-shek's plan to make his headquarters there, in the same way as he had done in Nanyang.

At eleven o'clock in the evening of February 12, the other members of the expedition and I left by train on the new line to Tungkwan. In the night we repeatedly met loaded troop trains going west. We changed trains at Tungkwan in the morning of the thirteenth. On our left we soon saw the great river Hwangho, whose blue waters, now free from ice, did not live up to the name "the Yellow River." It was often hidden by hills, but reappeared in fetching perspectives. Cultivated fields, villages, and farms were visible everywhere—a fertile, well-tilled country with a hard-working, patient population, a couple of years later to be plundered and ravaged by hostile armies and airplanes.

One of our fellow travelers told us that Chiang Kai-shek was still in Nanchang, the capital of Kiangsi. He was fairly certain that the government was prepared to sacrifice all Northern China and the country down to the Yellow River.

At Hsüchow on the Tientsin-Pukow line, we had to wait fully three hours for the train from Peking. Two years later that town was to become world-renowned. At Pukow we took the ferry which in fifteen minutes carried us across the Yangtse to Hsiakwan, a part of Nanking, where we spent the night at the Bridge House hotel.

I had hardly got out of bed in Nanking on the morning of February 15, when Mr. Suma, the Japanese Consul General, was announced. He was a courteous and good-natured man and strongly expressed Tokyo's wish to see me there and that I give some lectures on my latest travels, as I had done in 1908. He also gave me a letter from Marquis Tokugawa, whom I had known in Stockholm, where a few years earlier he had presented the King of Sweden with a precious gift. Suma assured me that I should be accorded a most hearty welcome in the Land of the Rising Sun. I replied that it would be a great pleasure for me some day to revive the bright and happy memories I still cherished of Japan from 1908, but that my first duty now was to report on our expedition to Marshal Chiang Kai-shek and his government, in whose service I had been.

On the following day I told Mr. Wang Ching-wei, the prime minister, of the Japanese invitation. He considered that after my stay at Nanking I certainly might accept the invitation to Tokyo. The Chinese would in no way consider such a visit inappropriate. When I replied that I preferred to postpone my visit to Japan until a later date, he admitted that this would be appreciated by the Chinese. And I did not make a trip to Nippon at that time.

During the eleven days I spent in Nanking, the government overwhelmed me with a hospitality and courtesy very rarely conferred upon foreigners, so the Western diplomats said. Banquets and receptions succeeded each other; upon request I gave a lecture on my trip before the whole Government and was honored on my seventieth anniversary with precious gifts from the ministers and a rare decoration from the President of the Republic. Preliminary reports were compiled by me and the two engineers, Irving C. Yew and C. C. Kung, who had been my companions. Our expedition had been under the supervision of Kuo Meng-yü, the railway minister, but as he was on leave on account of a neurosis, we negotiated mostly with the acting railway minister, Tseng Chung-ming, who spoke excellent French.

In Nanking I also had the pleasure of almost daily meetings with my old friend from the days of the Great War, General H. von Seeckt, now military adviser to Marshal Chiang Kai-shek. Seeckt was a profound admirer of the Marshal's. In reply to one of my questions he said: "Marshal Chiang is an extraordinary man. He is a judicious, wise, and prudent statesman, a skillful but careful strategist, and in addition a splendid and noble personality."

The General assured me that he was very happy in Nanking and could not dream of a more pleasant and profitable co-operation than that existing between him and the Marshal. According to von Seeckt, the Marshal's policy of uniting China was the only one possible, and during his stay in the country the General had strongly supported and encouraged the Marshal's plan for raising the people's standard of living, the abolishment of communism, the New Life Movement, and the economic advance. He also pointed out that the Marshal was perfectly right in saying that a new and powerful China could not be created unless these plans for uniting the country had first been realized. The plan for the definite extermination of the communists in Kiangsi had been outlined by von Seeckt, and in the strong hands of the Marshal it had also been a success.

Unfortunately von Seeckt shortly had to return to Germany on account of failing health, but I met him there several times toward the end of 1936. As late as the beginning of December, 1936, we had a long talk at his home in Berlin, and he then again emphasized his hopes of soon being able to return to China and the great Marshal. But death intervened and his wish was thus never granted. He was succeeded by General von Falkenhausen, who for two years served as adviser to the Marshal. In addition to his prominent military qualities he had the advantage of being able to communicate directly with the Marshal—in the Japanese language.

Upon my arrival at Nanking, the Marshal was staying at Kuling on the Yangtse, and on February 16 I telegraphed to him: "Have just returned with important results from motor-car expedition to Sinkiang—hope to have honor of seeing you before returning Sweden." Two days later I was informed by the staff that the Marshal, who had moved to Hankow, expected me there on the twenty-third of February.

At the last moment the matter became complicated. On the afternoon of the twenty-second, I had given a lecture at the university and had afterward been honored at a banquet. I then received a message that Lin Sen, the President of the Republic, desired to see me at ten o'clock the following morning. I told the person who delivered the message that I could not possibly be there, as that day was already fixed by the Generalissimo for me to be received at Hankow.

The reply was that the President's arrangement could not be altered and that his rank was higher than that of the Generalissimo. I therefore sent a new telegram to the Marshal, explaining the situation, and asking him to fix another day.

The twenty-third of February came, and I had no idea how the muddle would be cleared up. Just as I was departing to the President, an official arrived, stating that the regular airplane from Shanghai had arrived with only three passengers and that they had been requested to wait so that I might catch the plane at the end of the audience. They had said that they could wait until 10:30, but not a minute longer.

I hurried to the palace of President Lin Sen and did not have to wait many minutes. With old-world Chinese dignity, attired in the becoming dress of his homeland, and with a suave smile upon his lips, President Lin Sen entered the room and asked me to take a seat beside him on a sofa, which like the rest of the furniture was European. I sat there on tenterhooks, thinking of the waiting airplane. But the President of China was in no hurry. He made careful inquiries about the motor-car expedition and declared that highways to Sinkiang were absolutely necessary. The preparations we had made must be continued and pursued to the end. Then he began talking of other, more general subjects and was particularly interested in my seventy years, which had not kept me from making such a wearisome trip. He told me that he himself was only sixty-seven years of age.

All this and the usual tea ceremony took time. But I said nothing. I hoped that the three wise men from Shanghai would be so impressed by a person oscillating between the President and the Marshal that they would gladly wait.

But I had hardly left the palace when I learned that the airplane had been cruel enough to leave without me. I returned home philosophizing upon the impossibility of two audiences at the same hour in two different cities. As I was entering our villa, an official from the ministry of communications appeared as if sent from heaven, bringing a message from my friend Dr. Chu Chia-hua, the charming minister of communications, who had telegraphically ordered a special airplane from Shanghai on my account, probably at the request of the Marshal. It could be in Nanking at 12:30 and in Hankow at 4:30.

The spacious American plane did not leave until 2:14, piloted by Captain C. J. Sellers and a mechanic, and with Mr. Yew, whom I had asked to come along, and myself as passengers.

We rise slowly over the Yangtse, in many respects the world's most remarkable river—not least because two hundred million people, one-tenth of the world's population, live and work in its basin. The Yangtse and its shores are now rolled up before us like a map on a table, and beneath us lies this renowned country, irresistibly captivating in its ravishing, exquisite wealth of lovely details, where the water models the outlines of shores and islands and where pools and lakes sparkle like bright eyes. The earth's surface gleams in greenish hues. We see farms and villages connected by roads, along which people wander, carts roll, and coolies deftly balance their baskets on swaying bamboo yokes.

Canals from the river traverse the country in all directions and form reservoirs and lakes. Soon we lose sight of the river on the left, and yet we have more water than land beneath us—the flooded rice fields. But the river has only made a turn southward, while we have taken a short cut and again majestically approach its western bank.

The air is not perfectly clear but transparent enough for us to see the wide road extending from north to south and the small lakes connected with the Yangtse. We have crossed the river, which here forms one single bed and now flashes to the right.

From the west comes what appears to be a yellowish light between the hills. We have again lost sight of the river and there is little water below us. We fly between and above hills and scattered ridges; the landscape becomes more mountainous and at times we see no water at all. Now we soar above a labyrinth of irregular mountains and valleys. White clouds and cloudlets sail around us, and occasionally we dive straight through them, losing sight of the landscape below us. Sometimes we pass so close to a ridge that we imagine we graze its top.

Fields and villages are plentiful in one of the larger valleys. Then the mountains and hills fade away. At 4:38 we once again have the river on our left, its water as yellow as pea soup. There are large expanses of water along the banks. It is sometimes difficult to make out the course of the river itself in this confusion of waters. Finally we follow the left bank upstream, fly over the Yangtse, and descend upon its surface at 4:58 alongside the Bund.

One of the Marshal's adjutants, a colonel, met us at the landing place and welcomed me to Hankow on behalf of his chief. He also informed me that the audience was to take place the following day, on the twenty-fourth, at 10 A.M. He took Mr. Yew and me in his car to the Terminus, whose manager, a Swiss, Gerber by name, was a friend of ours from the Hotel Wagons Lits in Peking, where we had stayed on different occasions. We dined together with a few European correspondents. The party included Mr. Walter Bosshard, the well-known Swiss traveler in Asia, an excellent writer on travels and a splendid photographer, who in 1927-28 had participated in Dr. Emil Trinkler's daring explorations in western Tibet and Eastern Turkistan, and now on behalf of a couple of important German and Swiss papers was following and reporting the developments in China. For me, just having returned from the hazy deserts of Inner Asia and the provinces torn by unrest and civil wars, it was of great value to learn from Mr. Bosshard and his colleagues the news of the moment and the prospects for the future. As we have seen, the relations between Japan and China were just then rather promising; Hirota was working for an amicable settlement and the Nanking government had forbidden the boycott of Japanese goods.

The following morning the adjutant called for us and drove us to the house of the Central Bank, a villa in European style, which was at the disposal of the Marshal during his stay in Hankow.

Mr. Yew remained downstairs while the adjutant showed me up to the first floor, where the simply furnished reception suite of the Marshal and Madame Chiang was located. At a corner window in a middle-sized drawing room there was a small table between two armchairs—that is all I had time to see of the furnishing before Madame Chiang entered, small, dainty, sweet as a young girl, and bade me welcome in a most charming and kindly manner. She wore a dark dress with short sleeves, high in the neck. A gaily colored pattern of bamboo leaves formed a sort of wreath around her neck and also adorned the sleeves.

She seemed refined and at ease, and it was hard to believe that the preceding year and even quite recently this frail little lady had accompanied her husband on his lightning flights to first one and then another provincial capital, where with ruthless courage and boldness and without escort he had descended like a bomb and gone straight into the lions' dens, putting an end to the plots and intrigues of the insurgents and paralyzing them by this sudden and direct contact with Nanking's power, personified by him, the head of the government and commander-in-chief of the army. When he delivered glowing, patriotic speeches, admonishing officers and men in the ranks, reminding them that they all had the same fatherland as he and that they all were equally bound to fight for its future and welfare, she, too, addressed the throngs, who attentively listened to her words. They looked upon this apparently frail woman as an angel from the sky who could not personally rise higher than she already had done, but who beseeched the people to help her when at the

Marshal's side she fought to save China from suffering and ruin.

Thanks to their constant air trips back and forth across the huge country, Chiang Kai-shek and Madame Chiang learned to know China as no other Chinese did. Little by little, China's complicated and intricate geography became vividly clear in their minds, and that was not all; in the various provinces and districts they studied the prevailing local conditions with reference to agriculture, commerce, politics, material resources, and the most urgent needs. While the duties of the statesman, administrator, and warrior fell upon him, his wife concentrated on the humanitarian side and the work of moral restoration.

Madame Chiang Kai-shek, or Soong Mei-ling, is the sister of the wife of Sun Yat-sen and a member of the most remarkable and aristocratic Soong family. She is intelligent, clever, gifted, and stands at the peak of Chinese as well as Occidental culture. The latter she acquired during a few years of study in America, and she thus has a very good idea of what the time demands. In Christianity she found the road to the salvation of her soul, and she also made her husband a true Christian. Chiang Kai-shek himself considered that thanks to his marriage he would far better be able to devote his life to the realization of the revolution and to uniting China than when he stood alone. Now he had his clever and energetic wife at his side, and she would be his best support and strengthen his power of action. No doubt Madame Chiang Kai-shek is the most remarkable woman of our time. She finds ways and means even in the most difficult situations. Through pamphlets, broadcast talks, interviews, and appeals she turns to her own people and to the whole world, asking for help and sympathy for the Chinese in the terrible ordeal that has fallen to their lot. Long after the thunder of war has been silenced she will remain a blessed mother among her people, and her name will be mentioned with reverence and admiration.

At the time when I visited the Marshal and his wife in Hankow they had not yet started out on the narrow and swaying plank that led across the deepest abyss that can be imagined in this world. The task of uniting China was going on, the rival generals had been subdued, the communists were being ousted, and the New Life Movement was spreading over China like a steppe fire. Their main task was to strengthen and unite the whole people in strong resistance to the gigantic Japanese invasion which Chiang Kai-shek no doubt already divined and expected. He counted and made full use of the months, weeks, and days that he still had at his disposal to make the resistance to the invaders as strong and grim as possible.

When Madame Chiang and I were sitting in the armchairs on either side of the small table, a faint noise penetrating from one of the large concession streets of the town, and the sun of early spring peeping in through the window, it seemed almost fantastic to me that this charming, captivating little woman with kind and steady eyes under the straight-cut bang, not only ranked as the first lady of the largest country in the world, but also was the greatest woman in the world, considering her character and sense of responsibility and her ability to cope with superhuman situations. To be an uncrowned queen in a country thirty times the size of Great Britain, and to fill that position with the perfection and power of a born leader, is a feat unheard of, in the past as well as in the present. This lady is in a class by herself. History tells of many admirable women—heroines, rulers, philanthropists, but presents none who was at the same time a heroine, a ruler, and a philanthropist, so great as Madame Chiang.

And now she quietly and gracefully entered into conversation with a stranger, putting a number of intelligent questions, rather in the western way than in the Oriental manner with its courteous but empty and unnecessary phrases.

Madame Chiang first inquired about our expedition, if we were satisfied with the result, where the planned roads would cross the desert, and which towns and oases they would pass. I gave her brief and concise answers. It was evident that she had not only a personal interest in our expedition, but also wished to gain information in advance, for she was to act as the Marshal's interpreter. She waxed eloquent on the subject of the moral and material work of restoration which the Marshal and she had recently started, and expressed the hope that during my visit in China I would have a chance to see and study some of the things that had already been started.

The fragrant tea was served during our conversation, but no cigarettes, for smoking is one of the unnecessary luxuries that were to be abolished in modern China.

A door opened and the Marshal entered, courteously bidding me welcome. This time he was dressed in the aristocratic and tasteful Chinese dress, a long, gray coat and above it the black silk waistcoat with wide sleeves and buttoned up at the neck. He was thin and pale and nothing in his appearance betrayed his enormous power and energy. The Marshal's face was just as earnest as when I had seen him six years earlier, but also characterized by firmness and composure. His chestnut-brown eyes were full of life, and if the eyes are the mirror of the soul, a world of deep thought and great plans could be read in them.

No anxiety or desire to become rid of an intruding visitor as quickly as possible could be noted. On the contrary, he seemed happy and comfortable and appeared to have set aside a couple of morning hours for a talk about Sinkiang and the roads leading there. He took me into a larger room, evidently the dining room, and took down from a shelf V. K. Ting's and Wong Wen-hao's atlas of China, which he opened on the table. He found the map covering Suiyuan, Kansu, and Sinkiang. While we were bent over the sheet, he asked me to show him the course of the two suggested highways through the desert, and wanted my opinion about their prospects and capacity.

With Madame Chiang as interpreter, I gave him a report and pointed out, as I had done in 1933 in the plan approved by the Marshal, the importance of China's having convenient and fully up-to-date lines of communication with its westernmost and largest province, even though it is more sparsely populated than any other. As I had done before, I now emphasized that the geographical location of the province necessitated increased control, as otherwise it might be lost as was Outer Mongolia. Without touching upon the strategical problem, I spoke of the importance for China proper not to allow the trade of Sinkiang to go out of its hands. He nodded assent and from time to time asked more detailed questions. Little did we realize then the importance that these roads—and particularly the one following the old "Silk Road"—would have after only three years! Minister Sun Fo, who visited Stockholm in June, 1938, gave me to understand that the Marshal had not forgotten our conversation.

I told the Marshal that Mr. Irving C. Yew, the road expert and civil engineer, had accompanied me to Hankow, bringing along the detailed map of the course of the two roads that we had made up *en route*. Chiang Kai-shek then gave orders to a servant to ask Mr. Yew to come up. He came, showed the map, and explained it in Chinese.

The Marshal then asked a few quick questions about the political situation in Sinkiang and about the Russian influence in Urumchi. He spoke respectfully of Russia and seemed to harbor no fears about its growing influence in Sinkiang. Having said a few words about the necessity of improving the motor highways to Inner Asia, he went on:

"I have heard that you are an old friend of General von Seeckt. I am very fortunate in having such a capable officer as my adviser and hope that I may keep him a long time. Unfortunately our climate does not agree very well with him, and he is speaking of going home for a while, but if he goes, I hope he will soon return here."

Madame Chiang then said a few words about her affection for Mrs. Dorothée von Seeckt, who had accompanied her husband to the East. The two ladies often met when the Marshal and Madame Chiang had their headquarters in Nanking.

After a conversation lasting about an hour and a half, during which time the Swiss journalist, Mr. Walter Bosshard —who seemed as much at home as a tame cat—had taken several photographs of us, Madame Chiang expressed the Marshal's desire that I remain in Hankow the following day, as he wished to invite me to dinner. Although it certainly was tempting to accept such a kind invitation, I answered that I could not take more of the Marshal's precious time as I had heard that he was on the point of starting a new campaign, to Szechwan this time, but that I hoped to be able to avail myself of his hospitality on my next visit to China, hoping that peace and quiet would then again reign in the country.

With a smile he replied through his brilliant interpreter: "Yes, the next time you return to us you must feel that you come to dear old friends."

I then expressed my thanks and took farewell of this wonderful couple, who now, five years later, fill the whole world with even greater sympathy and admiration.

The adjutant accompanied us to the "Bund," where Captain Sellers awaited us. We boarded the plane and rose over the majestic river. There was a brisk wind, and the machine jerked and tossed with the gusts. Captain Sellers handed me a slip of paper containing the words: "I will fly within sight of the river all the way from here to Nanking." The wind had freshened, and he evidently wanted to be able to land the hydroplane at any point if this should be necessary. On the way out when we cut across the bends of the river, we had usually flown at about 1,000 meters and at a speed of 200 kilometers per hour. Now, on our way home, the maximum height was 400 meters and the average speed 188 kilometers.

The flight down the river to Nanking indeed provided a gorgeous spectacle of enchanting beauty, it being possible to observe the river's freakish bends, tributaries, islands, canals, and shore lakes. One never tired of the picturesque and decorative junks, which made the best of the eastern wind and sailed up the river against the stream, their brown or almost golden square-sails taut in the fresh wind.

I spent the evening with General and Mrs. von Seeckt, telling them of my unforgettable day in the home of the great Marshal.

XI

China and the Border States

WE HAVE SEEN HOW THE RELATIONSHIP BETWEEN JAPAN and China began to take on a peaceful aspect at the beginning of 1935 and how the two parties endeavored to come to an amicable solution of all unsettled problems. It was in the interest of Japan, however, that Northern China should act as a buffer between Manchuria and the rest of China, and at the initiative of Japan a demilitarized zone was established in the north. It was evident that this contained the seeds of new complications. And it was not long before the former Manchurian troops at Tientsin gave vent to their dissatisfaction with the pro-Japanese policy exercised by Hwang Fu, the Chinese political commissar in Northern China. Upon the demilitarized zone being violated by the Chinese and upon one or two Japanese being murdered, the friendly relations were once again disturbed. The autonomist movement in Northern China naturally aroused the suspicions of the Nanking Government against Japan, and all attempts to regulate the differences had been in vain. It was in October, 1935, that the autonomist movement began in Hopei, formerly called Chihli, where Peking and Tientsin are located. It was suppressed by the Nanking Government, which at the same time lodged a protest against the Japanese activities.

The result of these events was a strong and seething anti-Japanese agitation.

The prelude to possibly the greatest drama in the history of China had already commenced. Forces which for centuries had lain latent in the depths of the Chinese soul were aroused when the 450 million people were disturbed in their peace by

Japan's aggressive actions. In a few years the dangers threatening the independence of China and the liberty of its people were to become the force that would lash the heterogeneous throng of humans into unity and under the genial leadership of the Marshal unify it in streams of blood. The conquest of Manchuria was the first step on the road to China's consolidation. The autonomist affair in Northern China was the second.

Japan now demanded that the anti-Japanese agitation cease, that China should not appeal to the European great powers and the United States for assistance, that the government in Nanking acknowledge the independence of the new state of Manchukuo, and that China and Japan jointly make war upon communism. Chiang Kai-shek on his part declared that no infringement upon Chinese sovereignty would be tolerated, that in future co-operation the gains must be mutual, that everything would be done to maintain peace, and that China would deviate from the road of peace only if she were forced to do so.

There were new negotiations. When Hirota, the then Minister of Foreign Affairs in Tokyo, declared in January, 1936, that China had accepted the Japanese demands, this was denied by the Government at Nanking, and in China the agitation against Japan gained renewed vigor.

Chiang Kai-shek emphasized in a speech in July, 1936, that Manchuria could not be surrendered—it was thus absurd to try to persuade China to acknowledge Manchukuo as a state! He was equally emphatic in expressing his hope that it would be possible to solve the pending problems in an amicable manner. The Chinese Government would not tolerate any infringement on the sovereignty and autonomy of China. Negotiations continued between the leading men of the two great countries. Arita was Japanese ambassador in Nanking and later became Minister for Foreign Affairs in Tokyo. The Minister for Foreign Affairs in China was Chang Chun, later ambassador in Tokyo. It was with him that Kawagoe, the then Japanese Ambassador in China, negotiated in August and September, 1936. In these negotiations Japan presented several new demands. It was possible for the parties to agree on some points, and only with reference to the acknowledgment of Manchukuo as a state and of Northern China as "a special area," and of common action against the communists, would the Chinese Government not yield. As regards the last-mentioned question, the Japanese wished to take the lead and consequently at will interfere with the domestic and foreign affairs of China, and this demand could thus not be accepted. On no condition could Chiang Kai-shek sacrifice Northern China, and the Japanese on their part would not give in. Further negotiations were accordingly futile.

The situation was not improved by the fact that the conflict between the Mongol tetrarch Barun Sunit Wang (Teh Wang) and Fu Tso-yi, the governor general of Suiyuan, just then became acute. Ever since its beginning in the spring of 1927, our expedition had been on good terms with the former, and many of us had on different occasions been his guests. When our motor-car expedition visited Kweihwa at the end of October and beginning of November, 1933, we were very well and kindly received by Fu Tso-yi, whose duty it was to protect China's interests against the Mongol demands for liberty. The fact that the Minister of the Interior appeared in person at Kweihwa, where I had a talk with him, also illustrates how serious the Government at Nanking considered this question. At Beli-miao (Peiling-miao) we once more met Barun Sunit Wang, who had summoned the Mongol princes of Inner Mongolia and Ordos to that large monastery, and in his capacity of their spokesman energetically fought for the independence of the Mongols. He worked with vigor and authority for the ancient people of Chinghiz Khan, for their independence, liberty, and honor. We had long talks in his reception yurt and in my tent. In a clever and impressive manner he explained the demands and desires of the Mongols, saying that the arrangement he was about to propose to the Chinese Minister of the Interior would benefit both parties. But whatever agreements and decisions were made at that time, they did not turn out to be enduring. The Japanese had already taken possession of Jehol, and the invaders were threatening Chahar. Within eighteen months the sons of Nippon were to control Peking, Tientsin, and Kalgan, thus severing the ancient bonds between Mongolia and China. At the end of January, 1936, telegrams from Peking announced that Teh Wang had proclaimed Inner Mongolia to be an independent state, and now it only remained that he proclaim himself Emperor of the Mongols.

How well I remember him, that chieftain in his dark-blue, fur-bordered silk gown, authoritative and resolute, with distinguished and aristocratic features, a man of the type that must have made up the legions of the Great Khan, those semi-savage hordes that swept on horseback through Asia seven hundred years ago, conquering the greater part of the continent and part of eastern Europe, and who made all Christendom and the Occident tremble with fear. All that remained of the immense country of his ancestors was but a few shreds under Russian and Chinese rule. The flickering flame around Barun Sunit that had inspired Teh Wang with a vision of a flaming fire of greatness and honor was soon to be extinguished when the Japanese storm irresistibly swept over the mainland of East Asia.

In the past years Chiang Kai-shek had certainly proved himself a master in omnipresence, but even he had his limitations. When the Wang of Barun Sunit gathered the princes around him and, like young Temudjin, raised the nine-cleft flag, the Marshal of China could not possibly fly there in order to throw oil upon the waters. And then, when the storm broke out, he had no alternative, at least for the time being, but to listen from a distance to the peal of the death bells, tolling the death of an old Chinese possession, one of the four borderlands—Manchuria, Mongolia, Turkistan, and Tibet—that had been established and consolidated by the great Manchu emperors as a ring of buffer states around China proper toward northern, western, and southern Asia. The revolutionary year 1911 saw the loss of Tibet; in 1931 and 1932 it was Manchuria's turn, in 1936 Inner Mongolia's, and though when I left Turkistan in the autumn of 1934, that possession was officially still united with China, the thread attaching it to the Middle Kingdom was as frail as a spider's web.

According to the latest news, Sinkiang is now under Soviet influence but is not officially occupied. The hermit crab has lost its protecting shell, the fortifications have fallen; now comes the turn of China proper, and that, too, is nibbled at the edges in the north and east. Chiang Kai-shek now had to bank his defense against a vast invading army upon the precariousness of the terrain, the enormous area of the country, the lengthening lines of communication and fronts of the enemy, and most of all upon the people, this wonderful, tenacious, and patient people, with five thousand years of trials, suffering, and injustice behind it, and ahead of it a life of darkness and misery greater than any their forefathers ever had to endure.

Within three years, however, the day was to come when the dark clouds threatening the Middle Kingdom and its independence were to begin to disperse and when the fortifications around China proper would no longer seem hopelessly lost. We were thus to witness the help given China by Russia and we were to see how the new highway in the tracks of the old Imperial road and its continuation to the nearest Russian railway became a new connecting link between Sinkiang and China proper, how roads were built from Szechwan to eastern Tibet, and how in February, 1939, the loyalty of

Inner Mongolia to China and its highest leader was clearly expressed by a deputation, led by a Hutukhtu, a Lamaistic incarnation of a divinity, who handed Chiang Kai-shek a "pagoda of reverence and victory" cut in jade, symbolizing the loyalty of one million Mongols from the southern part of Inner Mongolia. This Hutukhtu expressed his people's feelings of gratitude to the Central Government for its support of the Mongol tribes in their efforts to resist the invasion. He reminded the Marshal that his people were descendants of Chinghiz Khan. The country he represented, western Suiyuan and the Ninghsia province, is important from a military and political point of view, as it is situated between Kansu, China's northwestern gate, and the eastern part of Inner Mongolia, to which belong parts of Suiyuan, Chahar, and Jehol, now occupied by Japan. The million Mongols represented by the Hutukhtu are under the rule of the two above-mentioned capable governors, General Fu Tso-yi in Suiyuan and Ma Hung-kwei in Ninghsia. It was thus not to take long for the descendants of Chinghiz Khan to realize that their lives on the steppes were happier under the white sun of China than under the red sun of Japan.

We seem to hear the rustle of the wings of time when listening to the tale of the young Mongol noble, Ki Pa-tsan, a direct descendant of Chinghiz Khan, the twenty-first generation, who visited Chiang Kai-shek at Chungking. Until 1934 he had studied at the Mongolian-Tibetan university at Peking, and was then sent to Tokyo by Teh Wang in order to study law. The Japanese intended to use him as an instrument, showered kindness upon him, and then sent him back to Teh Wang. The latter was leader and head of "The Federated Autonomous Government of Inner Mongolia," founded in December, 1937, which, according to the plans of the Japanese military, in time was to become a Mongol Empire. The young Mongol told how Teh Wang, now that it was too late, deeply regretted that he had allowed himself to be led

Teh Wang and His Son.

Photograph by G. Montell

Darkhan Beile, a Mongol Prince.

by the Japanese to betray his country and China, and that his greatest desire was to flee from the Japanese rule in the country of his ancestors. Attempts were made to mollify and demoralize him with opium and women.

There were formerly in Kweihwa, Kalgan, and Tatung domestic trading houses which exported leather, hides, furs, and wool. The Japanese now stop these lucrative enterprises and open brothels, gambling and opium dens in order to undermine the resistance of the people. The result is that the Mongols form their own guerilla bands, one of which numbers no less than 6,000 men.

Perhaps the unwise actions of the Japanese in time will have the same influence on the Mongols as on the Chinese, and arouse and unite them into a renewal of the days of yore when their mounted hordes conquered almost the whole of Asia.

But now it was the old Chinese people that was to be trained for the defense of its native land under the guidance of Chiang Kai-shek. The people seem to be conscious that they now have a leader in whom they may blindly trust, to whose judgment they may unhesitatingly entrust their fate, a man for whom they would gladly sacrifice their lives, for they know that he is sacrificing himself and is doing all in his power to promote their future existence, happiness, and liberty.

The Marshal in turn trusts his people. We know from his own statements how well he realizes what a terrible weapon he has in his people. He was just beginning to unite the masses and educate them in Spartan virtues when the avalanche started rolling down the Yangtse. The great national misfortune came to his assistance and would perhaps save both his work and China. If the loss of Manchuria was the first step toward a united China and the occupation of Northern China the second, then the great invasion of the south was the third, the decisive step toward the unifying of China in the spirit of Chiang Kai-shek. China had good soldiers, the Marshal's elite troops; the 19th Route Army had shown what it was worth at Shanghai. But generally speaking the Chinese army was no match for the Japanese forces, either in training or material. Their lines were soon to be annihilated. But behind the lines, behind the mountains and rivers, there were a hundred million people, a generation of hardened men, with qualities in their souls inherited from past generations, from forefathers who in the dawn of historic times cultivated their ground and fought their battles. For centuries these talents had slumbered; now they were to be aroused by necessity, knocking at the copper portal which so long and so relentlessly had concealed the secrets of the past. Now they were to be aroused from their slumber and come forward.

Rarely has humanity been afforded a more forcible and impressive picture of "a people" than now during the Chinese resistance to the Japanese invasion. It is not a military caste, nor certain exposed border provinces that are struck by the visitation; it is every man and woman, every child and every aged person in this enormous sea of humans, nearly one fourth of all the people in the world, who deep down in their innermost souls feel the effects of this war, see their beloved ones killed, their towns and villages burned, their homes plundered, their fields laid waste. And if they have been saved so far, misfortune will shortly be upon them. Everything precious and dear to them is trampled, annihilated: their family life, their homes, the yellow earth which for centuries has given them and their ancestors bread and where with sweaty brow they have worked behind the plow, the paths they have wandered undisturbed, and the peaceful groves where the wind sighed in the crowns of the trees above the graves of their parents and forefathers.

It was to this great people and to its inexhaustible latent

strength that Chiang Kai-shek turned on the nineteenth of February, 1934, when—in Nanchang, the capital of Kiangsi —he made known the moral code that he himself had written, and which he called The New Life Movement. It was at the same time translated into English by Madame Chiang, and distributed throughout the world in millions of copies. The day that Chiang Kai-shek presented his message to the Chinese people, I was in Turfan in Chinese Turkistan. It would no doubt take a long time for the Marshal's new gospel to penetrate that far into Asia. During the first months of 1935, when I was traveling eastward along the ancient Imperial Road through Kansu and Shensi via Suchow and Kanchow to Liangchow, Lanchow, and Sian, it was only in the last-mentioned towns that I heard of the New Life Movement from evangelical and Catholic missionaries active there, Swedes, Englishmen, and Germans. The Movement was received with ever greater understanding and sympathy by the common people the farther eastward we traveled. Once when I was in the company of a missionary in one of the streets of Lanchow, I started to light a cigarette, but was stopped by my companion and informed that it was not considered consistent with the strict principles of the New Life Movement to smoke in the open, and I naturally refrained from doing so.

XII

The New Life Movement

WALTER HAN-MING CHEN, WRITING IN THE DECEMBER, 1936, issue of the information bulletin published by the Council of International Affairs in Nanking, expressed the opinion that none of the European ideologies nor America's New Deal had so thoroughly and radically restored and rejuvenated a people as had Chiang Kai-shek's New Life Movement. It was spreading like a fire on the steppe. People believed in it because they believed in its creator and because they understood that the Marshal would never have created a doctrine that did not aim at the welfare of the people. It appealed to the masses that the new road to salvation went via the old classics, that the Chinese conception of morals was made a protection against corruption and disgrace, and that a purely co-operative life, based on voluntaryism, would give the people redress and revival.

Chiang's doctrine demands courtesy, consideration, obligingness, and respect for the rights of others. He demands honor and honesty and strives toward a social regeneration by molding the character. He uses no violent and harsh means to force the new doctrine on his people. His own almost ascetic life makes him an example for all. Everyone has his liberty. Without persuasion and commands all around him follow his example. The officers influence the troops, the farmers, the tradesmen, the well-to-do classes, the coolies, the man in the street—all join the Movement; from the center, where the stone fell into the water, the concentric rings spread farther and farther abroad until they reach the shore of the human ocean. From his very youth this up-to-date master had loathed the corruption of the Manchu dynasty, the rival generals, communism, and the bandits. His campaigns had taught him that military victories were not enough to uproot the communistic weeds. Other means were needed—moral education—the lessons embodied in his New Life Movement. It was not enough to liberate the people from injustice and oppression; it must also learn its duties not only toward home and family but also to its country and its God.

The national conscience and social co-operation should, according to Chiang, rest upon the four ancient Chinese virtues, *li*—courtesy, *i*—obligingness to everybody, *lien*—honesty and respect for the rights of others, and *chih*—magnanimity and honor. These four virtues had in ancient times made China a mighty nation, and now they were to serve as a basis for the New Life Movement, a doctrine unknown in the West.

Owing to the materialism of today and a steadily growing contact with the poisoned "civilization" of the West, China had lost touch with the virtues that in ancient times were the foundation of her moral strength. I need only go to my own recollections to find proof of this statement. The people I learned to know in Chinese provinces in 1890 and 1894 up to 1897 were certainly entirely different from and better than those I met in 1927-1935. Forty or fifty years ago one felt perfectly safe wherever one went. Straightforward, decent, and kindly people were encountered everywhere, and most of them could be relied upon to be honest—except a rogue here and there, as in all other countries. Forty years later the feeling of security had disappeared. The peasants, the great majority of the people, had not changed noticeably in character and loyalty, but bad elements could be found—spoiled by influence from without. It is against this depravation that the four revived virtues are to fight. They must elicit the good old qualities, teach the Chinese not to collect riches for themselves, but to share with those in need; induce an already corrupt class of public officials to impose just sentences, and to assist those who have no possibility of winning cases subject to dispute. All dishonesty in public life shall be made impossible.

The effect of Chiang's first address surpassed his most optimistic expectations. His message of a cleaner life, courtesy, punctuality, proper behavior in public life, honesty in government offices, good manners at gatherings, in schools, at docks and railway stations, and in the army, the extermination of theft, "squeeze" and tips, and of luxuries—all this was understood by the people, and the new commandments were obeyed. The weeds are to be pulled up by the roots and replaced with efficient and productive work to the good of the individual, the community, and the entire country.

Certain critics, although approving the ennobling effects of the four virtues, claimed that they were not sufficient to put the national economy and defense on a sound footing. But these pessimists forgot that once the people had learned to live according to the principles of the four virtues, the whole country would blossom in material prosperity and would be able to strengthen its defense.

Only ten or fifteen years ago corruption prevailed in many places in China to such an extent that we can hardly imagine it. The people were living in ignorance and the illiterates constituted an amazing majority. Organized hygiene was entirely lacking in small cities and in the country; epidemics and plagues raged unchecked; everything was left to the winds and nobody took care of the public good. The wealthy fleeced the people and led a dissolute life; judges were for sale; officials could be bought and racked peasants and townspeople; the governor and other high officials became millionaires; *likin* or domestic tariffs were imposed at will on all kinds of goods and had to be paid at all province frontiers, and also at the district frontiers, which paralyzed trade. Sons

and daughters of well-to-do families led a libidinous life.
Bandits harried everywhere. Everyone traveling in China at
that time must have observed the hopeless state of affairs,
which defies the most vivid imagination. Chin Shu-jen, the
governor general of Sinkiang, monopolized for his own account certain important wares, thus incurring the wrath of
both Chinese and Mohammedan tradesmen. In towns and
communities along the Imperial Road the people were racked
by twenty or thirty different taxes until they lost their land,
their property, and their daughters, thus being reduced to
the deepest misery. Among Europeans who had lived a long
time in China it was common belief that anything could be
had for money, concessions, antiquities, museum objects; indeed the most elementary feeling of shame could be nullified
by the jingle of silver and gold.

All this corruption and depravity were to be swept away,
the morals of the people and their standard of living was
to be raised, all mercenary and corrupt officers to be ousted.
That was the reason why Chiang Kai-shek started the reformation and the renaissance which has become known under
the name of the New Life Movement. He certainly did not
issue an edict to all China. He began very modestly in Nanchang, in the province of Kiangsi, where he had his headquarters, as if he wanted to feel his way and study the effect
of the message in his own city. New buildings were erected
on the sites of ruins and dilapidated houses; a new city grew
up; straight, clean streets were drawn; a number of schools
were opened; highways were constructed in various directions; and parks were laid out for the pleasure of the people.
The work of restoration and cleaning out thus effected in
Nanchang met with general approval and encouraged similar
measures in other towns and communities farther and farther
away from the original source, the Central Bureau, which
subsequently was moved to Nanking.

Bribery and corruption are disappearing. Gambling is prohibited, even the very poor are treated justly in court; a judge taking bribes is a dead man. The use of opium began to diminish after the introduction of the New Life Movement. The Chinese government had several times tried to fend off this vice, which for more than a hundred years has devastated the health of millions of Chinese and has made human wrecks of many of them. Once they heaved into the sea the stored opium of the British merchants. Then the Opium War broke out in 1840, which through the peace of Nanking opened China to the deadly poison and led to the occupation of Hong Kong. Epidemics and floods, the cases of local famine recurring yearly, and all the other misfortunes of China are, taken altogether, small compared with the constant ruin of men, women, and children through the opium vice. Unless my memory fails me, Lord Morley of Blackburn, in his capacity of Secretary of State for India, advocated the prohibition of the opium trade, which was one of India's best sources of revenue. However, the Chinese had learned to grow opium themselves. The law against cultivating poppies was simply disregarded, and anyone who has traveled in Suiyuan and Kansu knows what the smuggling opium caravans look like. A man of Chiang Kai-shek's capacity was needed to put a definite stop to the poppy growing. The Japanese cannot rejoice at seeing a vice extirpated which for more than one hundred years has undermined and enfeebled the Chinese people. Quite recently telegrams from China announced that Chiang Kai-shek had imposed penalty of death for growing poppies. The phrase coined by the author Edgar Snow, "In Russia religion is the opium of the people; in China opium is their religion" will, thanks to Chiang's intervention, no longer hold good.

"Enlightened" people, the intellectuals in the big cities, and "the upper ten," who light-heartedly enjoyed all the comforts of modern life, did not infrequently look upon "The New Life Movement" with a supercilious smile and found the Marshal's plan far too simple and childish. In the West, the same shallow and hollow criticism is also heard of "Moral Rearmament" and the Oxford Group Movement. "We knew all that before, it is too simple to be effective," is a widespread opinion. People forget that the great truths are often simple and that it is not enough to know; one must also practice what one knows to be right and true. It is said that Chiang Kai-shek and his wife very warmly embraced the message and principles of the Oxford Group Movement, and it is not improbable that this gave them the impulse for the New Life Movement, even though their propaganda for the improvement of morals and living naturally have been adapted to suit Chinese conditions. It is a sure thing, however, that the two movements in the east and in the west cannot but benefit humanity. If one has had an opportunity of studying at close range the destruction caused by opium in China, one must certainly come to the conclusion that even if the New Life Movement produces no other results but the abolishment of opium smoking, this means to China an added physical power and moral strength of the same value as a strong national defense.

In the beginning of his Chinese text about the New Life Movement Chiang Kai-shek says:

"A new national consciousness and mass psychology have to be created and developed, and with that intention what is called 'The New Life Movement' has been launched.

"Peoples of the outer world may not at first be able to understand the necessity for such a movement, but they will do so if they realize that they have grown up with national consciousness fully developed around and about them, whereas the Chinese people have been deliberately, forcibly bereft of it, and, therefore, know nothing of those sentiments and impulses that so quickly move the Occidental peoples when matters concerning their country come forward for consideration or action. It is to correct the evil consequences arising from this serious state of affairs that action is now being taken along a psychological and educational line.

"To correct, or to revolutionize, an age-old habit is a difficult thing, but, by using the simplest, and, therefore, the most efficient means, it is hoped that, in time, the outlook of the people will be entirely changed and they will be able with spirit and competency to meet the requirements of the new time and the new life. The aim of the New Life Movement is, therefore, the social regeneration of China.

"It is to this end that their thoughts are now being directed to the ancient high virtues of the nation for guidance, namely, etiquette, justice, integrity, and conscientiousness, expressed in *li, i, lien* and *chih.* These four virtues were highly respected by the Chinese people in the past, and they are vitally necessary now if the rejuvenation of the nation is to be effected.

"China has had a cultural history of some five thousand years with fine standards to guide the daily life of the people, and yet, owing to oppression and disregard, they have disappeared, and rudeness and vulgarity have supervened.

"China, with a territory of 1,896,500 square smiles, possesses abundant natural resources, and the only reason to account for the present degeneration and lack of development is that public virtues have been neglected.

"We have a population of over four hundred millions, yet, because we have neglected to cultivate our virtues, social disorder reigns and most of the people lead a life far below that which they should enjoy.

"We have, therefore, to learn that, to correct personal and national failings, we must fall back upon the influence of the old teachings. Rudeness and vulgar manners can be corrected by cultural and artistic training, and degeneration can be overcome by developing good personal character. It is difficult, however, to succeed merely through the ordinary processes of education and governance. If we are determined to reform we must start with the most fundamental question

—we must reform our habits first. This, therefore, is why the New Life Movement is regarded as the key to the salvation of our nation."

The Marshal then goes on to explain what he means by the New Life Movement. To begin with it must seek the protection of the Government to a certain extent, both as regards public education and economy. But when an old system vanishes and a new one appears in a revolutionary manner, it needs the understanding and support of the masses. A social movement goes hand in hand with politics and education. It is not dependent upon them; it may rather be said to lead the way.

Our people are poor in spirit, he says; they do not discriminate between good and evil, between private and public, between the fundamental and the selfish. The result is a chaotic disorder in all moral conceptions and a hopeless inability to meet domestic misfortunes or foreign invasions with resourcefulness. We must efface the past and begin a new life.

He then analyzes the meaning of the four virtues and shows how they are dependent upon each other. Finally he says that the aim of the New Life Movement is to make an irrational life into a rational one, a task that can be accomplished if we observe the four virtues in our daily life. He concludes with the words:

"The life of our people will be more refined when we have more artistic training; we will be richer when we are more productive; and we will be much safer when we are more patriotic, better-trained and equipped to defend ourselves. This rational life is founded on *li, i, lien,* and *chih.* The four virtues, in turn, may be applied to food, clothing, shelter, and action. If we achieve this, we will have revolutionized the daily life of our people, and we will have laid the solid foundation for our nation."

To us Swedes, used to quite different methods, the part played by Chiang Kai-shek seems almost fantastic in its boldness and wide perspective. With a magic wand, the like of which has never been seen in the world, he awakens a people that for ages has slept an enchanted, paralyzing sleep. Supported by the violent, revolutionizing events of the times, he makes the hundreds of millions wide awake; they follow him on the road to the new life; he is a son of China's yellow earth and liberates the greatest peasant stock in the world from unnecessarily heavy taxes and thus sweeps the peasants with him on his triumphal march and in the guerilla war against the invaders. He is a Christian and also shows his people the way to the throne of the Eternal God.

He appeals to this great people in words, in writing, and in action. Again and again he reminds them of the fundamental virtues that made the ancient Chinese a famous and honest people. He preaches loyalty, parental respect, kindness, faithfulness, integrity, peacefulness, harmony. He points out the inexhaustible resources, the history, and the richness and variety in civilization and art possessed by this people, and impresses upon them that if they turn their talents to account, they cannot be obliterated by any foreign nation. The activities of the new life must be "skillful, productive, soldierly"—those are the three watchwords.

In April, 1935, he introduced the "voluntary labor service," which appealed to the army, the party organizations, the schools, the women, and many other groups. Everything was to be utilized, the moral and physical strength as well as the material. With such a huge mass of people, that meant an enormous accession of strength and an inspiration toward unity. In his addresses he appeals to the sense of duty in the people and also turns to the women, who are to give the country sons and daughters, and he never omits to hold up before them his mother and his wife.

On October 10, 1935, the anniversary of the revolution, he instituted the "Politico-Economical Restoration Movement." Its aim is to improve the standard of living of the people and practically and effectively to utilize all the natural resources of the country. It also embodies the abolition of unemployment by creating new fields of labor. In connection therewith the lines of communication were to be improved and extended, a subject on which Sun Yat-sen already had written a book, though he certainly was no authority on the matter, which, however, Chiang Kai-shek was, thanks to his great personal experience. The two movements, the New Life Movement and the Politico-Economical Restoration Movement, would, according to the firm belief of their founder, raise China to a great power of the first order.

Chiang Kai-shek was faced with the task of raising his people out of a coma lasting a hundred years, under a terrible threat from without, which already had cost him several precious provinces, and of crushing the generals fighting each other for their own gain, the bands of robbers, and the communists. In a whirlpool of civil wars and foreign invasion he was to transform a slumbering people into alert and altruistic workers. And when he thought he had the goal in sight, the great war broke out, which was to demolish the peaceful restoration work and change the country into a battlefield where thousands of men were to be slaughtered and the fruits of labor destroyed. As a result of the events, and by necessity, he became dictator, although he himself does not wish to be looked upon as one.

Chiang Kai-shek's soldierly training and his military genius, which already in his youth had rendered him the highest rank in the army, made it perfectly natural for him to devote great attention to the development and perfection of the military force. During and after his work of unifying China, the troops of the former rival generals were dispersed. Many of these forces joined his. Already before the Japanese war, China had an organized army consisting of two hundred divisions, that is, two million men. The organization and training of the troops had been entrusted to German officers, veterans from the World War, in possession of the most excellent military experience in the world. No one could better than the Marshal understand the value of the air forces in a war, and he procured airplanes and experts from Italy and the United States. China thus had a respectable defense at the outbreak of the Japanese war, which the Japanese themselves have admitted.

On New Year's day, 1936, Chiang made a public speech, in which he pointed out China's precarious situation and emphasized that the future lay in the hands of the people themselves. Each and every individual was personally responsible for the common welfare of the nation. If every citizen did his duty, he believed that China could be pulled out of the mire within a year. A wise man once said, "A nation that knows no enemy and no outside danger may easily fall, and times of distress are clues to wisdom; constant dangers inspire a national awakening." Chiang himself is proud of his great people and asks what country in the world can hurt them, if only they are rejuvenated and improved. He always comes back to the four virtues as the road to salvation. If we stand at the height of moral perfection, he says, no one will dare attack us. No more of the old misery, laziness, indecency, dissipation—and we shall be able to vie with any other nation!

He summarizes the fundamentals of the country's domestic economy in eight points: the rational operation of agriculture; the exploitation of the earth; mining; compulsory industrial service teaching the people to gather riches by work of their own, this also comprising road building, draining, irrigation, and dam construction; industry; the control of consumption in connection with increased production; the facilitation of transports; and the organization of the country's finances.

For the realization of the New Life Movement the following twenty-one points were published: Punctuality, struggle against illiteracy, work and acquirement of knowledge, encouragement of sports and games, good all-round education, promotion of hygiene, increased production, encouragement of the defense, collection of refuse (struggle against prodigality), census, encouragement of voluntary help to the police, irrigation, building and upkeep of roads, protection of nature and tree-growing, encouragement of the use of domestic wares, insurance and savings-bank systems, establishment of sick-relief funds and invalid insurance, struggle against famine and disasters, fight against opium and gambling, assistance to the air force and air-raid protection, and finally support to the natural sciences.

All this work toward the regeneration of China was destroyed when the Japanese came and violently stirred the busy ant-hill. Everything then had to be reorganized—the industry, workshops, lines of communication—all was moved westward to the interior of the country. The New Life Movement drowned in a gigantic struggle that could be called the "Save Your Life Movement." The problem was no longer to improve one's living conditions and raise one's standard of living; it became necessary to save one's life for what it was worth, by enormous privations and hardships, to save the native country, sacked by strangers. If the sedulous, patient, and tenacious people could but endure the years to come, the New Life Movement would in time continue to grow, but then out of earth so drenched in blood and tears—and thus so fertile— that it would blossom into a never-dreamed-of perfection. And if old Mencius was correct in saying that a state which is not continually threatened by new enemies from without cannot endure, the Chinese should live on for thousands of years.

XIII

The Fiftieth Anniversary

IN A BOOK ON MARSHAL CHIANG KAI-SHEK, HIS LIFE, HIS work, and his character, it would be a mistake to omit "Some Reflections on My Fiftieth Birthday," which he wrote on the twenty-ninth of October, 1936.

It is always difficult, indeed, almost impossible, for a Westerner to probe a Chinese, to sound the depths of his soul, to make out his thoughts, and form an opinion of his character, and on the whole to distinguish between what may be simulation and truth in his utterances and actions. It has been said that the Chinese are the best diplomats in the world because they do not betray by their expression, by a glint in the eye or a nervous movement, what they are thinking; even in the most difficult situations they are in absolute control of their bodies and their facial expressions, and can seemingly say in dead earnest things that have very little to do with the truth. The same servants may for years have accompanied you on long, dangerous expeditions to innermost Asia, loyally and patiently sharing your hardships, without your ever having had any reason to complain about their conduct, but you do not know them nor what they think of you and your activities.

Chiang Kai-shek is a Chinese and in certain respects he is puzzling. But the world knows the essentials about him. His whole life and career, his patriotism and self-sacrifice, his speeches, writings, and proclamations, his courage and dauntlessness—in one word, his actions, clearly disclose his spirit and the stuff of which he is made.

In the above-mentioned small autobiography he has written

down his thoughts concerning the first fifty years of his life. On but a few pages it gives us a clearer conception of his character than volumes written by outside observers. He gives his mother all the honor for his success and shows that her memory has been his guiding star through life. His first concern is his country and its welfare. Personally he is very modest. His "Reflections," or rather memoirs, leave the reader with the impression that they are out of all proportion to his real genius. He says:

"Having devoted a good portion of my life to the cause of the Revolution, but before accomplishing one-hundredth part of the work I wish to do for my country, I find myself at the age of fifty. Educated and maintained by the State for more than thirty years, I have since manhood enrolled myself in the Army and dedicated myself to the cause of the National Revolution.

"During all these years, what I ate, what I wore, and what other things I needed daily, were derived from the State, in other words, from the sweat and toil of the people. My debt to the country is great indeed.

"The hearty and inspiring spirit with which my compatriots, both at home and abroad, men and women, young and old, have contributed toward the purchase of the airplanes as a birthday present for the Government made me deeply conscious of the profound trust and great hopes that are reposed in me. Unworthy as I am, it awes me even more to think that I should be the recipient of such an honor which I know not how to repay.

"I recollect now the counsel of my teachers, the assistance of my comrades, and the heroism and sacrifice of my colleagues. They are as vivid as if they were before my eyes, and I reflect upon them with extremely mixed feelings.

"Among such deep impressions is the indelible memory of my mother who endured so much in educating and bringing up the fatherless boy. Now, while the trees by her grave have grown tall and thick, I cannot but realize how little I have accomplished and how I have failed to live up to the hopes that she had placed in me.

"The difficulties confronting the Party and the State are numerous, the misery of the people is still great, and the road to recovery is long. It makes me ashamed to think that I have allowed time to slip by without accomplishing my duty.

"While my mind is full of these unrestful thoughts, I choose at this time to make public the hardships and difficulties which my mother endured in bringing up her family, so that the world may better realize and appreciate the position of the helpless and the poor. I also hope that this may serve in some measure as an incentive for us to practice self-restraint and self-training, and to remind us of the great task of national salvation.

"I was born in a little village where my grandfather and my father maintained a farm and pursued their studies. Through diligence and frugality they had acquired a little wealth. My father died when I was nine years old. After that, my family had to undergo all sorts of difficulties and tribulations.

"It will be remembered that the then Manchu regime was in its most corrupt state. The degenerated gentry and corrupt officials had made it a habit to abuse and maltreat the people.

"My family, solitary and without influence, became at once the target of such insults and maltreatment. From time to time usurious taxes and unjust public service were forced upon us, and once we were publicly insulted before the court. To our regret and sorrow none of our relatives and kinsmen was stirred from his apathy.

"Indeed the miserable condition of my family at that time is beyond description. It was entirely due to my mother and her kindness and perseverance that the family was saved from utter ruin. With an iron determination she boldly undertook to save the family from its threatened fate and, with the same determination, she resolutely undertook to bring up the children in the proper manner.

"Her task was neither light nor enviable, for she had to look after everything herself. As a boy she loved me very dearly, but her love was more than the love of an average mother; she was a very strict disciplinarian. She never failed to hold me to strict account whenever I was unusually mischievous.

"Upon returning home she would ask me where I had been and what I had been doing, and when I got back from school she would question me on the lesson of the day. She taught me how to conduct and behave myself. She would make me do manual labor in order to train me physically. In a word, all her time and energy were devoted to my well-being.

"Having reached manhood, I determined to go abroad for a military education. At first many of our kinsmen and neighbors were quite surprised at, and some of them were hostile to, my decision. They certainly would have prevented me from carrying out my wish had it not been for my mother's resolute will and her efforts to supply me with the necessary funds. Later, when the general principle of our National Revolution became more deeply rooted in my mind, I decided to dedicate myself to the Party and the nation—a step which involved much difficulty and subsequent dangers. At that time, all my relations forbore from communicating with me. The only one who still believed in whatever I had undertaken to do, and did everything to help me, spiritually and materially, was my mother.

"At the time of the establishment of the Republic, I found myself at the age of twenty-five. By then I had been able to improve our home for my mother and to gratify her wishes a little. Unfortunately, the establishment of the republican form of government was not followed by the establishment of perpetual peace.

"Already internecine conflicts among warring militarists had occurred all over the land. In such circumstances, the application of Party principles was absolutely impossible, and for a time the cause of the Revolution seemed hopelessly lost. At this critical time, my mother again came to me with valuable advice. For a period of seventeen years—that is, from the time I lost my father at the age of nine till I was twenty-five years old—my mother had never spent a day free of domestic difficulties. Though often anxious about my fugitive life during that period, she remained persistently calm and self-confident and regarded the reconstruction of our home as her only responsibility.

"Once she said to me: 'I had become such a poor widow since your father's death, and sometimes the conditions were so unbearable that I really did not know how to preserve ourselves. My sole conviction was that a fatherless child like you must be carefully brought up before we could expect any success in this world. Our house must be carried on by an heir who could keep untarnished the good reputation of our family.' At another time she said: 'Such things as misfortunes, dangers, and human sufferings are of daily occurrence in every corner of the world, but in the face of these we must practice self-reliance and self-betterment in order to find a way out. Hence, the greater our domestic difficulties, the more important it is to uphold our family traditions; the worse our domestic disaster, the stronger we have to make our will. For a poor widow and a poor orphan, or anyone who is trying to support himself in this cruel world, there is nothing better than the strict observance of self-reliance and self-betterment.'

"At the first disappointment I encountered in the early days of the Revolution, my mother again came to my aid. She taught me how to make the principle of filial piety applicable to the whole nation. She told me to recall to mind how we overcame our home difficulties in the earlier days, and wished me to apply the principle in a broader sense—in a national sense—so that injustice and oppression might forever disappear from human history. She impressed upon my mind that to be merely a dutiful son does not fulfill all of the exacting conditions of the principle of filial piety; the principle demands also an unflinching devotion to the cause of the nation.

"All these good counsels were given by my mother with the purpose of guiding my life in this world. Although it has always been my ardent desire to do everything in accordance with my late mother's wishes, yet so far I have not been able to live up to her great expectations. Whenever I reflect on the conditions in which we two—a widowed mother and a fatherless son—lived in the shadow of cold realities, I cannot but pray for the day when I should be able to fulfill my mother's wishes in a worthy manner.

"Such is the great debt I owe to my country, and such is the great debt I owe to my mother. In some of my leisure moments, I have reflected upon my experiences during the past fifty years. I cannot but confess that the first twenty-five years of my life were beset with great difficulties. I suffered the loss of my father, I was handicapped by the want of means, and again I was handicapped by my limited knowledge in the struggle for a better life.

"The latter twenty-five years were equally difficult, for upon my shoulders has fallen the great task of national salvation. All these long years of hard struggle appear to me as if they had happened yesterday. Fellow countrymen and dear comrades, it all depends upon one's own endeavor to bring back one's old glories, and, as the reflection on things gone by inevitably throws light upon the things to come, I take this opportunity to dwell a little further on the principles whereby a nation may establish itself.

"There is a proverb which says: 'From the family is built a nation.' The cause by which a family rises or falls can be equally applied to a nation. Just as with a family, a nation may be powerful at one time and weak at another. Whether a nation perishes or flourishes depends upon the endeavor and determination of its people. The past one hundred years have witnessed a number of nations establishing themselves after years of hard struggle, and these nations have set us a noble example to follow. No crops can be harvested without a due share of labor, and no labor is ever denied its due reward. If we can keep on struggling with singleness of purpose, we are sure ultimately to triumph over our difficulties.

"At this point I would like to draw an analogy from my own experience. During my childhood, as I have just related, my family was in a most difficult situation, but, difficult as our situation was, and oppressed as we were by those in power, yet my mother went on boldly with her noble task of safeguarding the sanctity of her home and the supreme duty of bringing up her children. From this we may learn a profitable lesson. In our march toward national salvation, there is no difficulty too great for us to overcome if we have the courage and resolution, but I must point out that our success depends entirely upon our own efforts.

"Ever since the death of Dr. Sun Yat-sen in 1925, China has encountered numerous disasters both within and without. The country was first overrun by communists, who almost succeeded in overthrowing the Republic and the Kuomintang. Following came a series of foreign aggressions which resulted in the loss of the Three Northeastern Provinces. In the midst of these disasters and sufferings, which covered a period of ten years, and which endangered the very life of the nation, the people began to lose confidence in their leaders and, in turn, to lose confidence in themselves. The situation undoubtedly was critical, and the crisis confronting the nation was unprecedented in our history, but in spite of this I still cherish great hope; I find despair neither in the defeat of international justice nor in our own apparent impotence.

"My hope lies in the revival of our old national traits of self-reliance, self-improvement, temperance, and self-consciousness.

"Should each and every one of us devote himself to the cause of national salvation with the same persistence and endurance as my mother showed in raising her family, it will not be long before China takes her place once more among the great powers of the world. Should the women of the nation do their best to have their homes well-managed and their children properly brought up, I am sure their effort will contribute immensely toward the upbuilding of the nation.

"Our late leader, Dr. Sun Yat-sen, once said that the existence of China as a nation depends entirely on following the line of her destiny. We should not imitate the superficialities of the West, nor plagiarize the Doctrine of Might of the imperialistic nations. The eight great virtues—loyalty, filial piety, kindness, love, faithfulness, righteousness, peace, and justice—are in accordance with the true spirit and time-honored characteristics of the Chinese race. Filial piety is particularly emphasized in the testaments of our late leader. We should, therefore, observe filial piety as one of our fundamental principles in rebuilding the nation.

"In practicing the virtue of filial piety, we must strictly observe two fundamental codes of conduct. The one is to do honor to our parents, and the other to conduct ourselves without disgrace. In order to do honor to our parents we must endeavor to improve ourselves and to follow the teachings of our forefathers. To conduct ourselves without disgrace, we must be fair and honest in our daily dealings, in order not to bring humiliation upon our parents. The Chinese nation has had a very long history and a glorious civilization. No nation can ruin us unless we first ruin ourselves. If each one of us recognizes his own weakness and endeavors to correct himself accordingly, he will have no difficulty in removing any obstacle he may encounter in life, and, if we can do this collectively, we can remove all obstacles confronting the nation. . . ."

XIV

Dramatic Days at Sian

IN CHIANG KAI-SHEK'S FANTASTIC CAREER WE HAVE NOW reached the dramatic episode at Sian, an occurrence that for a few weeks kept China and the rest of the world in intolerable tension, a dazzling one-act play in which two of the actors played their parts with such fortitude, personal courage, patriotism, and self-sacrifice, that a parallel can but rarely be found in the history of China. The Sian incident is a legend full of loyalty and romance at the same time that it embraces an intermezzo with the destiny of a great people at stake, while the life of its leader was in the gravest danger. I willingly admit that in those days I read the cables from China with greater interest than ever, and that I was most apprehensive about the life of the Marshal. Surrounded as he was by enemies, the remains of the communist troops and officers which he had chased through China, it seemed as if nothing less than a miracle could rescue him from that hornet's nest.

We remember that in 1929 Chang Hsüeh-liang, the "Young Marshal," hoisted the blue-and-white flag of the Kuomintang in Manchuria. In 1930, when Yen Hsi-shan and Feng Yü-hsiang conspired against Chiang Kai-shek, Chang Hsüeh-lang had attacked them from the rear and helped Chiang to victory. Chiang then appointed him his right-hand man, second in command of the army. When Chang Hsüeh-liang in 1931 lost Manchuria without lifting a finger in its defense, Chiang Kai-shek was the only one who took his part and protected him. In 1933 Chang Hsüeh-liang lost Northern China and found that he then needed a recreation trip to

Europe, where he was honored everywhere. After his return he was made first in command of the anticommunist armies in three provinces with headquarters at Hankow. He advised Chiang to introduce fascism but to no avail. At the unveiling of Chiang's statue in Hankow he made a speech in which he declared Chiang to be the greatest man in China and Sun Yat-sen's successor. He said that all Chinese must follow the Marshal. When early in 1935 the communists had withdrawn to northern Shensi and Kansu, where they had their headquarters and lived according to Soviet rule, Chang Hsüeh-liang and his 130,000 men, the Tungpei Army, were removed from Manchuria to southern Shensi and ordered to extirpate the Reds. Instead of obeying orders, he fraternized with the communist generals and finally went over to their side. When Chiang Kai-shek appointed Chiang T'ing-wen first in command against the communists, Chang Hsüeh-liang regarded this as lack of confidence in him and he lent a willing ear to his officers who advised him to utilize the anti-Japanese mood in China and make common cause with the communists. They wanted to put a stop to the civil wars and fight Japan. They mistrusted Chiang Kai-shek and did not realize that he also regarded the Japanese as his worst enemies, although he did not wish to go to war against them until he had made all necessary preparations.

Yang Hu-ch'eng, a onetime bandit general who had 40,000 men at Sian, was the Pacification Commissioner of Shensi. At Tungkwan, east of Sian, the Central Government had ten divisions. Chiang's best general, Hu Tsung-nan, was completely defeated by the communists in northern Kansu.

This was the right setting for Chiang Kai-shek's bold and determined flight on December 8, 1936, from Loyang to Sian to put things right and to find out Chang Hsüeh-liang's attitude. Here, too, he evidently applied his old principle of settling problematic situations by appearing in person and using his great authority. He would descend upon the lion's den, and then by scratching the lions behind the ears, he would tame them without resistance. But this time he had gone too far and depended too much on his lucky star. The dissension was too great. He wanted war against the Reds; Chang Hsüeh-liang and the Reds wanted war against Japan. At Sian the Marshal was thus alone with enormous odds against him, consisting of his own countrymen. He was "between the devil and the deep sea." What would then have been more natural than that his opponents, if they considered him the greatest obstacle to their anti-Japanese plans, had simply had him removed, and then continued along their own lines! Is it any wonder that his friends within China and without were in deadly fear for his life, when all they knew was that he was a prisoner in a hostile camp! This is the dramatic part of the Sian episode. The romantic issue is the immortal part played by his wife, Soong Mei-ling. If a detailed account of the happenings during those critical days is desired, the diaries of the Marshal and his wife may be studied. Let us start with the essay written by Madame Chiang Kai-shek, which she calls *Sian: A Coup d'État.*

"What happened at Sian during the fortnight beginning December 12 last was not a rebellion as we know such politico-military upheavals in China.... In it were involved explosive elements of personal, national, and international problems and policies of first magnitude."

The terrible news that her husband had been taken prisoner by mutineers at Sian came as a bolt from the blue. The message was delivered by her brother-in-law H. H. Kung, the Minister of Finance, when she was attending a meeting in Shanghai of the Commission for the Air Defense, of which she was general secretary.

"No news of the Generalissimo" were words that had a dire sound. She admits that even for her the message was almost too much, although she had gone through many things in her life. The telegraphic communications from Sian were partly cut off. Wild rumors circulated, were believed, and printed. Together with Dr. Kung and Mr. W. H. Donald [1] she hurried to Nanking and found the government circles paralyzed by this unexpected blow. Chang Hsüeh-liang had been deprived of all military titles and he was severely criticized in his capacity of leader of the mutiny.

Earlier in the day a telegram had arrived from Chang Hsüeh-liang and several others, stating that they had tried to tender the Marshal good advice, but that they were treated with harshness. They guaranteed his personal safety and had drawn up eight points for the salvation of China. They hoped that these points would be accepted by the Nanking Government.

Madame Chiang arrived in Nanking on Sunday morning, the thirteenth of December. The suspense there was terrible, and wild suggestions were made. She realized that she herself must take charge in order to form an acceptable plan of action. The officers wanted to mobilize all forces available for a punitive expedition against Sian. She opposed this suggestion with all her might and wanted to find a peaceful solution without bloodshed. She talked to all the leading men and entreated them to refrain from all rash actions and first of all to await reliable news. They might be right in their accusations. If so, these must be investigated and things put right. "We are all Chinese—don't let's fight if we can find a way out of it."

She sent Mr. Donald by air to Loyang with a letter to the Marshal, saying that she knew that everything he did was for the best of the people, that she was praying for him, and commended him into the hands of God. She also wrote to Chang Hsüeh-liang reminding him of his duty.

Feelings became more and more pessimistic. To deaden her anguish she continued her work as general secretary. She wanted to be impartial and just. She never condemned the

---

[1] An Australian, and an intimate friend of the Chiangs.

Photograph by G. Montell

The Luanho, the River Connecting the Province
of Jehol with the Sea.

Photograph by William Allen Dunn

A Mixed Team—Mule and Water Buffalo—Plowing through the Dust near the Temple of Heaven in Peking.

mutineers. She could reach her goal only on a foundation of truth and justice. No violence, no attacks! All efforts must be concentrated on liberating the Marshal—otherwise his life was in the greatest danger. The military still urged that violent measures be taken and also criticized the Marshal for having exposed himself to such a grave danger. She replied, "If he thought of his personal safety above everything else, then he would not be worthy of being the leader of the country."

The Government wanted to act in order to save its own face. "Aside from him," she replied, "just mention the name of a man among you who has the qualities and character of a national leader?"

He is already dead, one of them said. You are a woman begging for her husband, said a second. "I am speaking not as a wife trying to save her husband's life," she answered. "If it is necessary that the Generalissimo should die for the good of the country, I would be the first to sacrifice him, but, to my mind, to use military force and to attack and bombard Sian would not only endanger the life of the Generalissimo . . . but would also cause untold misery and suffering to thousands of innocent civilians, as well as waste our military force which should be conserved for national defense." In the ensuing discussion she particularly reminded the officers that not only China's unity but also the existence of the country as an independent state were dependent upon the life of the Marshal, and for that reason nothing must be left untried that could lead to his liberation without violence.

"If peaceful means fail, then it is not too late to use force. I believe that time will prove that my envisagement of this situation, and my idea of how it should be solved, will prove correct."

When she said that she would fly to Sian herself, she met with unanimous opposition. She was told that she would only be complicating the situation, be tortured, and retained as a hostage.

The pessimists gave no encouragement. She wondered if all the efforts, all the work that she and her husband had expended on the welfare of the people should have been in vain. But she held her ground. It chagrined her that this was the first time in many years that she had not accompanied her husband. She was beset on all sides by people offering her consolation, news, or advice, and upon special request she gave a lecture to cadets and young officers at the Whampoa Military Academy. She then reminded them that the Marshal looked upon them as his own sons. It was their duty to act and live in his spirit. There was no excuse for the actions of the insurgents at Sian, but they could be forgiven if they repented and realized the danger of their behavior.

The first ray of hope came on the fourteenth. Mr. Donald, who had gone to Sian, telegraphed that the Marshal was alive and in good health. Chang Hsüeh-liang vowed that no harm would come to him and expressed the wish that Madame Chiang Kai-shek and Dr. Kung would go to Sian. No one believed in the sincerity of this message. It was claimed to be a trick on the part of the insurgents in order to make Madame Chiang a hostage and Kung prisoner, which would make it so much easier for them to accomplish their aims. Madame Chiang Kai-shek believed implicitly in the message and looked upon it as proof that her friendly policy was the only right one.

On December 15, Mr. Donald telephoned from Loyang and was able to relate all that had happened in Sian, that the Marshal had had a talk with Chang Hsüeh-liang, and that on no condition did he wish his wife to come to Sian.

The following day Madame Chiang again spoke over the telephone to Mr. Donald and admonished Chang Hsüeh-liang to take good care of the Marshal, otherwise Chang would not be worth much. In roundabout ways she learned that her husband had given the insurgents to know that he would rather die than allow himself to be forced into making any concessions. The Marshal was evidently prepared to die, for in a letter to his wife he had expressed a wish that she should carry out certain commissions for him after his death.

She was splendid in her inexhaustible efforts to obtain reliable information from Sian. She made inquiries and investigations like a detective, she picked up news, drew conclusions, and became convinced that Chang Hsüeh-liang had only his bodyguard within the walls of Sian and a handful of troops outside the city, and that he thus was powerless. And in the midst of it all she had to use all her wits to keep the military from attacking Sian, for in that case her husband would never have gotten away from there alive. And she said that his life was more precious to China than his death, even if his death would serve the country.

General Chiang T'ing-wen, one of Chiang Kai-shek's most trusted men, arrived in Nanking with a letter from the Marshal, and he entreated the war agitators in Nanking to refrain from making threats and spreading rumors, and begged them to observe self-control and quiet—all of which indicated that Madame Chiang had judged the position quite correctly.

On the nineteenth of December, her brother, T. V. Soong, former Minister of Finance, went by plane to Sian, and on the twentieth of December he wired that the Marshal was in good health. On the twenty-first, T. V. Soong and Mr. Donald came to Nanking by air. The brave woman describes the intolerable suspense in which she lived during those days. But she was beginning to gain new hope and felt convinced that if she were only allowed to speak to Chang Hsüeh-liang, she would be able to save her husband.

Accompanied by General Chiang T'ing-wen, Madame Chiang Kai-shek boarded an airplane and flew to Loyang. She knew the country and, from earlier flights, the difficulties of landing; she knew the value of the troops that had revolted at Sian, and she was very well aware of the terrible risks to which she was exposing herself. But she never wavered. Modestly, but also with national pride, she says:

"People think I am brave, but I know I am not exceptional, for I am certain millions of other Chinese women would act exactly as I did. . . ."

She landed at Loyang; the airport was full of bomber planes ready to attack Sian. She impressed upon the commander that not a single plane must approach Sian until the Marshal himself had given orders to that effect. The dauntless woman gave orders to the officers in command in a very delicate situation as if *she* had been the commander-in-chief —and she was obeyed!

In a state of growing excitement she flew across snowclad mountains and into the mouth of the valley leading to Sian.

She flew over Lintung, the town where the Marshal had been captured. Her heart was thumping. In another minute she would be at the Sian airport! In that minute she handed Mr. Donald a revolver and asked him to shoot her if the troops captured her and refused to obey orders. Even if they should be impudent she would control herself and "speak to them like one man to another."

She landed. Chang Hsüeh-liang arrived in a motor car and entered the plane, tired, embarrassed, ashamed. She greeted him as if nothing had happened. He must have felt like a guilty schoolboy before the firm look of this staunch, manly woman. Another hero appeared, Yang Hu-ch'eng, the Pacification Commissioner in Sian, looking very nervous but more at ease after Madame Chiang's greeting.

They drove to Chang Hsüeh-liang's quarters and had tea. Then they proceeded to the house where the Marshal was held prisoner. It was well guarded by sentinels and machine guns.

She entered his room. He was in bed. His hands, feet, and legs were covered with wounds made by rocks and bushes

when he fell down a hill in an attempt at flight. His eyes
filling with tears, he cried:

"Why have you come? You have walked into a tiger's lair."

She answered calmly, "I have come to see you."

He was emaciated, worn, and sorrowful. Although he had
implored his wife not to come, he had known that she would.
He said, "I opened the Bible this morning and my eyes lit on
the words [Jer. 31:22]: 'Jehovah will now do a new thing,
and that is, He will make a woman protect a man.'"

He then told her of his fortunes and declared that he would
not sign anything as long as he was a prisoner.

She then told him of the commotion that his capture had
created all over the world, of how children wept and grown-
ups prayed for his salvation, and of soldiers who had committed suicide when they heard of his death.

He said several times that he was prepared to die for the
welfare of the people, but she encouraged him and said that
he certainly should not die now when he was needed more
than ever. The two of them should continue to work together
for the future of their people.

The Marshal was still angry and insulted by the treatment
to which he had been exposed. She tried to placate him and
read aloud from the Book of Psalms until he fell asleep.

She was in Sian, "the cradle of the Chinese race," sitting
beside her sleeping lord and master, wondering if this was to
be their grave. No, that must not be! As a result of the drama
at Sian, the people were to be welded together more strongly
than ever.

But nothing was certain. Sian might also prove to be a
death trap. They were surrounded by unreliable troops. And
beyond them lay the Red hordes, which the Marshal had
fought for years. And others lurked outside the boundaries
of China. Never has a woman single-handed had to face such
a terrible situation; never was a man in greater danger at the

very moment when the welfare of hundreds of millions of people depended upon his destiny.

She summoned Chang Hsüeh-liang and he now asked her to appease the Marshal, and assured her that they would not force him to do anything, not even to sign any agreements. She retorted that he must prove his statement by having the Marshal released unconditionally. China's regeneration would not be accomplished by dramatic episodes at Sian; common efforts, patience, and the elevation of the whole people were needed for that.

"I know I have done wrong," Chang Hsüeh-liang admitted. "It would never have happened if you had been here with the Generalissimo as you usually are. I tried again and again to speak to the Generalissimo, but each time he shut me up and scolded me violently."

She retorted, "The Generalissimo only scolds people of whom he has hopes. If he thinks people are useless he just dismisses them."

"You know I have always had great faith in you, and my associates all admire you. When they went through the Generalissimo's papers after he was detained they found two letters from you to the Generalissimo which caused them to hold you in even greater respect. They saw by those letters that you were heart and soul with the people. . . . If he will only let us explain our ideas everything will be satisfactory, and that you can get him to do."

In reply to her question as to which letters he meant, Chang Hsüeh-liang replied that in one of them she had suggested that money be collected for the defense of Suiyuan; in the other she had said that they had done too little for the salvation of the people, that they must exert themselves still more and pray that God might help them not to make more mistakes than those they already had committed. This last confession had particularly impressed Chang's accomplices.

She told him point-blank that he had violated law and justice, failed in his duty as an officer, and that by his actions he had struck a blow at the very foundation of the unity of the nation, which had cost so much work to build up. His statement that he in no way wanted to hurt the Marshal was certainly not in accord with what had happened in the morning of December 12, when the Marshal on the snow-clad mountain had been a target for the fire from the machine guns.

"But let us not talk about that, the thing to discuss is how to bring this incident to a rapid conclusion.... How shall we go about this?"

He assured her that if it only depended on him, the Marshal would be set free immediately. But there were others who wanted to have a word in the matter. She asked him to send them to her. He promised to do so and departed.

He finally returned at two o'clock in the morning. Yang and the others refused to let the Marshal go. They had said that since T. V. Soong and Madame Chiang were friendly toward Chang, his head would be safe. But how about theirs! They had reproached him for having involved them in this tangle. If they were to set the Marshal free, they would place themselves in an extremely dangerous position.

Madame Chiang gives a masterly description of the terrible strain under which they were living those days. There were sentries in every room. When she and her brother, T. V. Soong, walked back and forth on the paths in the snow-covered yard, soldiers with machine guns stood staring at them, and without the house was guarded like a prison in order to prevent the Marshal from escaping and strangers from approaching him. T. V. Soong had constant conferences with the conspirators. Chang Hsüeh-liang was suspected by his fellow conspirators. They considered him to belong to the Marshal's, Madame Chiang's, and T. V. Soong's group. The Marshal was dead tired of everything and did not care what happened to him. The situation was aggravated by the approach of the Nanking troops.

The attitude of the Red troops was uncertain. They seemed to have changed their policy. Madame Chiang kept her husband advised of all that took place. Her servant noticed that the guards were always eavesdropping. Madame Chiang had long talks with influential men. One gentleman told her they all understood that there was no one in China but the Marshal that could be their leader, and that their reproach was that he did not act quickly enough. She then retorted that all evolution was slow in China, and that it was not possible for the Marshal to rush ahead at such a speed that the great masses could not follow him. She asked them how they could think of taking over the responsibility for the whole nation when they had not even been able to bring this little coup to a successful climax. The best they could do would be to follow the Marshal. The Reds should also participate in the work for the good of the people, and the road to follow was that indicated by the Government.

On Christmas Eve she reminded Chang Hsüeh-liang that the truce expired on Christmas Day. The release of the Marshal should thus be a Christmas gift to the people. Chang suggested that he take the Marshal out of the city in disguise, but Madame Chiang knew her husband well enough to be able to assert that he would never agree to such a trick, but would expect to leave the city openly. She vehemently demanded his immediate release:

"The whole of China demands it, and so does the whole world. Chinese everywhere are . . . denouncing you as a traitor and worse."

The Marshal did not surrender to the demands of subordinates to whom he said, "Theirs but to do and die, theirs not to reason why." In his campaigns against the Reds his tactics had always been to persuade them in a peaceful manner to change their point of view. Many had also gone over to him.

The living conditions of the people had been improved in the former communist districts, and the effects of the Red poison had thus been neutralized.

Christmas Eve drew to a close; the atmosphere was anything but gay. There was an agreement between the Marshal and his wife that the one who woke up first on a holiday was to decide the program for the day. Before the break of dawn she heard from the depths of her husband's bed, "Merry Christmas," and answered, "Merry Christmas to you."

She missed the Christmas tree. But presently there was a knock at the door and two servants entered, one carrying a portable typewriter for her, the other a warm plaid for the Marshal. They suspected Mr. Donald.

Nothing more happened. She was torn between hope and doubt. The rebellious officers demanded a written order from the Marshal before they would let him go. He refused to sign anything. The hours passed. She longed to go away from there. "If we pray hard enough I am sure our prayers will be answered somehow." Confusion reigned, people came and went. Luncheon was announced. They ate and found new hope.

Finally at two o'clock T. V. Soong arrived. The commanding officers in the city had consented to the Marshal's departure. But it was late. It was hardly possible to reach Loyang before dark. "Would it not be better to wait till the morning and go direct to Nanking," asked Chang Hsüeh-liang.

"Wait?" cried Madame Chiang. "Wait till these people change their minds again? No, indeed! We leave while leaving's good."

She was told her *amah* must remain behind.

"What, leave her to the mercy of mutinous troops! No, I have not the heart to let her run any risk when she has been so faithful."

It is not necessary to hear more than this short dialogue between Madame Chiang and Chang to understand which of the two was a man, a real man, a fine and splendid personality!

When she informed her husband that there was no longer anything to prevent their departure, he said that he first wished to talk to Chang Hsüeh-liang and Yang Hu-ch'eng at the same time, before closing the two most critical weeks of his life. Yang was sent for. The Marshal was told that Chang Hsüeh-liang wanted to accompany them to Nanking. The Marshal refused and ordered him to remain with his troops. But when he had explained that he and his friends had agreed that he alone was to shoulder the responsibility for what had happened, and that he wanted to be tried before the government court, the Marshal yielded and promised him he could fly with them. As a result, the verdict of the Central Government was lenient—"a pact which many foreigners could not understand," says Madame Chiang.

The Marshal was still in bed on account of his aching back, when General Yang Hu-ch'eng and Chang Hsüeh-liang entered and stood at attention at his bedside. After much fussing they were finally persuaded to sit down.

And now Chiang Kai-shek lectured the two malefactors. Having been held a prisoner for two weeks at the mercy of rebellious generals, he was again highest in command, and he had not yielded an inch. He laid down the law to them. But he did not do it as "a great and stern and revengeful prophet," but with mild and forgiving words. He dwelt on their crime, but praised their repentance, and took upon himself his share of the responsibility. His speech is a human document. And it will be remembered and ever connected with the name of the town where it was held, Sian, the famous capital of the Han and Tang dynasties, where a line of great emperors sleep their last sleep.

We are indebted to the alert and quick-witted Madame

Chiang for the exact wording of this speech. Word for word she took down her husband's statements. "He was gentle and earnest with them; they were visibly moved," she says. This is the speech, somewhat abbreviated:

"This *coup d'état* is an act which gravely affects both the continuity of Chinese history of five thousand years and the life and death of the Chinese nation, and it is a criterion whereby the character of the Chinese race may be judged. . . ." The consideration shown by them in releasing the Marshal without any conditions or compulsion makes the incident a turning point in the life of the nation, and gives proof of the moral and cultural standard of the people.

"The present outcome of the *coup d'état* shows that you are both ready to correct your own mistakes, and that is creditable to you as well as auguring a bright future for the Chinese race. Since you are now so convinced by my sincerity toward you that you have the courage to acknowledge your wrong-doing, you are entitled to remain as my subordinates. Furthermore, since you can be so readily converted it will certainly be easier for your subordinates to follow suit.

"Formerly you were deceived by reactionaries [2] and believed that I did not treat the people fairly and squarely and that I was not loyal to our revolutionary ideals. But now you have read my private diary for this whole year, the public and private telegrams and documents . . . that have passed through my hands . . . , you must now know that there is not a single word which could condemn me of any self-interest or insincerity on my part.

"In fact, since I took military command and began to take charge of military training, there are two principles which I have always emphasized to my students and subordinates, namely:

"(1) That if I have any selfish motives or do anything against the welfare of the country and the people, then any-

---

[2] He had the communists in mind.

body may consider me a traitor and may shoot me on that account.

"(2) If my words and deeds are in the least insincere and I neglect the principles and revolutionary ideals, my soldiers may treat me as their enemy and may also shoot me.

"From my diary and the other documents, you can see whether you can find one word which is to the detriment of the Revolution. If you can find one such word here, I am still in Sian and you are at liberty to condemn and kill me. On my part, I am glad that I have always done what I have taught other people to do.... I have done nothing of which I need be ashamed.

"The responsibility of this *coup d'état* naturally rests with you two, but I consider myself also responsible.... I have not paid any attention to my personal safety. I have taken no precautions on that account and have therefore tempted the reactionaries to take advantage of the situation.... My own carelessness was the remote cause of this *coup d'état* and gave rise to this breakdown of discipline.... I feel I am to be blamed and must apologize to the nation, the Party, and the people.

"A country must have law and discipline. You two are military officers in command of troops, and when such a *coup d'état* has taken place, you should submit to the judgment of the Central Government. However, I recognize that you were deceived by propaganda of reactionaries and misjudged my good intentions to be bad ones. Fortunately, immediately after the coup you realized that it was harmful to the country and expressed your deep remorse to me. Now you have further realized your own mistake in listening to reactionaries and are now convinced that not only have I had no bad intentions toward you, but that I have always had every consideration for you.

"I have always told my subordinates that when they make mistakes their superiors must also be blamed for not having given them adequate training. As I am in supreme command of the army, your fault is also my fault, and I must ask for punishment by the Central Authorities. . . . As you have rectified your mistake at an early stage, the crisis has not been prolonged, and I believe the Central Authorities should be able to be lenient with you.

"I have always impressed upon the people the importance of ethical principles and integrity to cultivate a sense of probity and of shame, to bear responsibility, and to obey discipline. If a superior officer cannot make his subordinates observe these principles, he himself is partly to be blamed. Hence in connection with this crisis, I am ready to bear the responsibility as your superior officer. On your part you should be ready to abide by whatever decision the Central Government may make, and your subordinates need not have any fear for themselves.

"We must always remember that the life of the nation is more important than anything else. We should not care for ourselves although our personal integrity must be preserved in order that the nation may exist on a firm foundation. Our lives may be sacrified, but the law and discipline of the nation must be upheld. Our bodies may be confined, but our spirit must be free. My own responsibility to the country and the Central Government will always be willingly borne as long as I live. That is why I have repeatedly refused to give any orders or sign anything you wanted me to give or sign while under duress. It is because I consider life or death a small matter compared with the upholding of moral principles."

He leaves his words and actions to the verdict of posterity. Acquiescence to the demands of his captors would have meant the downfall of the nation. If he had yielded to violence, he would have risked the independence of the nation he represented. To a nation as well as to an individual the loss of liberty is equivalent to death. For the morale of the people he was prepared to sacrifice anything. He felt that if he did not practice what he preached, the nation was lost. This *coup d'état* would teach them that the freedom of the soul is more important than anything else and that the welfare of the nation comes before the welfare of the individual. Dr. Sun Yat-sen preached that the moral backbone of the nation must be re-established before the nation can be roused.

"Honesty, righteousness and love of peace are important moral characteristics of our country. For more than ten years, I have devoted myself to uniting the nation, politically and spiritually, for national salvation and honesty and righteousness are of particular importance. . . .

"The policy of the Central Government for the last few years has been to achieve peace in and unification of the country, and to increase the strength of the nation. . . . You are responsible for bringing about warfare in the country. But as you have expressed remorse, I shall recommend the Central Government to settle the matter in a way that will not be prejudicial to the interests of the nation. . . .

"I always give first thought to the life and death of the nation as well as the success or failure of the Revolution and do not pay any attention to personal favors or grudges. Questions of personal danger or loss are of no interest to me. I have had the benefit of receiving personal instruction from Dr. Sun concerning broadmindedness, benevolence and sincerity, and am not vindictive with regard to things that have passed. As you felt remorse very early it shows that you know that the welfare of the nation is above everything else. That being the case, you ought to obey unreservedly the orders of the Central Government, and carry out whatever decisions it may make. This is the way to save the nation from the dangers it is facing and this is the way to turn a national calamity into a national blessing."

When the Marshal had finished his speech, everything was ready for departure. The Marshal, Madame Chiang, and

Chang Hsüeh-liang departed in one motor car, T. V. Soong and Mr. Donald in another. They drove right up to the airplane. The engines were already running. They went on board. The plane lifted and Sian soon disappeared in the distance. Madame Chiang heaved a sigh of relief as if she had awakened from a terrible nightmare. And it is easy to imagine the Marshal's thoughts. With teeth clenched he sat looking down upon the country which he now could continue to unify. He dreamed of happy years that would carry China toward a new period of greatness.

XV

The Marshal's Diary from Sian

IN FEBRUARY, 1937, CHIANG KAI-SHEK DECIDED TO PUBLISH
extracts from his diary describing the two critical weeks at
Sian. He did it partly to explain his actions, and partly to be
spared the countless questions that Chinese and foreigners
put to him.

He began with a few introductory remarks, telling how on
the fourth of December he departed from Loyang for Tungkwan, where he had summoned the leaders of the troops that
were to suppress the freebootery in Shensi and Kansu. He
questioned them one by one and reminded them of their
duty. He believed in the loyalty of the Manchurian troops
and had no thought of the possibility of a mutiny. And yet,
a revolt broke out, and he blames nobody but himself for not
having taken the necessary precautions.

He takes the revolt very seriously and says that the restoration work of the past eight years in the northwest has been
frustrated by it. If the rebels have any conscience, he says,
they will realize that their action is unpardonable. "I am
ashamed of my shortcomings and have no wish to appear to
justify myself. . . . People may suspect that I have exaggerated
my own merits and the wickedness of others."

In his diary the Marshal tells of how he heard rifle shots
while he was dressing at half past five in the morning of
December twelfth. He suspected, and it was soon confirmed,
that the northeastern troops had mutinied. The head of his
bodyguard, Lieutenant Mao, begged him immediately to go
up on the mountain behind his quarters. He and a couple of
his men climbed over a wall at the foot of which was a moat

ten meters deep. He missed his step in the dark and fell into the moat. He managed to get away from there, however, and some of his men led him up the mountain. They climbed to the top and took a rest. Suddenly the firing recommenced. The bullets whistled around Chiang Kai-shek. Some of the men in his bodyguard fell. He realized that it was a general mutiny and that he was surrounded.

He decided to return to his headquarters. On the way down he fell into a hole hidden by bushes, and could not get up. The whole mountain was surrounded by rebellious troops. They were looking for him. Shots were being fired around his headquarters, and his bodyguards were defending themselves. A couple of times rebel troops passed without seeing him. Shortly afterward he gave himself up and was taken prisoner. A couple of Chang Hsüeh-liang's officers asked him to accompany them to Sian in their car. Angrily he went with them. They took him to Sian, where the new town hall, Yang Hu-ch'eng's headquarters, was to be his residence.

He summoned Chang Hsüeh-liang. A violent dispute ensued. The Marshal said:

"Do you still call me the Generalissimo? If you still recognize me as your superior, you should send me to Loyang; otherwise you are a rebel. Since I am in the hands of a rebel you had better shoot me dead."

Chang replied, "If Your Excellency accepts my suggestions, I shall obey your orders."

The Marshal replied with a rebuke. Negotiations were superfluous. "Why do you still disclaim any previous knowledge of the mutiny?" he cried. Chang suggested negotiations in spite of their enmity. Blind with rage the Marshal replied that he had no intentions of negotiating with rebels. He would never allow himself to be forced to yield.

Chang admitted that he was not alone: he believed that he had the people behind him and it was for them that he was fighting. The Marshal ought to consider the matter and retire from his post. He thus wanted to make use of the mob to get rid of his chief. Furious, the Marshal shouted that he was a rebel, and reminded him that when he lost Manchuria, it was he, the Marshal, who had saved him from those who wanted to punish him, and that he also had made possible his trip to Europe. But where could he seek refuge now? There was no place in the world where he could go, and if he died, not a piece of the earth where his grave could be dug.

"You are a rebel. . . . You . . . deserve not only reprimand but also punishment. . . . Do you think that by using force you can compel me to surrender to you rebels . . . ? I shall not bring shame and dishonor to this world, to the memory of my parents and to the nation. . . . You mistake my firm stand on the principles of law and order for obstinacy. If you are a brave man, kill me; if not, confess your sins and let me go. If you do neither, you will be in a dangerous position. Why don't you kill me now?"

The picture of Chang Hsüeh-liang is not a very pleasing one. He wavers, too, in his part. He feels his guilt, blushes, loses courage, makes excuses like a schoolboy. He then invites the Marshal to move over to his house, as he would be safe there, but Chiang answers, "I shall never enter the enemy's camp. I need none of your protection."

Confused and nervous, Chang got up to leave several times. He ordered a servant to lay the table, but the Marshal refused to eat the food of an enemy. After renewed visits and on account of his being so closely guarded, Chiang understood that he was to be a martyr for the revolution, and wanted to communicate his last will to his wife. He told an officer that he would never sign any agreement.

"If I yielded on any point for my personal safety, I would forfeit the confidence placed in me by four hundred million people."

Early in the morning of December 13, Chang returned. The Marshal said that he was far too tired to speak to him.

The servants purchased food with their own money since the Marshal refused to touch the food of the authorities. The staff said that the welfare of the nation depended upon the personal safety of the Marshal. Renewed discussions—always surrounded by guards.

As Chang dared not talk to Chiang Kai-shek in person, he sent an officer asking the Marshal to move over to another, better house, belonging to a divisional general. Chiang answered that he would rather remain in the house of the Pacification Commissioner of Sian, as that official served the Central Government, the Marshal himself being chief of the executive committee. His idea was that Chang had allowed himself to be deceived by others:

"He should awake from his dream of a Sino-Russian Alliance. He should not be under the delusion that even if he fails in this coup he can still go abroad to enjoy himself. . . . If he commits such folly without any feelings of repentance, . . . he will lose the respect of the whole world." Chang had double-crossed his leader, Chiang said. His disobedience would lead to his death. He ought to remember what was the result of Chen Chiung-ming's treachery in Canton. He raised an open mutiny against Dr. Sun Yat-sen.

The Marshal continued in his diary:

"I am determined to fight them with moral character and spiritual strength and with the principles of righteousness." He thought of the heroic deaths in the history of China. "The martyrs of the former ages always defied death. . . . I must maintain the same spirit which led Jesus Christ to the Cross. . . . This will justify the teachings I have received from my mother, and will fulfill the expectations of my comrades."

In the morning of December 14, Chang returned, despondent and irresolute. He said,

"We have read your diary and other important documents, and from them have learned the greatness of your personality." They admired his loyalty to the revolution and his self-sacrifice for the good of the people. "If I had known one-tenth of what is recorded in your diary, I would certainly not have done this rash act. Now I know very clearly that my former views were wrong. Now that I realize your qualities of leadership I feel it would be disloyal to the country if I did not do my best to protect you."

He entreated the Marshal to move, as it would be easier to effect a secret flight from General Kao's house. But the Marshal refused. He was going to leave openly. "One's character is more important than one's life."

Chang showed the Marshal Mr. Donald's telegram stating his intention to fly to Sian. Chiang Kai-shek asked Chang immediately to show Mr. Donald to his room upon his arrival.

The Marshal then sent for Yang Hu-ch'eng, the Pacification Commissioner, who was one of the insurgents, and pointed out to him how wrong their behavior was.

To the Marshal's great joy Mr. Donald arrived in the afternoon, bringing Madame Chiang's letter. At Donald's request he moved over to Kao's house. Chang also appeared. In reply to the Marshal's request to go to Nanking, he replied that all the insurgents would have to agree upon a solution. They had made a list of eight demands. If any of them were not accepted, Chang's friends were not prepared to let him go. The eight demands were:

1. Reorganize the Nanking Government so that members of other parties and spheres may become members and participate in the work for the salvation of the nation.
2. End all civil war.
3. Release immediately the "National Salvation" leaders arrested in Shanghai.
4. Pardon all political crimes.
5. Guarantee liberty of assembly.

6. Give the people a free hand to join patriotic movements.
7. Carry out loyally the will of Sun Yat-sen.
8. Call a conference immediately for "national salvation."

Chiang answered: "You are a military officer, and cannot enjoy the same privileges of a common citizen. All those who try to endanger the fate of the nation are my enemies, as well as the enemies of the people. . . . You have taken part in a mutiny, feel no remorse about your wrongdoing, and try to cover up your own tracks by making these so-called proposals. . . . Before I go back to Nanking, there can be no discussion."

Then followed a discussion in which Chang accused his chief of having too old-fashioned, heroic, and Christian ideas of sacrifice instead of accepting modern ideas of politics and diplomacy.

"I think you are the only great man of this age," said Chang, "but why won't you yield a little, comply with our requests, and lead us on in this revolution so that we may achieve something instead of your merely sacrificing your life?"

Chiang Kai-shek's opinion was that his sacrifice would be the work of his life.

"If I should try to save my life today, . . . the nation will be in a precarious position. . . . On the other hand, if I stand firm and would rather sacrifice my life than compromise my principles, I shall be able to maintain my integrity till death, and my spirit will live forever. Then multitudes of others will follow me, and bear the duties of office according to this spirit of sacrifice. Then, though I die, the nation will live. So if anyone wrongly thinks that he can manipulate national affairs by capturing me and endangering my life, he is a perfect fool."

In his diary the Marshal gives Chang Hsüeh-liang what he deserves. On the tenth of December he had deserted the Marshal and joined the insurgents. On account of his attitude in 1928, when he supported the Central Government, Chiang Kai-shek had always supported him, in order to give him a chance to blot out the earlier stain, i.e., the loss of Manchuria. By his treachery he had now exposed northwestern China to the risk of meeting the same fate as Manchuria.

On December 16, Chang once more visited the Marshal. He was ghastly pale and very nervous. He said that the conspirators had decided that the Marshal should be allowed to return to Nanking in a few days, but that matters were complicated by the fact that Central Government troops had begun to advance, bombing as they approached. This information cheered Chiang Kai-shek. It meant that his people were doing their duty. It mattered not one bit that his own situation became more precarious. The loss of one man means nothing; the welfare of the people everything.

On December 17, Chang asked the Marshal to put into effect the suggestion he had made the day before, which was to order the Central Government troops to postpone their attack for three days. The Marshal agreed although he suspected new intrigues. He writes in his diary:

"Sincerity and righteousness have no place in the conduct of rebels, so I can only let them do as they like."

The first truce expired on the 19th of December. Chang once more urged the Marshal to accept at least four of the eight demands.

The Marshal replied that that question would be discussed in Nanking.

On December 20, T. V. Soong arrived. He brought with him a letter from his sister, the Marshal's wife, in which she wrote that if her brother did not return within three days, "I will come to Shensi to live and die with you." Her devotion touched him.

T. V. Soong demanded that he be allowed to see his brother-in-law in private. His request was granted. Previously there had always been witnesses. The Marshal emphasized that the country could not be freed from the crisis caused by the mutiny unless a punitive expedition were sent to Sian immediately. "Do not take my personal safety into consideration. We must put the welfare of the country first."

The following morning Soong arrived and whispered to the Marshal—for there were eavesdroppers outside—that the Government's military plan was identical with the Marshal's own. The Marshal replied that if they surrounded Sian within five days, he might be saved; if not, he harbored no fears. Soong was to return to Nanking the same day. They were greatly moved when parting—perhaps forever. Chiang Kai-shek asked Soong to tell Madame Chiang that on no condition must she come to Sian. He also asked him to take care of his wife and children.

On the twenty-second of December Madame Chiang Kai-shek arrived in Sian. When he saw her and thought of her courage, self-sacrifice and devotion, he nearly burst into tears. It worried him to know that she was in danger. "She is so courageous, wise, kind, and affectionate that I always have been confident that her contribution to the Party and the country will have far-reaching results. She and I have always been of the same mind and we have unceasingly exhorted each other to fight to the end...."

In his diary he wrote: "If my wife had not very strong faith in God, how could she brave such great dangers to come to me?"

His wife told him the names of seven members of his bodyguard and personal staff who had been killed in the attack on the twelfth of December; many others had fallen. He grieved over their fate but rejoiced at their brave readiness to sacrifice themselves for their country.

On the twenty-third of December Chiang Kai-shek and his

wife had a talk about the necessity of imperturbable firmness. "Only then can one not be ashamed before heaven and earth, and remain consistent whether in danger or in safety." He showed her how much more valuable it was for him that his wife had come to share his dangers than if his former comrades or pupils from the Whampoa Military Academy had sacrificed themselves for his sake.

T. V. Soong reported that the leaders of the rebellion most likely would release the Marshal unconditionally. There seemed to have been a psychological turn of current. But on the twenty-fourth of December they once more demanded that the Central Government troops should withdraw to Tungkwan. Soong became excited; Chiang remained calm, for he had never expected to leave the lion's den alive.

On December 25, there were renewed intrigues by Chang Hsüeh-liang. He tried to persuade Madame Chiang to fly to Nanking before the others.

At two o'clock T. V. Soong appeared, announcing that Chiang Kai-shek and his wife could fly to Nanking whenever they wished. Everything was prepared. But just before departure, Chang Hsüeh-liang and Yang Hu-ch'eng were summoned and had to listen to the Marshal's speech quoted above. At four o'clock they departed for Loyang and spent the night there. On December 26, they were in Nanking. The Marshal was received at the airport by President Lin Sen, the whole Government, and the commanding officers of the army. The streets were crowded with people who cheered when the Marshal drove past. Finally Chiang Kai-shek writes in his diary:

"The *coup d'état* was due to my inability to teach and discipline my subordinates, as well as to prepare for such unexpected contingencies.... A *coup d'état* which had shocked the whole world passed without causing any great disturbance.... Henceforth I must exert myself more strenuously than ever, and be doubly loyal to the nation in order to repay their kindness."

XVI

The Obscurity around the Sian Incident

SUCH IS THE FINAL ENTRY IN CHIANG'S DIARY COVERING the two black weeks at Sian. Unconsciously he proves himself to be a man of rare nobility, with an iron character and will power, a clever and prudent statesman, conciliatory and kind, with no hateful and revengeful feelings, a patriot who gladly sacrifices his life for his country, a hero of the classical type in old China, a leader with the welfare of his people always before him, modest, humble before God and man, a great and harmonious personality; one of the finest figures in history's motley gallery.

A mysterious fate seems to have lured him into a trap. The Marshal himself looked upon the Sian incident as an expression of the will of the Almighty. His soul was certainly hardened during that fortnight's purgatory. He was given more strength to withstand the far greater trials that awaited him within the next few months.

The morning service on Christmas Day, 1936, in the capital of Shensi will in times to come range among the immortal moments in the history of China. When the tolling of the bells of the Christian missionary churches at Sian was heard over the yellow earth, it foretold a new era in the Middle Kingdom, the dawn of an epoch that would be christened in blood before it was ready to develop into unity and power. Solemn and silent, but with head erect, the great leader of the people returned to his capital. He alone was equal to the new times; he alone had power to inspire the masses with hope and faith; and he was the first to defend his country when the storm broke out from the north, east, and south, spreading death and destruction among the poor and patient people of China.

I have discussed at some length the Marshal's and Madame Chiang's accounts of the happenings at Sian, but to obtain a still better picture of this so important event, I have deemed it suitable also to include a few extracts from Edgar Snow's work *Red Star over China:*

"They [Chiang Kai-shek and his wife] saw the events at Sian as an outrage inflicted upon their own highly emotional assertions of personal destiny, and have given us the subjective account of their experiences. But the heavy impingement of those events on their own lives naturally imposed great restraints, and privately they would probably be the first to admit that reasons of politics and the necessity of maintaining the dignity of office, obliged them to omit much material of value. . . .

"Communist policy throughout the Sian incident has never been clearly explained. Many people assumed that the Communists, in triumphant revenge for the decade of relentless war which Chiang Kai-shek had waged against them, would now demand his death. Many believed that they would use this opportunity to coalesce with the Tungpei and Hsipei armies, greatly enlarge their base, and challenge Nanking in a great new struggle for power. Actually they did nothing of the sort. They not only urged a peaceful settlement, and the release of Chiang Kai-shek, but also his return to leadership in Nanking. Even Mme. Chiang says that, 'quite contrary to outside beliefs they [the Reds] were not interested in detaining the Generalissimo.' . . .

"Despite all the temptations which the situation obviously presented to them, they gave a demonstration of Party discipline which must profoundly impress any candid observer. From the very beginning they recognized that the central meaning of Sian was for them the opportunity to demonstrate the sincerity of their program for the United Front.

They had nothing to do with the arrest of Chiang Kai-shek. It astonished them as much as the rest of the country. But they had much to do with its *dénouement....*

"As is well known, Chiang at first refused even to discuss the rebels' program. But as he remained isolated from the environment provided for so long by his own satellites, as news came of the intrigues going on in Nanking, as his fears increased of the consequences of a big civil war, he became more convinced not only of the sincerity of his immediate captors, but also of the Reds, in their opposition to civil war and their readiness to assist in the peaceful unification of the country, under his own leadership, provided he defined a policy of positive armed resistance to Japan. Here in these meetings also the four points may have been discussed which eventually became the basis of a truce between Nanking and the Soviets.

"Chiang naturally does not record the details of these discussions in his diary, for his position was, and had to be, that he never 'bargained' for the peace that was achieved. There could be only 'submission to the Government.' The full content of these two weeks must remain obscure until Chang Hsüeh-liang and others record their versions of the interviews—which, in view of present political formations, may not be for some time."

After the Sian incident Chiang Kai-shek did not have many months to devote to the resumption of the work of regeneration he so resolutely and successfully had begun in the interior of the country; after only six months the enemy from without again knocked with mailed fists at the doors of the country. The Marshal's career had reached its most fateful stage, and now as never before he was to be put to the test to show his people, his enemies, and the whole world whether he really was able to solve the problem that the Chinese nation had confidently left to him. To him it was first of all a question of saving China from destruction, from the loss of its age-old independence, and from being made into a vassal state by the Japanese.

But in reality the issue was much greater. The future of East Asia was at stake. The war that broke out on July 7, 1937, would perhaps decide the fate of the Philippines, Australia, the Sunda Islands, French Indo-China, Burma, and British India. In recent years Japanese statesmen, generals, admirals, and authors had made repeated solemn declarations, orally and in writing, that they followed no other principle in their active policy than "Asia for the Asiatics," or in other words, Japan's absolute supremacy of entire Asia and of the commerce on the Pacific (i.e. Asia for the Japanese).

The war that on July 7, 1937, began spreading death and devastation over the world's largest people and most densely populated areas, was not only a war between two nations and two states, directly influencing five hundred million people, Chinese and Japanese, but a war which according to open and unmistakable statements by the Japanese was intended to expel from the Asiatic continent and its islands all representatives of the white race, and to end forever the supremacy of the white race over the colored peoples. The white man was no longer to be allowed to treat Asia as his private gold mine, from which in centuries to come he might collect inexhaustible wealth.

Frightful perspectives opened in the background of the raging Sino-Japanese war, a racial war, a struggle between the yellow and the white race. Whatever the end, it is most probable that this war between the two great peoples of East Asia will denote a boundary in the history of mankind between an old and a new world. The white man's time is up in East Asia.

In the center of this historical drama we find Chiang Kai-shek, resolute and firm as a rock in agitated waters. The whirlwinds sweep around him; the Chinese put all their faith in him; the Japanese rage against him in their hatred, well knowing that he is the soul of the strong resistance the invaders have encountered for more than two years during their toilsome advance over the yellow earth. He knew Japan and could interpret the signs of the times well enough to divine what was in store, and it was his hope to lead the country that he had aroused from its sleep to such strength and firmness that the enemy would refrain from an invasion. When Chiang Kai-shek came into power, he did not lose a minute in commencing his unifying work. The Japanese, on the other hand, made a mistake in their calculations and lost valuable time. If they had taken their chance ten years earlier when the fifty generals were still fighting each other, making China into a puzzle of more or less independent states, which might easily have been inflamed against each other, the invasion of China would have been a comparatively simple matter, a military promenade which certainly would not have required an army of a million men and a struggle lasting for years, as now is the case.

In our description of Chiang Kai-shek's life we have reached the trial of strength between the two great powers in East Asia, a gigantic struggle which in the subversive drama of the history of the world may gain the same importance as the appearance of the Huns and the Mongols once had on the colossal stage of the old world.

PART II

XVII

Japan's Road to Greatness

EUROPE FIRST LEARNED OF THE EXISTENCE OF THE GROUP of islands whose rocks and volcanoes emerge from the waters of the East China Sea through Marco Polo's descriptions of the vast domains of the Great Khan, the Emperor of China. The immortal merchant of Venice who traveled through Asia in 1273 and for about twenty years was in the service of Khubilai Khan, the grandson of Chinghiz Khan, at the Imperial Court in Cambaluc (Peking), tells how Khubilai Khan sent an army of horsemen and infantry through Korea and then in a big fleet to Chipangu, "an island eastwards in the open sea, 1,500 miles from the continent, a very large island." The expeditionary corps was overtaken by a violent gale which wrecked many vessels, while others—with 30,000 men on board—were driven to an island. The greater part of the fleet was able to return to China. The shipwrecked army found nothing to eat on the smaller island. But the Emperor on the large island sent an army to capture the newcomers. Having anchored their ships off the shore, the army began to pursue the enemies, who cunningly drew them up into the mountains and then made a detour down to their ships, manned them, and sailed across to the large island, where they took possession of the capital.

Marco Polo's description agrees in the main with Chinese annals, translated by the Jesuits of the courts of K'ang Hsi and Ch'ien Lung, but it is also embellished with thrilling adventures created by the imagination of the Venetian or those who had told him the tales. The fact remains, however, that from his first year as emperor, 1268, up to 1280,

Khubilai Khan sent expeditionary forces from Korea across the Tsushima Sound to Japan, which country he wanted to subjugate or at least force to pay tribute money. They all failed, incurring great losses. Finally, in 1283, the Emperor decided to make a final conquest, but the Chinese regarded his plan with such reluctance that he had to refrain from it. That was the first time a foreign power tried to conquer Japan. It was to be 625 years before the next hostile fleet steered toward Nippon, and that, too, was to be a failure.

Hideyoshi, the Japanese autocrat, had no greater success, when, 1592-98, he on two occasions landed on the coast of Korea and had to retreat with great losses. On his deathbed he ordered that the Japanese troops should be withdrawn from Korea. That was the first time that Japanese armed with swords, bows, and spears set foot on the mainland of Asia for the purpose of enlarging their dominion toward the inner part of the continent. Three centuries were to pass before they renewed the attempt in an era that inaugurated a number of victorious wars in the history of Japan.

Just as the British Isles in the Far West flank the continent of the Old World in the eastern part of one ocean, so does the Japanese group of islands occupy a similar position in the Far East in the western part of another ocean. Centuries have passed since the British people became conscious of the part they were destined to play as rulers of the sea, on account of the geographical location of their islands. The Portuguese, Spaniards, Dutch, and French who had preceded them as conquerors, were soon surpassed by the British, who annexed enormous territories in foreign lands and finally built up the empire which now embraces the oceans and one fourth of the surface of the earth.

Right now, before our very eyes, the Japanese, and above all their military caste, the descendants of the Samurai, are driven irresistibly ahead in an action whose aim is the supremacy over Asia and the Pacific and whose sequel is a

threat against the continued existence of the British Empire.
It is thus very late that the Japanese have become conscious of a mission similar to that of England, of which it is
but an imitation—like so many other things in Japan. What
had been possible for the islanders in the Far West could,
according to the Japanese, just as easily be accomplished by
the islanders in the Far East.

Some of us will remember the different stages that step
by step, in forty-five years, gave Japan the rank of one of
the world's strongest powers. On the boundary between the
largest continent and the greatest ocean in the world the
Japanese have thus in less than half a century risen from a
humble station to such power that they can dictate terms to
European powers and create a new order in the Far East.

We have seen that Marco Polo was the first to make
Japan's existence known in Europe. But to him and his time
Japan was nothing but a conception, an island, a name. He
had heard the Chinese speak of it. They called it Jih-pen-kuo
(Chipangu), or "The Land of the Rising Sun," the islands
being located in the ocean at whose eastern horizon the sun
rose.

Long after the death of Marco Polo, Toscanelli, the learned
mathematician of Florence, figured out that since the earth
is spherical, a ship sailing westward from Europe would
arrive at the coast of Japan, China, or India, the countries
described by the traveled Venetian. It was thus Toscanelli
(1474) who furnished the theoretical suggestion resulting
in the discovery of America, but it was Christopher Colum-
bus who, after a careful study of Toscanelli's maps, realized
the plan and discovered the New World and some of its
islands. He thought he had discovered Marco Polo's India,
which name embraced also China and Chipangu. That is why
the islands between the North and South American continents to this day are called the West Indies.

Exactly fifty years after the discovery of America, some

Portuguese landed on the shores of Japan and opened commercial establishments and missionary stations. And so Japan became incorporated with the rest of the world and in the following centuries became more and more important in the eyes of the western merchants, missionaries, and explorers. Carl Petter Thunberg, the pupil of Carl von Linneus, is one of the best known among the latter.

The origin of the Japanese people beyond the impenetrable twilight of prehistoric times is unknown and puzzling. But thanks to its isolation on the islands, this people has developed its unique characteristics. Except for Khubilai Khan's and Hideyoshi's expeditions, it had been spared all wars with outside enemies until Russia advanced to the coast of the Pacific. Then the Japanese woke up in earnest. They had been aroused already, fifty years earlier, when Commodore Perry in 1853 landed on their coast with his American squadron and demanded a commercial treaty just as England ten years earlier had demanded ports in China, in the peace of Nanking after the Opium War 1840-42. Japanese ports were subsequently opened to American as well as European trade.

Japan had great and far-sighted men. Ito Hirobumi, of Samurai nobility, one of the best heads, realized that the West with its superior culture and technique and its conquests in foreign continents might some day became dangerous also for Japan. Although trips abroad were still prohibited at that time, he and a couple of patriots sharing his views signed on as sailors on a British ship. In England he and his comrades saw quite enough to understand what would have to be done. More than a hundred years before, England had conquered India and acquired a firm footing along the coast of China. If Japan was to have any future at all in East Asia, she must be reformed according to European pattern.

In 1867 the Shogun rule of the Tokugawa family came to an end after a reign of two hundred and fifty years. The

Shoguns, the Daimyo or feudal lords, and the Samurai fighting knights were abolished, and in 1868 the Emperor Mutsuhito took the Imperial Oath. That was the beginning of the great period called Meiji, or "enlightened rule." Japan armed herself according to European patterns and engaged German and French instructors.

Three hundred years after Hideyoshi's futile attempt to make conquests on the mainland of Asia, Japan in 1876 again found an excuse to extend her arms toward Korea. A Korean fort near Fusan fired on a Japanese warship and this gave rise to certain demands. It was as yet too early to think of annexation. Korea had belonged to China under the Manchu dynasty. Through a treaty dictated by Japan, the peninsula was now severed from China and declared an independent state where Japan opened a legation and a consulate.

Ito, confidant of the Emperor, a minister, and possessor of the highest dignities of the country, managed Japan's politics throughout the proudest period in its history. He added to the greatness of his country by the war with China in 1894, when the Chinese were defeated by this new great power which until then had been their harmless neighbor. During that war, General Hassegawa, under command of Marshal Oyama, captured the Chinese fortress Lü-shun-kou, which ten years later was to become famous under the name of Port Arthur. Through the peace of Shimonoseki in 1895, China surrendered to Japan Formosa, Liao-tung, and the southeasternmost part of Manchuria as well as the Pescadore Islands, and in addition had to pay a war indemnity of two hundred million taels.

Japan had finally secured a firm footing on the Asiatic continent and could at liberty extend her dominion at China's expense. At any rate she could make sure of the bulwark which was to protect the Empire from Russia, about which they still spoke thirty-seven years later, after the conquest of Manchuria.

For the first time the world now obtained distinct presage of the deadly rivalry that in years to come was to grow up between Russia and Japan on the Pacific coast north of China proper, which rivalry in 1938 and 1939 repeatedly found expression along the Manchurian boundary toward eastern Siberia and Outer Mongolia.

The Russian, French, and German ministers in Japan, who jointly represented a preponderant power, in 1895 "advised" the government in Tokyo to give up Liao-tung and Port Arthur, as a Japanese seizure of these districts would mean a direct threat against Peking and the integrity of Korea.

With clenched teeth the straight-backed and prudent Japanese statesmen, headed by Ito, had to swallow the humiliation and follow the advice. But they as well as the officers in command of the army and navy had been given a lesson which in due time would turn out expensive for the European great powers. As a compensation for the loss of their conquests the Japanese received the ridiculous sum of thirty million taels!

Thirty pieces of silver for the most excellent location imaginable on the Asiatic mainland from which to start new expansions! Anyone who was personally acquainted with some of the great men of Japan at that time, Ito, Togo, Nogi, Yamagata, Oku, Oshima, Fukushima, and others, will understand their wounded pride, their hurt *bushido*, their bitter sorrow and their hatred of the white people, who but a week after the signing of the peace treaty at Shimonoseki tripped them up and deprived them of the fruits of their victory.

It was now perfectly clear to the Japanese leaders that the white people could not be budged without power, violence, and blood. Their attitude toward Russia became extremely aggravated when the Czar only one year after Shimonoseki acquired a concession to build the Chinese Eastern Railway from Manchuli via Harbin to Vladivostok, straight through Chinese Manchuria. The Japanese leaders, and particularly the army, must have felt indescribable mortification when Russia in 1898 "leased" the fortress of Port Arthur for twenty-five years, which the Japanese had conquered and which in the hands of the Russians, could be made practically inexpugnable. The excellent harbor of Dairen, which the Russians called Dalni (Distant), was also included in the Russian lease. They were allowed to build a railway from Harbin to Port Arthur and Dalni. Through new agreements they also obtained the right to keep troops in Manchuria.

Russia had "advised" Japan to withdraw from the mainland as their occupation of Port Arthur and Liao-tung would be a threat against Peking and Korea. The fact that the Russians immediately afterward obtained possession of these strategically extremely important places was naturally a far greater threat not only against China and Korea, but most of all against Japan. The history of diplomacy and international politics is responsible for many maneuvers based on military violence, but Russia's treatment of Japan in the years 1895 to 1898 surpassed all records of cynicism, and if Japan at that time had been sufficiently armed, a war would have been inevitable. But her war apparatus was far too inferior to the Russian, so with ostensibly well-suppressed wrath Japan had to put up with losing face and swallowing her humiliation before the eyes of the peoples of East Asia, indeed before the whole world.

If the year 1868, when the Meiji period began its triumphal march in the history of Japan, was the first milestone on the road to the greatness of the new empire, 1895 was the second, for then the islanders first came into direct contact with a great European power and realized that Russia was a rival on the Pacific coast who did not even try to hide her intentions. With her two fortresses, Vladivostok on the coast of the Sea of Japan, and Port Arthur on the coast of the Yellow Sea, Russia controlled the two seas that wash the shores of Nippon. Russia thus held a strategic position directly threatening the life and independence of Japan, and raised a barrier to her future development, with regard to commercial as well as territorial expansion.

The second milestone is thus denoted by Japan's awakening to the realization that she had to choose between being smothered and enfeebled in the grip of the Russian eagle, or forcibly beating the eagle, compelling him to drop his prey and chasing him back to the Siberian forests north of Amur. With their ability, patriotism, Samurai spirit, and *bushido,* the Japanese did not hesitate in their choice. With an energy that knew no bounds they began their armament, which particularly after 1900 grew to dimensions never before seen in history. They worked day and night in the army as well as the navy. After the treaty with England in 1902, Japan began to feel more confident. It was in the interests of both England and India that Russia's advance into Asia be arrested. Upon Japan's suggestion of an amicable settlement by Russian concessions being rejected, the Japanese navy, without any declaration of war, made its devastating attack on the Russian navy under Admiral Makarov's command, which was then in the roadstead of Port Arthur. On January 2, 1905, Port Arthur fell. Kuroki and Oyama defeated Kuropatkin's armies at Mukden, and Roshestvensky's fleet was demolished by Togo in the Tsushima Sound. Through the Treaty of Portsmouth, Japan obtained Port Arthur, Dairen, the southern part of the Manchurian railway, and the southern half of Sakhalin. Japan took charge of the protectorate of Korea, but, as Russia had done, agreed to evacuate Manchuria and to return these provinces to Chinese sovereignty.

Through the treaty Japan probably did not obtain all that she had desired—the northern part of Sakhalin and reparations—but nevertheless her war with Russia was of vast importance in history and for her own future. For the first time since the Mongols and Turks invaded eastern Europe, a great European power had been defeated by an Asiatic people.

With one stroke Japan had risen to the rank of one of the strongest powers in the world. She had in all respects recovered face and her prestige which was shaken ten years earlier. Through the war against Russia Japan had gained her coveted goal, a foothold on the Asiatic mainland. It had also removed the Russian threat from Port Arthur. The other claw of the eagle still has a grip on Vladivostok. This naval port is not ice-free the whole year, but it is only a couple of hours' flight to Osaka, Tokyo, Yokohama, and other large and industrial towns in Japan. Vladivostok is in the geometrical center of the Japanese Empire, between Manchukuo, Korea, the islands of Nippon, and southern Sakhalin. In the spring of 1935, Shiratori, the then Japanese minister at Stockholm, smilingly assured me that his people would not forever tolerate the reigning conditions.

The Russo-Japanese war was followed with intense interest the world over and practically everywhere the sympathies were with Japan. The Russian minister in Stockholm complained to our minister of foreign affairs that the crowds before the windows of the newspapers loudly expressed their delight at the telegrams announcing Japanese victories. Great admiration was aroused by the young lieutenant and the crew of volunteers who, at the order of Admiral Togo, undertook to operate an obsolete man-of-war at full speed straight into the narrow opening between the batteries of the "Eagle's Nest" and the "Tail of the Tiger," the intention being to stop up the passage with its sunken hull and to shut in the Russian warships that were still intact and lying in the inner basin of the harbor. People were amazed at this proof of true heroism, and with tear-dimmed eyes the telegrams were read quoting the parting speech of the Admiral of the Fleet to those destined to die. Had they been Romans, they might have cried with conviction, *"Morituri te salutant!"* Young and hearty, they were called up and gathered around Togo on the deck of his ship, the *Mikasa*. All glasses were filled with—

water. With complete composure the Admiral raised his glass: "I drink to you, not in champagne, but in water. Go to your graves!" They threw their glasses into the sea and hastened on board the doomed vessel. "Full speed!" Straight toward the entrance of Port Arthur. The batteries of the forts began to thunder. But the fire soon ceased. The vessel had then sunk in the middle of the narrow passage, and the Russian ships were locked in until the fortress surrendered on January 2, 1905. None of the crew was saved.

The war correspondence and telegrams at that time reported numerous incidents of a similar kind. White men all over the world were amazed at the fanatic patriotism and exaltation that drove the soldiers of the front lines to sacrifice their lives to the murdering fire of the Russian forts, that their dead bodies might fill the trenches and pave the way for those behind them. Sixty thousand Japanese, among them the two sons of General Nogi, fell, before the Commander, General Stössel, surrendered.

It was easy to understand that a nation displaying such bravery and splendid endurance day by day throughout a whole war in order to preserve the independence, liberty, and honor of its country must have a glorious future, and during the thirty-five years that have elapsed since that time Japan has strengthened and developed her position as the strongest power in the western part of the Pacific, the best-armed country on Asiatic ground.

XVIII

My Visit to Japan Thirty Years Ago

NOW, MORE THAN THIRTY YEARS AFTER MY FIRST VISIT TO
Japan, the experiences and impressions I then gathered in
the Land of the Rising Sun stand out in my memory in a
dreamlike yet memorable radiance of Oriental splendor and
as an echo of a saga or a song that long since faded away.
Everything was so different from the Japan of today. I
learned to know a people who less than three and a half
years earlier had fought a war against a great European power
to a victorious end, but who still did not boast of its achievements and the high rank it had acquired among the mightiest
nations of the time thanks to its own ability and readiness
to make sacrifices. It aroused admiration, this people that
one previously had learned to know mostly through Pierre
Loti's and Lafcadio Hearn's poetical descriptions. One admired the picturesque kimonos of its native land, the graceful dance of the geishas to the tunes of string instruments,
the monotonous, melancholy song with its Asiatic coloring,
the enchanting landscape, the temples and pagodas between the trunks of the Japanese cedars, and the small,
dainty houses in the shade of blossoming cherry trees or the
flame-colored arbors of the maple trees in the autumn. Although the thunders of war so recently had died down on
the neighboring continent and on the seas around the islands
of the fairyland, the stranger but rarely saw anything to
remind him that he was visiting a warrior nation of the first
order. Peace and security reigned and the people sauntered
carefree under the red arches of the maples, conscious of

their own physical strength and ability to keep anyone away from their isolated insular world.

Often one became lost in contemplation at the sight of this people whose daily pursuits and efforts were elegant and artistic, whose harvest feasts were full of charm, and whose religious processions around the Buddhist and Shinto temples were characterized by dignity and artistic refinement. One stood amazed to think that these islanders, who from time immemorial had lived their isolated lives under despotic Shoguns and Daymios, and in feudal times had witnessed the struggles between the Samurai, whose peasants grew their rice in poverty, and whose craftsmen could spend a year in making a lacquered box or a group of monks in ivory, also could build battleships and cruisers and mobilize armies with full modern equipment when the welfare of the country was concerned.

The Emperor Mutsuhito's regime was at its height. The Japanese had experienced their baptism of fire and had a right to rest, to recover from their exertions, arrange their finances, and repair their military forces. The memory of the six weeks I spent as a visitor in Japan at the close of 1908 forms a colorful, enchanting background—like the reflection of a sunset—to the noisy events of present times and to the radical change that denotes the beginning of a new era, not only for the Far East but for the whole life and development of the old world.

My recollections from the past, and not least the circumstance that most of my own activities have been concentrated to Asia, make it quite natural that my interest in the blood-drenched drama now being enacted in Asia is greater than that of many others, and that I embrace with sympathy and admiration the central figure of this drama, Chiang Kai-shek.

The courteous invitation I received from the Imperial Geographical Society in Tokyo to speak on Tibet was not only dictated by a desire to honor me personally, but also a proof that the cultured and far-seeing Japanese whenever possible wished to increase their knowledge of the geography of the Asiatic continent, its nature, habitation, and roads—in other words to become familiar with that part of the world which might be called their neighborhood and on whose ground they were perhaps some day to play an important part. With a few outstanding exceptions, Japanese explorers and inventors have not made any very great contributions to international science, nor have the Japanese to any great extent increased the fund of human knowledge. As adepts in the quest of the laws of natural science and the possibilities of the technical sciences, the Japanese, like the Chinese, are so young, however, that it would be unreasonable to expect a contribution from them comparable to the experiences gained by the peoples of the West during a couple of centuries.

Considering the expansive aspirations of present-day Japan to supremacy in China, it is remarkable that their leaders as recently as thirty years ago did not give more attention to the exploration of inner Asia. The geographical, ethnological, and physical reports submitted by a few Buddhist priests such as Kawaguchi and Narita are of but little value. Count Otani's expeditions to Sinkiang, where Tachibana even visited Lou-lan, seem to have had chiefly archaeological aims, while the geographical results are unknown. This, however, does not preclude the possibility that in recent times the Japanese may have sent expeditions to Central Asia with scientific as well as political aims in view, though we are not familiar with any such expeditions. During my stay in Urumchi in the summer of 1934 I met a Japanese who stated that he was a Chinese professor, and who was traveling in disguise together with four Chinese students. He was subsequently arrested.

In hardly any other country, not even in England, did my discovery of Trans-Himalaya and its orographical significance arouse such great and understanding interest as in Japan. Upon request I gave one lecture after another, not only before geographers but also at the universities in Tokyo and Kyoto and before societies in other cities. I was overwhelmed with hospitality, honors, gifts, sympathy, and kindness, which after about sixty banquets began to become quite a strain on my physique. When I addressed four thousand students at Waseda University, I was greeted by its chancellor, the old experienced statesman Count Okuma. On the evening of my lecture to the students of Tokyo university, the enormous hall was filled to the last seat by the general public, which caused the students who arrived later to drive out all outsiders, then taking the seats themselves. In schools to which I was invited, the children had been taught to bid me welcome in unison in the English language and to express the hope that I should preserve a pleasant memory of them and Nippon. I replied by congratulating them on being the sons and daughters of this proud and splendid country, which it would be their mission to honor and improve. Many of those boys have perhaps now lost their lives on Chinese battlefields!

Prince Tokugawa of the last Shogun family presided at the Peers' Club, the meeting place of all Japanese aristocracy at that time. In the Nishi Hongwan-ji temple at Kyoto, where I spent several days visiting Count Kozui Otani, the high priest of the Buddhists, I had an excellent opportunity of studying at close range the organization and sacred rites of a Japanese Buddhist temple. In his palace, Prince Kanin surrounded me with a *corps d'élite* of famous men, and I was always accompanied by a staff of scientists, many of them known and esteemed also in Europe—for instance Omori, Inouye, Hori, Ogawa, Yamagama, Yamasaki. Some of them had met me already at Shanghai and accompanied me to Yokohama on the *Tenyo Maru,* while others accompanied me through Korea to Port Arthur and Mukden.

The most remarkable of all the receptions at which I was

the guest of honor and which seems so strange in the light of the past years, was undoubtedly the one at which Mr. Gustaf Wallenberg, the Swedish minister, Captain Charles de Champs, our naval attaché, and I were the only guests and twelve generals our hosts. The one that presided was old General Oku, former chief of the Second Army in the Russo-Japanese war, who had had his share in the glorious victories at Liao-yang and Mukden over my old friend, General Kuropatkin, the Russian commander-in-chief. Like an old fir tree, with gray hair, gray whiskers, and a gray uniform, General Oku arose and made a speech to me in Japanese. With a hissing sound he sucked in the air through a narrow crack between his dry lips and ejaculated his words slowly in a loud voice with a strangely squeaking and grating sound. He roared like a furious tiger in the tone of one commanding troops on a battlefield. But what he said was beautiful and far too kind—I was given an English translation. My answer was brief and consisted of the only words I had learned in Japanese for this occasion: *"Konnicheva omaneki kudasare arrigato sonchimasu"* (I thank you for the hospitality shown me tonight).

None of our hosts ranked lower than major general, and their number included General Oshima, the governor general of Kwantung, whom I later met at his post, General Hasegawa, who had taken Port Arthur in two days in 1894 and now was commander-in-chief in Korea, and General Fukushima, whom I had met in Berlin in 1892, then a major and military attaché at the Japanese Legation. Upon completing his service in the German capital, he rode home on horseback all the way from Berlin, through Siberia, Manchuria, and Korea, and acquired a personal knowledge of these countries and their roads which was very valuable to him during the war, when he held a high post on the General Staff. He was awarded the large gold medal of the Geographical Society for his feat on horseback.

When I look back upon that dinner, given by a few of the army's victorious officers, it seems almost symbolic. Perhaps those gentlemen had a feeling that their successors to the high military posts in the next generation would become interested in the inner parts of the large continent and in the knowledge of it, to which I had been in a position to contribute.

I spent a few hours with Prince Yamagata, the field marshal, who was seventy years of age and who had been chief of the General Staff during the war with Russia, and in charge of the operations. I wandered beside him up and down the paths in the small garden, over arched bridges and artificial miniature mountains.

After the autumn maneuvers Admiral Togo took a well-earned rest at his house. He received me most courteously. He was reticent and serious, but smiled charmingly when I congratulated him on the victories that had made his name immortal. It seemed almost like a paradox that this small, inconspicuous man, wearing an ordinary kimono and sitting on the floor in his doll's house had annihilated the iron-clad giants of the Russian navy in two of the most decisive naval battles in history.

Count Nogi, the general who had seized Port Arthur after seven months' siege, sat with a bandaged leg when I visited him in his home. He was jovial and witty and literally fired questions at me regarding Tibet. Four years later the Emperor Mutsuhito died, and Nogi and his wife then committed harakiri in order to accompany and serve the great Mikado on his journey in the underworld.

I once expressed to some Japanese friends my surprise that they and people generally apparently showed so little respect and admiration for the great men who had saved their country from the Russian grip. They answered, "There is nothing remarkable in doing one's duty to one's country—that is what we all must do."

One day the Empress had invited the diplomatic corps and a number of other guests to a garden party in one of the gardens of the Palace. Her Majesty appeared, small and pale, and graciously greeted the white strangers. She was accompanied by a number of ladies-in-waiting, and after her came a small group of lovely, happy, and graceful princesses, two of whom spoke French and could not hear enough of my Tibetan adventures. The mild autumnal winds rustled in the red crowns of the maples above us, and outside the wall around "the forbidden city" life hummed in this strange metropolis, which thirty years ago more resembled a gigantic village than an imperial city.

Another incident from my visit to Japan is vivid in my memory. Just as my stay in Tokyo was drawing to an end, I received a telegraphic invitation from Prince Ito Hirobumi to visit him at Seoul. I traveled via Fusan through Korea and everywhere had a definite feeling that the newly acquired country was being thoroughly modernized at the hands of General Ito. The Koreans wished to retain their old traditions, family customs, and habits, and dissatisfaction with the Japanese rule was seething among them.

Ito governed Korea with dictatorial power, and found pleasure in telling of his past life and of his plans for the future. He stated that Japan would become one of the greatest empires in the world, that eastern Siberia would be occupied as far as Lake Baikal, and that the Korean people would die out.

One day he said to me:

"The last Emperor of Korea, who has for some time been detained in his own palace here in Seoul, will be dethroned in two days' time and taken in custody. But he will be free tomorrow and I have arranged an audience for you, which will be the last one of his reign. Tomorrow will thus be an historical day in Seoul, and it may be of interest for you to return home with the memory of an historical episode, a conversation with this last Emperor on the last day he still wears his crown. For the day after tomorrow the Korean Imperial crown will be crushed forever."

Two of Prince Ito's attendants drove me to the palace, where I was courteously received by the unfortunate monarch, dressed in the customary white Korean costume. He was a man of middle height, pale and serious. The audience was short; he asked me a few questions, handed me the Grand Cross of "The Eight Elements" and wished me a pleasant journey back to Sweden. But what could I wish the Emperor, knowing that the prison gates would close behind him the following day! And I could not very well express my pity. The great reconstruction of East Asia had begun and the Japanese Empire had been enlarged by incorporating an empire on the mainland. Thirty years were to pass before the Empire was to be enlarged by yet another "empire"—Manchukuo.

It was evident that the aged, white-bearded Prince Ito did not feel safe in his residential town. I remember the atmosphere at a banquet there on the fifteenth of December, 1908, when the Prince returned from an inspection outside of Seoul. The tramp of horses' hoofs was heard in the frozen street. A couple of torch bearers dashed past on horseback and a yellowish red light played on shops and warehouses. Then came a cavalry detachment and a small black closed carriage drawn by two black Russian trotters and escorted by a few more horsemen. Prince Ito sat inside the carriage, and it was the duty of the soldiers to protect him from attempts on his life. Absolute quiet reigned in the room and the Japanese stood silent until the light from the torches had died away in the distance. It could be felt that an autocrat, a man of iron will, had rushed past.

On October 26 the following year, Prince Ito was killed at Harbin railway station, hit by the bullet of a Korean assassin. A man of the people wanted to revenge the lost independence of his country.

In 1910, when General Terauchi resided at Seoul, Korea was renamed Chosen, a state of the Japanese Empire. Finally I also visited General Oshima, the governor general of Kwantung, and chief commander of Port Arthur, and for three days had the opportunity of carefully studying the famous fortress under expert military guidance, and following the whole process of investment up to the surrender. Almost four years had passed since that time and nothing had been done except to remove corpses and rubbish. We visited the various forts, in whose casemates the wild battles had been fought man to man, and where the dead had served as barricades for the living. There was no indication that the fortress was once more to be put in repair; for the Japanese the important thing was that no one else occupied it.

My round trip in the Empire, which for two reasons could be called the Land of the Rising Sun, ended in Mukden, the capital of Manchuria, already then coveted by the Japanese.

XIX

Japan during the Last Three Decades

IT REMAINS FOR US TO RECALL THE MOST IMPORTANT MILE-
stones on Japan's road from the time of the Russo-Japanese
war up to the great war she is at present waging against
China. On August 23, 1914, Japan declared war on Germany.
On November 7 the Japanese captured the fortress of Tsingtao in Kiaochow, the German Shantung colony.

On January 18, 1915, while Europe was busy with the
Great War, Japan submitted to China the Twenty-one Demands which among other things declared that Japan was to
have the German rights in Shantung, on which point the
Allies gave Japan their secret support. Japan also demanded
special advantages in Manchuria, Shantung, the Yangtse Valley, and Fukien. The fifth group of the Twenty-one Demands
meant such an interference in China's sovereignty, from a
commercial, military, and administrative point of view, that
if China had accepted it, she would have been reduced to a
vassal state or a protectorate under Japan. Thanks to England, Japan had to waive these far-reaching demands, but
after a Japanese ultimatum, the others had to be accepted.
Through the Versailles Treaty of 1919, Japan took over Germany's rights in Shantung.

During a short period in 1918 Japan as well as the United
States had occupied certain parts of eastern Siberia, but had
to give them up when Kolchak was defeated by the Bolshe-
viks. The Japanese kept the Amur district until 1922.

Through the Five-Power Treaty in Washington in February, 1922, Japan agreed to limit her naval armaments. In the

same year Japan was party to the Nine-Power Treaty which guaranteed China's inviolability and equal rights for all powers in the Middle Kingdom. Anglo-American pressure at the same time induced Japan to return to China all former German possessions in Shantung. The old treaty between Japan and England was replaced by a new one between England, the United States, France, and Japan, agreeing to status quo in the Pacific.

On September 1, 1923, Japan was shaken by an extremely violent earthquake which reduced the whole of Yokohama to dust and ashes, and destroyed more than one third of Tokyo. The earthquake, which lasted a minute and a half, occurred at noon, when fires were burning for the midday meal in all the small inflammable houses. Expressed in lives and property the loss to Japan through this earthquake was just as great as that incurred by the Russo-Japanese war. I was at that time in San Francisco where collections were started on a large scale, and I contributed the receipts of a couple of lectures—a drop in the ocean. Money and clothes for the distressed were also collected in China. On October 6 I arrived in Yokohama, where the smoke still hung over the ruins. In Tokyo I received a deep and indelible impression of the misfortune that had struck the great nation.

During the following years, the Japanese emigration to California was restricted by the tightened immigration laws of the United States, and this may have contributed to the growing desire for more territorial space in Asia. But the time was not yet ripe to put such thoughts into effect, and when the new National Government in China ascended to power in 1928, it was acknowledged by Japan.

Japan has changed in many respects since my first visit there. The atmosphere of delicacy and charm about these people and their streets has largely disappeared; since the earthquake Tokyo and Yokohama have grown into large, modern towns of a Western, mostly American style.

When I last visited Japan, in 1933, I distinctly perceived the effects of the invasion and occupation of Manchuria, which had begun sixteen months earlier. A couple of obstinate generals and a number of bandit hordes were still offering resistance, and at Kobe and Moji I saw some of the transport vessels that carried new troops to the mainland. Once when such a vessel was leaving the quay, I looked in vain for signs of enthusiasm. But it may be natural that silence reigns when soldiers set out for unknown destinies, and for those remaining at home it can be no pleasure to see them go. The masses of the people did not understand much of what was happening. Now, six and a half years later, when greater and greater masses of soldiers are sent away from Japan, the causes for rejoicing are fewer than ever. Far too numerous are those who will never again see their sons, brothers, and husbands, but will receive instead a small urn containing the ashes of a fallen soldier.

XX

The Causes of the War

CHIANG KAI-SHEK WORKED INDEFATIGABLY AT HIS GREAT
unifying task and the regeneration of China. The years
passed and his work advanced. The Japanese could not help
seeing that something unusual was going on in China.
They evidently began to feel nervous in Tokyo, unexpected reports having been received from the ambassador in
China, telling of growing determination and nationalism,
and of increasing unity. Reliable Japanese observers had noticed great activity in the Yangtse Valley, the defense being
strengthened, active patriotism, a social cleansing called the
New Life Movement, a revival of the old Confucian virtues,
improved finances, an improvement of the banking system,
and a willingness to co-operate with Japan—no anti-Japanese
tendencies, but resistance to Japanese penetration.

Co-operation with China on grounds of equality! Never!
The Japanese leaders had already announced clearly enough
that their aim was the subjugation of the whole of China,
making it a vassal state. And now strong forces were at work
to cross this proud scheme!

The Middle Kingdom was beginning to develop into a military power which in time might grow in strength and become
superior to Japan's. China might prevent Japan's expansion
on the continent. Chinese industry showed signs of flourishing to such an extent that it might become a dangerous com-
petitor. Supported by foreign loans and investments, China
was able to face the future with confidence. The administration was being consolidated, and no one could deny that
Chiang Kai-shek's government was the strongest and most

honest that China had had for a hundred years. The wise rule expressed by Prince Yamagata in 1916 was remembered: "A strong emperor is the most essential factor for the regeneration of China and to enable her to surpass Japan. Consequently Japan does not want a strong emperor in China. Still less does Japan desire a successful republic in this country. What Japan wants is a feeble and powerless China. A weak China under a weak emperor under the influence of Japan would be ideal."

The Japanese propaganda advanced other excuses. It said that communism, anarchism, and disorder made it a mission and a duty for Japan to bring order into the Chinese house. It was considered opportune always to blame the invasion of China on communism. For ten years Chiang Kai-shek had fought the communists in China and finally got the better of them. None the less the Japanese propaganda claimed that the Marshal was a communist and that Japan would liberate China from him as well as from the communist plague. Chinese communism, however, was entirely different from the Bolshevism preached in Canton by Joffe, Karakhan, Borodin, and Galen (Bluecher) during Sun Yat-sen's time. It was and is an agrarian revolutionary movement to the good of the peasants, and strives to liberate some hundreds of millions of practically enslaved peasants from the tyranny of blood-sucking landowners. If Chiang Kai-shek had been allowed to carry out his work, the life of the agricultural population would have taken a different turn. And now the Japanese were talking of exterminating a communism which in reality did not exist.

We have seen that the Sian incident paved the way for understanding between Chiang Kai-shek and the communists in the northwest, who turned out to be some of the Marshal's best troops in the war. At the large annual meeting of the Kuomintang in February, 1937, immediate resistance to Japan was decided upon—not as before: "Unification before everything else."

During the war whose threshold we have now reached, the Japanese have proved to be excellent soldiers, but impossible psychologists and propagandists. When they announce that they fight the Kuomintang because it is communistic, but not the people, the question arises: Then why this cruelty to the people? When Japan demanded the extirpation of communism and the installation of a strong government in China, why then start a war just when the anticommunistic Chiang Kai-shek had risen to power and formed his strong Central Government at Nanking? Ever since the revolution in 1911 up to his accession to power in 1928, the Chinese government had been very weak indeed. Why was not the Japanese attack made at the time when China was weakest, instead of after its awakening to new life? Prince Konoye had declared: "Our aim is not to acquire land, nor to divide China." As late as January 16, 1938, the Japanese government solemnly declared that they would respect China's territorial integrity and sovereignty—at the very time when the Japanese armies were busy laying Chinese provinces under the Imperial scepter.

The gentlemen in Japan who invent and organize a propaganda of this kind must believe that the rest of the entire world is far more stupid than they are. It would be much simpler and more comprehensible if they said: "We fear nothing from China's military power, and a preventive war is thus absolutely unnecessary. But financially, morally, and nationally, China is threatening to surpass us, and that is why she must be crushed before it is too late."

Those defending Japan's occupation of Chinese territory find still another excuse for the expansion on the Asiatic mainland in the rapid growth of the Japanese people and an overpopulation necessitating emigration to the continent, particularly since the United States has introduced restrictions for the immigration to California, and Mexico and Brazil have taken similar steps. Japan's population, now 71 millions, is increased by about one million a year. Furthermore the industrialization requires raw material and markets. The Chinese reply that their country with its 450 millions is also overpopulated and cannot be burdened any further. In seven years from 1932, it is estimated that 6,000 to 7,000 Japanese emigrated to Manchuria. More than half of Japan's population consists of peasants working under feudal conditions for a million land-owners. The peasants decline with thanks the offer to settle down in Manchuria with its endless, naked plains and, in winter, frozen ground. The Japanese are not made for such a severe climate, while to the Chinese emigrants Manchuria is an ideal country, and 35 million Chinese have moved there and cultivate the soil with success. To them the frozen ground is in no way frightening.

It had been promised that the iron, coal, and agricultural products of Manchuria should be shared by the entire Japanese people. In reality it is Mitsui and the other large commercial houses that have appropriated all the revenue from Manchuria. As far as the masses are concerned, the conquest of the Three Northeastern Provinces has meant nothing but increased taxes, in addition to the one milliard yen that the struggle with the bandits had already cost the State a couple of years ago. The excuse now is that Manchuria will not be a paying proposition until the whole of China has been occupied.

Since 1932 Manchuria and the armaments have caused Japan an annual deficit of 40 million pounds sterling. When the war started in 1937, Japan had no monetary reserves, but a national debt of 11 milliard yen. In the budget year, 1938-9, the Government had to borrow 6.5 milliard yen (541 million pounds).

When the Japanese refer to anarchy and communism in China and the overpopulation in Japan as the three foremost

causes of the war, it must be remembered that the two first
are mere excuses, while the third is not entirely unreasonable.
There is no doubt but that Japan with her scant area, inexorably limited by the sea, lacks space for her ever growing
population. From 1875 to 1925 Japan's population was
doubled, the industrialism at the same time giving birth to
the labor proletariat. The demand for raw material became
greater and greater every year.

The inhabitants of the British Isles at the extreme west of
the old world, whose position is similar to that of the Japanese islanders, had released themselves centuries earlier than
the Japanese from the bondage placed upon them by the sea,
and they had made the sea their obedient servant, which
opened the roads to distant, unknown worlds. Thanks to their
domination of the seas the British have placed one fourth of
the surface of the earth under their rule.

The overpopulation and industrialization of Japan naturally tend toward a similar development. We can follow this
process day by day. The foundations of the British Empire
are economic and commercial, those of Japan military and
aggressive. Consequently the Japanese development must take
place far more quickly than the British, perhaps in just as
many years as England required decades to attain her present
position. Otherwise Japan would suffer financial death. With
ruthless energy and power she has started on her road toward
the stars, and she will not stop until she has reached her goal.
And it is believed that this goal can be reached mainly at
England's expense. We have already witnessed the first stages
—Shanghai, Canton, Kulangsu, and Tientsin. While Japan's
determination must be admired, the English statesmen must
also be regarded—if not with admiration, at least with astonishment and surprise, considering the stoical calm with which
they have awaited the fate that has threatened Hong Kong,
Singapore, and India. What is really revolutionizing is not
Japan's war with China, but the prelude betraying Japan's

desire to change places with England as the greatest maritime power in the world. The slogan, "a New Order in East Asia," is but a faint variation of the relentless maxim, "Asia for the Asiatics," which also embraces the demand that the white people be banished from that continent.

The fact that the war broke out in the summer of 1937 was perhaps due less to the impulse the extremists received through the financial difficulties of Japan than to the general unrest in Europe. On account of the civil war in Spain and other troubles Great Britain and France were prevented from helping China. The execution of high Russian officers indicated domestic troubles in the Soviets. America was certainly not inclined to disturb her lucrative trade with Japan. The Anti-Comintern Pact meant additional strength for Tokyo. No great power would lift a finger if Japan took possession of Northern China, which enterprise would be facilitated by Chinese traitors.

The opportunity was excellent. Hesitation and procrastination might spoil everything. And in the night between July 7 and 8, 1937, the war broke out.

XXI

The Outbreak of the War

JUST AS MARCO POLO'S NAME WILL FOREVER BE CONNECTED with the discovery of Asia, the monumental bridge, Lukouchiao, across the Hun-ho, not far from the southwestern corner of Peking, which foreigners to this day associate with Marco Polo's name, will forever be remembered and mentioned in connection with the war between Japan and China. For it was near this bridge that the great war kindled, a war that may influence human history for centuries.

This bridge impressed Marco Polo as much as it does the traveler of today, for he describes it in detail and also fairly accurately, although the bridge has been partly rebuilt since his time. Strangely enough he gives it a Persian name, Pulisanghin (Pul-i-Sangin), the Stone Bridge, probably because foreign merchants used that name, or because he got it from a Persian interpreter.

Having described Cambaluc (Peking) and the pompous court and wealth of Khubilai Khan, Marco Polo goes on to say:

"When you leave the City of Cambaluc and have ridden ten miles, you come to a very large river which is called Pulisanghin, and flows into the ocean, so that merchants with their merchandise ascend it from the sea. Over this River there is a very fine stone bridge, so fine indeed, that it has very few equals. The fashion of it is this: it is 300 paces in length, and it must have a good eight paces of width, for ten mounted men can ride across it abreast. It has 24 arches and as many water-mills, and 'tis all of very fine marble, well built and firmly founded. Along the top of the bridge there is on either side a parapet of marble slabs and columns, made in this way: At the beginning of the bridge there is a marble column, and under it a marble lion, so that the column stands upon the lion's loins, whilst on the top of the column there is a second marble lion, both being of great size and beautifully executed sculpture. At the distance of a pace from this column there is another precisely the same, also with its two lions, and the space between them is closed with slabs of gray marble to prevent people from falling over into the water. And thus the columns run from space to space along either side of the bridge, so that altogether it is a beautiful object." [1]

The great merchant of Venice little dreamed that the bridge to which he had devoted so much attention was to become famous among Europeans more than five hundred years later, under his own name, and still less could he foresee that 664 years after his trip to China one of the most fatal wars in history was to burst into flames near the very bridge described by him.

It happened in the night between the seventh and eighth of July, 1937. At Fengtai railway station outside Peking, the Japanese had erected barracks for several thousand men—in a country that was not theirs! A Japanese detachment carried out night maneuvers by the Marco Polo bridge, and in a feigned attack on the small town of Wanping shots were fired. A Chinese post at the bridge thought it was an attack and fired some shots. A skirmish ensued. A couple of Japanese and many Chinese fell. The Japanese demanded that the Chinese army stationed in the neighborhood should be removed. When Japanese reinforcements had arrived, Chiang Kai-shek sent a couple of his divisions from Hankow to Paoting, one hundred and forty kilometers southwest of Peking. At the same time he explained that he desired peace but would defend

---

[1] Yule's edition of *The Book of Ser Marco Polo,* which, besides, contains other information regarding the Marco Polo bridge.

One End of the Marco Polo Bridge, Near Which the First Shot in the Present Sino-Japanese War Was Fired.

Photograph by G. Montell

Street Scene in Peking.

himself if forced to fight. Shortly afterward bombs were dropped over Tientsin and on July 30 the Japanese were masters of that town and its harbor, Tangku. On August 8 the Japanese marched into the old Imperial city of Peking. On August 20 Kalgan was occupied, that historical gateway from China to Mongolia and Siberia; on September 12 Tatung was taken, and on October 3, Techow, on the boundary between Hopei and Shantung. When Taiyuanfu, the capital of Shansi, had been conquered on November 8, almost the whole of Hopei and the railway in Shansi were in the hands of the invaders. As a result of treachery and inability on the Chinese side, the Northern Provinces were lost in the course of four months. The valleys, mountain ridges, and passes of Shansi offered every possibility for an effective defense. If the Chinese had taken warning from Manchuria's fate and been prepared to offer resistance, the Japanese would have found Shansi a hard nut to crack, as pointed out by Professor J. G. Andersson. Two years later the Chinese made several successful counterattacks in Shansi and recovered parts of the province. Chiang Kai-shek could not risk going there—he had more important tasks south of the Yellow River. But in order to alleviate the Japanese pressure in the north, he concentrated his best troops in Shanghai, where five years earlier the 19th Route Army had withstood all attacks for two months.

On August 13 action began in Shanghai. Before the war Japan had 4,000 marines in her concession and just as many on board the fleet on the Hwangpu. Three thousand marines were then sent over from Tokyo as reinforcement. Thirty warships constituted the base of operations. At the end of August the Japanese invading corps had at its disposal forty airplanes and eighty or a hundred tanks.

The Chinese defense consisted of 6,000 men under General Wang Fu, 10,000 police, and a civil guard. On August 12 the 87th and 88th Divisions arrived. The Northern Railway

Station was put into a state of defense, and the lower Yangtse was blocked by mines. On the morning of August 13 the Japanese went to the attack with armored cars, and artillery set to work in the afternoon. New Japanese reinforcements suffered losses when landing. Three days later the Chinese made a counterattack and drove back the enemies. Up to September 13 the Chinese were successful in warding off the attacks. The Japanese then had at their disposal one hundred warships and four hundred airplanes. The Chinese were no match for such forces, and their losses were great. But their sacrifices were not made in vain, for this was the first opportunity Chiang Kai-shek's young army had had to show its country, the enemy, and the rest of the world what it could do. The Yo Regiment, which defended Paoshan on the mouth of the Yangtse against overwhelming odds from September 5 to September 12, held out until the last man fell. At Shanghai the army of the new China received its baptism of fire.

The Japanese fleet was ready in time for this new deathblow to China's largest city. General Matsui, the Governor of Formosa, made an inspection flight to northern China and continued from there to Shanghai, which became the center of operations, with Matsui commander-in-chief.

Prince Konoye, the prime minister, a liberal pacifist, had to yield completely to the will of the military dictatorship. Heavier taxes were imposed upon the Japanese people, and they were to be drilled into rapture about the war with China —which was no easy matter. The Japanese peasants, peaceful and industrious, had no reason to hate their Chinese brethren, who had never wished to touch a hair of their heads.

After three months the Japanese had 250,000 men at Shanghai. Chiang Kai-shek hoped that the foreigners who had their interests there would not tolerate the effrontery of the Japanese, but become involved in the war on his side. It was also of vital importance for the Chinese to safeguard the customs revenues, the most important source of income of the Nanking Government. When the fight began the foreign concessions, belonging to England, the United States, Italy, and France, were defended by their own troops, and for three months the foreigners succeeded in protecting their Western communities. Under the pretext of wanting to defend their part of the international settlement, the Japanese army and navy had made the northern part of the settlement their base. The Chinese crack troops resisted the Japanese for months, causing them severe losses. Foreign officers declared that the Chinese soldiers were equal to the Japanese both with regard to endurance and courage. Other experts stated that they had never seen or heard of anything that could be compared with the bravery of the Chinese divisions in their defense of Chapei. But as the Japanese leadership and equipment were superior, they pressed the front line farther and farther west until it extended 30 kilometers northwest, from Chapei and the Northern Railway Station to the shore of the Yangtse at Linho. Along that front about 250,000 Japanese were ranged against half a million Chinese.

In the night of October 27 the Chinese withdrew from Chapei, having set fire to that part of the city. It was a gigantic fire. A million people lost their homes. Throngs of unfortunates swarmed out of the burning districts, poor, aged and sick, women and children. Japanese flags were already fluttering from houses not yet reached by the fire. An heroic battalion of Chinese soldiers stood its ground for another four days, as no order to retreat had reached it.

In his book, *China Fights for the World*, Professor Andersson gives a vivid description of the horrible destruction in Shanghai, which he witnessed in person:

"From dawn on the twenty-seventh (of October) throughout the whole day we saw from our lofty look-out fire after fire flare up and spread, till we had before us a continuous front of fire the length of which was estimated by different observers at from four to six miles. I cannot even guess at the depth of this conflagration, and it is quite likely that here and there in the sea of fire there were islands which escaped destruction; but it appears probable that four square miles would be a very cautious estimate of the urban area that was wiped out by fire. As this was one of the most thickly populated quarters of Shanghai, it has been conjectured that something like a million people lost their homes, even if large numbers had fled at an earlier stage from this inferno of street-fighting.

"There is no doubt that night of burning of Chapei will be reckoned as one of the great conflagrations in the history of the world. On me personally the sight of the unparalleled zone of fire made a strangely nauseating impression. My thoughts were split up into tens of thousands of little pictures of all the poor, thickly clustered homes where only a few months ago an industrious peace-loving population went about its daily work. Where are they now, all these small tradesmen and workers who have lost all? How many old people, pregnant women and little children were left to be roasted to death among the glowing ruins?"

On November 5th the Japanese navy set ashore new reinforcements, about 30,000 men, on the northern shore of the Bay of Hangchow, eighty kilometers southwest of Shanghai. With the right generalship the Chinese would have been able to stop them, but missed the opportunity. The Japanese could therefore advance toward Shanghai. At the same time they introduced a number of armored motorboats on the Yangtse and on the canal to Lake Taihu. The Chinese retreated or fled.

On November 19 the famous and picturesque town of Soochow, the Venice of China, was occupied, and at the beginning of December the advance began toward Nanking, the capital of China since 1928. The Chinese retreated, but burned and destroyed all material that could not be removed.

On December 7 Chiang Kai-shek flew to Nanking where General T'ang Sheng-chih was in charge of the defense. On December 13 Nanking fell, and the Chinese crossed the Yangtse to the northern shore. Japanese warships went up to Hsiakwan, Nanking's port on the river, and airplanes bombed the British and American gunboats stationed there, killing and wounding several members of the crews. President Roosevelt demanded that the Japanese Emperor be informed.

The Japanese arrogance toward the Westerners has been startling all the way along. Their triumphal march through the international settlements of Shanghai was nothing but pure provocation, an expression of their contempt for the foreigners. Even before Shanghai was taken, the Japanese had dropped bombs over Nanking and Canton and other cities, and had blocked practically the entire Chinese coast.

Now, Nanking had fallen, that old city roused from a long sleep, the city where Sun Yat-sen, the "Father of the Revolution," reposed in his magnificent mausoleum on Purple Hill. Here General Matsui let loose all the powers of Hell. The hounding of the wild animals onto the Christians in the arena of the Colosseum in the time of Nero was a fairly harmless spectacle compared with the orgies of bestial cruelty which were considered the well-deserved reward of the Japanese soldiers after the courage they had displayed in fighting the Chinese. The unfortunate city became the scene of murder, plunder, rape, and cruelty defying all description. The soldiers practiced bayonet attacks on innocent Chinese. The victims were tied together, drenched with kerosene and burned. Everything of value, industries, factories, institutes, was burned down. The magnificent building of the Ministry of Communications with its red-lacquered columns, its exquisite mosaics, and its modern application of old and beautiful art, a creation which I always shall remember as a fairy palace, was leveled to the ground.

Why? Who had anything to gain by this mad rage toward humans and inanimate objects? The war could not possibly be furthered by the fact that desolate, defiled women in desperation jumped into the river. If the intention of these victors without a trace of chivalry was to take over the inheritance from the Son of Heaven and Chiang Kai-shek, they could have nothing to gain by all that destruction. Did they perhaps have a feeling that some day the Chinese would return to their capital? But the fact remains that this vandalism created a hatred of the Japanese soldiers that was to spread all over China and enhance the rage of the masses and the dauntlessness of the guerilla bands. The cruelties after the fall of Magdeburg are remembered with horror to this day; and when Skobelev, having taken Gok-tepe, had the entire Turkoman garrison shot to regimental music, the widows and children of those killed could for years after the outrage not hear Russian Cossack music without weeping.

General Matsui was recalled, perhaps less on account of the cruelties in Nanking than on account of the two weeks spent to no avail, which time Chiang Kai-shek used to arrange for the defense of Hankow.

A month before Nanking fell the Marshal had decided to change from tactic defense to strategic operations, and to use the whole of China proper as a field of operation. As a result of this splendid and bold plan, he moved his own and the Government's headquarters further inland. By this action China and her great leader showed that they were prepared to stake their country and their national independence on one card, to risk everything except their honor, to hold out until death, and to make the utmost sacrifices for their liberty.

XXII

The War Spreads

THE FIRST OF THE THREE PHASES OF THE WAR HAD BEEN going on from July 7 to December 13, 1937. The second lasted from December 14, 1937, to May 19, 1938. The second phase primarily embraced the struggle for the three most important railways, Tientsin-Pukow, the Lunghai line, and Peking-Hankow, and also the operations in Northern China. The Japanese had taken the Nankou pass and the Shü-yün pass west of it, where the defenders were killed to a man. In northern Suiyuan the Japanese had tried to win the Mongol Prince, Teh Wang (Sunit Wang), but the Mongols did not turn up, and a Japanese expeditionary corps which had ventured as far as the outskirts of the desert, was forced back by guerilla troops. They were thus not successful in driving a wedge between Inner and Outer Mongolia. Before the outbreak of the war the Japanese had tried to start an autonomous movement with the assistance of Teh Wang, but the Mongolian troops had been defeated by the Chinese and the lamasery Beli-miao (Peiling-miao) had been taken on November 24, 1936, which had stopped the advance of the Japanese in that district.

The Japanese advance had ceased in Shansi and northern Honan. Chinese communist troops had joined Chiang Kai-shek's army and appeared in strong guerilla bands, irritating the enemy like swarms of hornets.

The Japanese suffered great losses in attempts to break through to the Yellow River, the province of Shensi, and the Lunghai line, which were in vain. Shensi was the most coveted of the occupied provinces, and finally the Japanese withdrew their troops to the northern point of Honan. Their goal there was Chengchow, the important junction of the Lunghai-Hankow and Peking-Hankow lines. At the same time the attacks began, from the northeast and southeast, on the strategically important Hsüchow, where the Lunghai line crosses the Tientsin-Pukow line.

The war of destruction that the Japanese had planned and begun changed into more sporadic and planless actions, which did not seem to follow a fixed line of operation. They made attacks here and there and often met violent counterattacks. In the north the Chinese no longer tied their troops to the defense of certain points, and by obstinate flank attacks they prevented the enemy from reaching the northern bank of the Yellow River. In the south they stopped the Japanese on the River Hwai. When the enemy had taken the entire northern shore of the Yellow River, he penetrated through Tsinan into Shantung, whose governor and commander-in-chief, Han Fu-chu, did not even trouble to offer resistance, which cowardice cost him his life. He was shot.

Chiang Kai-shek himself then intervened at Yenchow. The furious struggles that had been going on there for a couple of months resulted in a decisive battle at Taierhchuang. The Japanese had advanced from Tsinan, while another army advanced from the south. The Chinese were also threatened by Japanese troops from the west, but these were stopped from crossing the Yellow River. The attack on Hsüchow was thus made from three directions. The aim of the Japanese drive was to obtain the whole Tientsin-Pukow railway and to unite the puppet administrations in Peking and Nanking into one single government under Japanese control. And the Chinese fought doggedly to prevent the realization of such plans.

The battle of Taierhchuang took place on the sixth of April, the Chinese under command of the generals Li Tsung-jen and Tan An-po, and the Japanese under General Itagaki, later minister of war. It is believed that the Chinese on that occasion had 800,000 men in the field. Their patrol service and reconnaissance were unsatisfactory and the artillery was insufficient. But the artillery that did exist was of great value and the battle resulted in a glorious victory for the Chinese. Twenty thousand Japanese were killed or wounded and large quantities of war material fell into the hands of the victors. It is said that this was the worst defeat that Japan had suffered since its rise as a military power. At Taierhchuang the Japanese learned that strength and warrior spirit lay dormant in the armies of young China, which properly directed, could be roused to accomplish respectable feats. The victory inspired the Chinese with confidence, courage, and hope, and taught them that the Japanese invaders were not unconquerable. Military experts are of opinion that the battle of Taierhchuang marks a turning-point, for there the Chinese demonstrated on the battlefield that they could deprive their enemies of supremacy in East Asia.

It was only after the invader had obtained large reinforcements that they could take Hsüchow, on May 19. But the Chinese did not lose their self-control in the face of this defeat. They retreated in the direction of Kaifeng, the capital of Honan. The Japanese had hoped to seize that important city at about Christmas, 1937, thus disheartening the Chinese with a parallel to Cannae, but there, too, their calculations went amiss. The Chinese retreat was carried out in exemplary order, and when the pincers closed they caught nothing.

East of Hsüchow the Japanese had cut off the Lunghai line and west of the Tientsin-Pukow line they were penetrating southward, while the Chinese still held Hsüchow. At the last moment the bulk of the Chinese forces broke through the embrace of the Japanese armies and advanced toward Kaifeng and Chengchow. Near Kaifeng the Chinese generals defeated the pursuing Japanese troops under Doihara, while the Chinese rearguard pushed southeast and formed guerilla troops, which soon became annoying to the enemy's lines of communication and centers. The Japanese had evidently intended to advance to Chengchow at the crossing of the Peking-Hankow and Lunghai railways. They had instead become involved in fights in Shantung, a province that they had believed could be taken in one week from the incompetent Han Fu-chu, but the fighting lasted six months. The Chinese had shown strategic as well as tactical ability. After the trying days between Shanghai and Nanking, when they concentrated on the tactical defense of certain points, they had switched over to operations on a larger scale. The second phase of the war developed into a front war in a curve toward the southeast around Nanking and toward the northwest along the Grand Canal. There the Chinese fought deftly and well, giving the Japanese no chance to break through. True are the Chinese reports saying that it would not have been possible to achieve such successes unless the leaders had had soldiers willing and able to march, to fight with the utmost intrepidity, and to fall at a hopeless post after firing their last bullet.

The third phase of the war began on May 20, 1938, and ended with the occupation of Hankow on October 25.

The southern curve of the front covered Hankow, the northern shore of the Yellow River, the Lunghai railway, and Chengchow. By conquering Hsüchow the Japanese had not definitely taken the Lunghai railway any more than the Tientsin-Pukow line. As long as the guerilla troops carry out their night attacks, burn or demolish bridges and railway stations, break up the rails and attack night trains, the value of possessing such railways in the occupied parts of China is problematic. In the spring and summer when the *kaoliang* fields are two to three meters high, guerilla bands can hide anywhere among them without being observed.

The goal of the Japanese was now Chengchow and the Peking-Hankow railway. When advancing westward they en-

countered just as great difficulties as in the areas west of the
Tientsin-Pukow railway, where the Chinese made several
flank attacks.

However, nature intervened, coming to the aid of the
Chinese, and at one stroke the situation at Kaifeng was
changed.

Near Chengchow the majestic Yellow River flows out over
its enormous alluvial plain, and by depositing the suspended
loess, it raises its furrow more and more, as much as nine
meters above the surrounding country, the furrow being reg-
ulated and directed by elevated banks. During the high-water
period in the summer, 23,000 cubic meters of water flow
through its bed every second. The Hwang-ho waters the
fields of the Chinese farmers, but is also a constant threat.
If the river should overflow its dike at one place only, enormous areas of the surrounding fields would be placed under
water. Frightful devastation and great loss of human lives
would be the result. It is these changes in the river bed that
cause the Hwang-ho to wander and make it disembogue into
the Yellow Sea sometimes north of the Shantung peninsula,
sometimes south of it—the same phenomenon as is found, on
a much smaller scale, in the case of the lower Tarim, although instead of flowing into the sea, that river forms a
wandering lake at its mouth, Lop-nor.

On the eleventh of June, 1938, the Hwang-ho broke
through its banks between Kaifeng and Chengchow and
flooded enormous areas in Honan, Anhwei, and Kiangsu,
when the water sought a new course down to the valley of
the Hwai. The population fled. The overflowing water ran
200 kilometers toward the southwest and in the south its
front was 100 kilometers wide.

This time the Yellow River played the part of a mighty
ally to the Chinese military command. The Japanese advance
was stopped in the district now that a whole lake obstructed
their passage, and the Chinese gained time. The attackers

consequently had to remove their operations to the Yangtse Valley and Hankow.

They needed Chengchow and the western part of the Lunghai railway as points of support for their operations in Shensi. From the Yangtse River they could make effective use of their heavy naval artillery. The Yangtse was a first-class artery for the Japanese advances toward inner China, for on its mighty waterway they could bring their warships and transport vessels not only to Hankow, but far above that town. In addition they sent considerable forces westward from Nanking via Lake Taihu in the direction of Sinyang.

The Chinese operations and counterattacks there were most unpleasant for the Japanese and often interfered with their plans. As far as Hankow was concerned, the Chinese military command was of opinion that its fall or stubborn defense would have no influence on the situation in general. The nearest aim of the military command was to defend the road to Hankow, and Hankow itself only until the water of the Yangtse—when the southwest monsoon was succeeded by the northeast monsoon—had begun to sink to such an extent that no large men-of-war could go farther up than to Hankow. The Chinese hoped that the Blue River would also come to their assistance. They evacuated Hankow on October 25 without offering resistance, having first burned everything that could be of value to the enemy and could not be taken away.

Like Hsüchow, Hankow proved to be no walk-over for the Japanese, who are considered to have made use of just as powerful war material here as the Germans and the French did on the western front during the Great War. It was said that the Japanese infantry showed signs of fatigue, while the Chinese war apparatus and organization worked perfectly. Chiang Kai-shek had no choice but to leave the defense of Canton to the provincial troops. He could not split up or enfeeble his forces in the vital areas, compared with which Canton must be considered of secondary importance. The Japanese had used six months advancing from Nanking to Hankow.

They began their attacks on June 20 along three lines, north and south of the river, and through the Chinese mined areas in the Yangtse. The resistance was more energetic and tenacious than before and caused the attackers many repulses. The Japanese reports stated that 200,000 Chinese had been surrounded west of Lake Poyang. In reality they themselves suffered a couple of defeats, which caused disorder in their plans. In the Taihu section the Chinese made an attack on August 26, recaptured several towns, and cut off the enemy's communications on the northern shore of the river. On September 8 the generals Li Ping-sen and Sun Lien-chung had a violent engagement with the enemy and took about forty of his guns. Northeast of Hankow General Ch'en Ch'eng on Sept. 28 beset the 13th Japanese division on all sides, scattering it entirely, and taking 30 guns, 200 machine guns, and more than 200 armored cars and tanks. On October 10 the generals Sih Toh and Chiang Chin-kuo, the Marshal's son, won an equally splendid victory at Teian. It was estimated that two million soldiers participated in these operations and that 400,000 of them were Japanese. The Chinese troops were too numerous, too pliant, and under too good leadership to allow themselves to be led into traps similar to those at Sedan or Tannenberg.

It must also be remembered that the Chinese were favored by fighting on their own ground. Even though the military units consisted of various elements from different provinces—which to a certain extent contributed to the realization of Chiang Kai-shek's dream of transforming the Chinese into a homogeneous people—these millions of men were working on ground they knew from their childhood, where they had grown up and lived their whole lives. They were also morally supported by the knowledge that the country belonged to them and that they, while defending their fields, farms, homes, and families, were fighting for their liberty and against the frightening prospect of becoming slaves under a foreign yoke.

To the Japanese armies, on the other hand, the country was *terra incognita* and the terrain was entirely different from theirs on the islands. They must have felt giddy at the thought of the ever growing distance from their native country and the vast expanses of land without end. A day's journey in Japan almost always meant encountering a coast. Here in China false hopes were created by lakes and obstructions were caused by rivers such as had never been heard of before. And the Japanese were compelled to penetrate farther and farther westward until they were lost among hills and mountains. Perhaps they even heard of labyrinths of rocks and ridges where they would be caught by the innumerable Chinese and shot like wild animals.

No high ideals can have inspired the Japanese soldiers on their march southward and westward. They are not fighting for the liberty of their country, for that has not been threatened by anyone, and in the long run it is impossible even for the most licentious soldiery to feel elated by the murder of innocent people and the looting of their property. They must at last grow tired, and symptoms of flagging have been observed.

During this third phase of the war, the Chinese army gave many proofs of better training, quicker operation, and more flexibility in their movements than at the beginning of the war. At the same time the leaders became bolder and more confident. The army and the whole people of China confidently hoped that the fourth phase of the war would develop to their advantage. In Japan propaganda was made in the press and by speeches. In China no other propaganda was needed than the one offered by the cruelty of the Japanese soldiers and the murdering effects of the bombs. The Chinese would stand firm as long as the bloodshed and violence lasted.

The Japanese military began this war with a contempt for the Chinese military which was quite comprehensible and even justified, being based on experiences from the years of 1894 and 1931. The defense of Shanghai, the battle of Taierhchuang, and the ever growing resistance and difficulties in conquering new land and in keeping what has been conquered, has caused the Japanese to change their minds. One of their generals has stated that the Japanese army is the best in the world, the German comes next, and the Chinese third, and he does not even mention the military forces of other nations. He seems to be of opinion that only Japanese and German soldiers surpass the Chinese in the art of war, and that is really very flattering for the latter, even if it is not actually true.

Two of the conclusions arrived at by the French author, Jean Escarra, in his book *L'Honorable Paix Japonaise*, are worth quoting in this connection:

"1. The Sino-Japanese war broke out two years too early for China but two years too late for Japan.

2. It has shattered many illusions: about the mediocrity of the Chinese soldier, about the invincibility of the Japanese army, and about the chivalry of the soldiers from Nippon.

"The Chinese has proved that he can be an excellent soldier—'an admirable soldier,' as stated by German officers serving in the Chinese army—just as brave as the Japanese, more intelligent, and better disciplined.

"The battle of Taierhchuang ended in the most crushing defeat ever suffered by a Japanese army. Foreign military observers claim that this battle constitutes a turning point in the history of Asia."

There is no exaggeration in this statement, for if it has been proved on more than one battlefield that the Chinese soldiers are superior to the Japanese, it is reasonable to conclude that if the army of a million men that Chiang Kai-shek is now drilling in the west and southwest provinces is energetically and patiently developed to the same capacity as the heroes of Chapei and Taierhchuang, the Japanese troops will no longer be victorious and their days in China will be numbered. The Rising Sun will then no longer rise in a sea of blood—the dawn in the east will promise the beginning of a new day, a new era, in old Asia.

Travelers in China who still remember the conditions prevailing in Northern China ten or twenty years ago, when the warlords were fighting each other and most of the battles were fought with "silver bullets," must have changed their opinion of Chinese warfare if they read a short news release from Chungking issued on the third of February, 1939. It stated that more than a million soldiers in Szechwan were under the command of some of China's bravest and ablest generals, real daredevils. To begin with they fought each other. Now they were fighting a common foe and their fame was being carried from west to east throughout their country. At least two divisional commanders from Szechwan and a number of brigade and regimental officers had been killed on the battlefield, and many others wounded. While suffering from the illness that finally sent him to his grave, General Liu Hsiang, Governor of Szechwan and chief of the seventh war area, led his troops to battle. He was one of the most enthusiastic spokesmen for the guerilla war. On his deathbed he cautioned his subjects "never to return to their native provinces until the Japanese had been chased away from Chinese ground."

Those to whom General Liu's last message was directed are now spread over all the fronts in China. General Yang Shen, chief of the 20th Army, is the most prominent of the Szechwan generals. He offered heroic resistance near Shanghai and obstinately defended Nanking at the beginning of the war.

Before the outbreak of the war he was directly under Chiang Kai-shek's command. When the war started he was stationed with his troops in western Kweichow, where he was Pacification Commissioner, and from there he was ordered to Hankow. In 24 days he and his army covered a distance of 1,500 kilometers which otherwise took the infantry 59 marching days. He demanded that each and every one of his soldiers should fight to the last bullet. After one week, 75 per cent of the 20th Army were killed or wounded. He immediately ordered reinforcements and fought with splendid bravery in the rear guard when the Shanghai sector was evacuated. Then he drilled his troops in guerilla tactics and taught them to utilize the terrain. After nineteen months of war the 20th Army was once more beginning to grow. In February he held his positions in Anhwei.

In the fight for Hsüchow, the army commander, Sun Tsong, and his Szechwan troops were engaged in one of the most blood-drenched battles of the war, at Tenghsien. His divisional general, Wang Ming-tsang, also displayed brilliant bravery. He fell when he and his men attacked the Japanese machine gunners, while Chen Lih, another general from Szechwan, was severely wounded. Tenghsien was taken by the Japanese, but the great intrepidity shown by the Szechwan people and the severe losses they caused the enemy was much spoken of in the neighboring sectors and helped to encourage other armies, particularly those who won the glorious victory at Taierhchuang.

But the most renowned and admired of all the generals from Szechwan is Sun Yuan-liang who led the famous 88th Division of regular troops in the fights at Shanghai. "The Lone Battalion," which aroused such great admiration all over the world when several hundred of its soldiers preferred death to retreat from Chapei, was under command of General Sun Yuan-liang, whose troops were famed for their remarkable discipline and strength. General Sun is thirty-six years old and is known for his amazing bravery in the field. He is considered to be one of the most promising generals of the new China. In Shanghai people were in great anxiety for his life. After the battle he became army commander. During Marshal Chiang Kai-shek's northern campaign he was wounded several times. In 1927 he went to Japan and went through the Military Academy in Tokyo. In 1929 the Japanese Minister of War had him removed from the Academy, as it was feared that his interest in politics was too great.

I have mentioned but a few of the generals from Szechwan. No doubt the other provinces can also present long lists of heroes who have fought and died in this war. And countless privates have died like heroes. Innumerable graves on innumerable battle fields in China hide the remains of the unknown soldier, whose act of heroism deserves a better fate than oblivion.

The surviving millions trained in the Marshal's rigid school already form the nucleus of a soldiery which, emanating from the people, will raise the prestige of this caste, leaven the nation, and teach the people the importance of military service and constant preparation. The laxity of the old Manchu system belongs to the past. The Japanese war has opened the eyes of the Chinese to how serious are the times, and one day China will be so well armed that no power will dare venture upon a new invasion. For that reason it is safe to say that this war is of universal importance, and that its blood-stained banners proclaim the dawn of a new era in old Asia.

XXIII

Direct Reports on the War in China

ANYONE WISHING TO FOLLOW THE COURSE OF THE WAR IN East Asia and its dramatic events can of course do so by reading some of the extensive literature on the subject—books, brochures, and periodical publications—not to mention the innumerable articles and telegrams in the daily press and the news bulletins. But it is not often that we have the opportunity of receiving oral information from persons who have come direct from the fronts and can relate what they have seen with their own eyes. Such an opportunity was offered me on November 6, 1938, when I had the pleasure of receiving a visit from Robert B. McClure, M.D., Field Director of the International Red Cross Committee for Central China, who spent a few days in Stockholm in order to have a conference with H.R.H. Prince Carl, who is Chairman of the Swedish Red Cross. Dr. McClure is a Canadian who has spent most of his life in China and speaks Chinese.

He told me that as late as December, 1937, the spirit of the Chinese people was depressed and almost desperate. The Japanese were looked upon almost as a kind of superior beings, unconquerable, bold and daring, in possession of inexhaustible supplies of murdering machines on the ground, on the seas, and in the air, a superhuman people, whereas the Chinese were mere humans.

But in February and March, 1938, a sudden change in feeling took place. An effective information system was started. Specially drilled and trained patriots, mostly communists, were sent out as apostles among the civil population, to farmers and peasants, villagers and workmen, coolies and paupers, in other words to this ocean of people who had no greater desire than to be allowed to help to obstruct the path of the invading armies, and with sword in hand reduce their numbers. The Chinese Government had founded a number of temporary military schools, where young, strong, and brave men received instruction, each of them subsequently to become the leader of a guerilla band. The course was neither long, nor difficult. It consisted of a catechism with about ten commandments, each of which taught the chosen adepts of the brotherhood the art of effectively combating some certain manifestation of the enemy's military resources. There was a special stratagem for nocturnal attacks on hostile infantry, a second for the cavalry, a third for motor lorries, a fourth for transport columns, a fifth for troop and material trains, a sixth for patrols, sentries, bivouacs, stations, etc.

The scouting service was developed at the same time. The guerilla war burst into flame from the different cells. The Chinese have always been good at this kind of fighting, which they have developed to a real art, and in which they can vie with Cooper's red Indians. With indefatigable patience they lie in wait for their opportunity. They slink like leopards through the grain fields, through ditches and ravines, making good use of all the irregularities of the terrain. In the deep silence of the night in some occupied area they steal up and demolish or burn the bridges, or break up the rails in a sharp bend for a distance of some fifty meters, then replace them with rails made of black, polished wood. When the wooden rails are fastened to the sleepers they bear a striking resemblance to iron rails. The guerilla band then hides in a field close by or behind a hill. The train approaches, runs off the track, is "telescoped" and wrecked. Drowsy and little aware of their whereabouts in the dark, the hostile soldiers are lost. The guerilla men crawl out of their hiding places and put a bullet or a blade into every Japanese they can get hold of.

If someone then says to a guerilla home from such an experience: "But you yourself might have been shot by a Japanese!" he replies, "What of it? That would have meant nothing compared with the pleasure of destroying a troop train!"

When I ask my authority: "If such a catastrophe takes place once, the Japanese of course take such precautions on the night trains that it cannot be repeated?" he answers. "Not a single man survives to tell the tale. The line is blocked for a few days by the wreckage, but there are other lines where the same maneuver can be tried. Moreover, the guerilla war is chameleonlike. The Chinese are prudent and ingenious. The struggle for their families and native country sharpens their wits.

The remarkable thing, according to Dr. McClure, is that after March, 1938, the whole people seemed to have been struck by an electric shock and became wide awake. No longer were the Japanese superior beings and unconquerable in war. Thanks to our tricks and night attacks, the Chinese said, we can annihilate them, wreck their troop trains, set fire to their transports, stations, and bivouacs, demolish their bridges, attack their small units, surround them and defeat them. Not even in the towns of the occupied areas are their troops safe. If small groups of the garrison go outside the city wall, for instance at Peking, they never return at all. They are shot by guerilla patrols. But they dare not go ten *li* (five kilometers) from the city. In reality the Japanese own the railways in the occupied areas only in the daytime. At night the guerilla bands are the masters. The so-called safety on even the most frequented lines in the parts of Northern China that have been longest and best occupied by the Japanese, is illustrated by the fact that trains between Peking and Tientsin have been attacked and plundered.

The old deep-rooted local patriotism, the love of the home community, explains why the guerilla bands do the best work in their home districts—a trait that surely is not characteristic of China alone. And this means a great deal when the *whole* people is fired by a common interest—to rid itself of a common foe.

The Japanese soldiers are the objects of burning hatred. The invading army made a disastrous mistake by laying hands on the wives and daughters of the peasants. This is the revenge for those outrages. On the other hand, the Chinese harbor no hatred toward the Japanese civilian population. According to Dr. McClure, the Christian Chinese follow the example of the Marshal and his wife and include the Japanese people in their daily prayers. If the Japanese leaders had been wise, they would have been able to find a formula for good co-operation between the two peoples, to the advantage of their mutual interests in East Asia.

The following incident, related by the Canadian physician, illustrates the relationship between the two fighting peoples, and also the Chinese cunning and the Japanese imprudence and haughtiness.

In a town near Kaifeng on the Hwang-ho there lived a man who had devoted his life to research work. After the revolution in 1911 he lost everything he possessed and was neglected and ignored. His ambition was aroused. He decided to make a career as a business man and to rise to a respectable position and become one of the rich and mighty in his neighborhood. He succeeded. His fortune grew. In order to make himself still more esteemed in the eyes of the people he built several watchtowers at the gates of the city and outside the wall. Being very smart, however, he used his watchtowers as warehouses for grain, peanuts, and other products from his fields.

Then came the Japanese invasion which also swept over Kaifeng and neighboring districts. This gentleman, whom we may call Wang Lung, like the hero in Pearl Buck's book, then thought that his chance had come and that he would be able to do wonderful business with the invaders with his large stores of grain. He prepared his approach to the enemies by incessantly praising the Japanese. They were coming as liberators who would save the Chinese from despotic governors, undisciplined generals, treacherous usurers and tax collectors, and heralded a new period of wealth and order in China. The Chinese ought to declare undying friendship with them.

A division of the invading army approached. The new "Wang Lung" donned his holiday clothes of black silk, and when the advance guard marched into the city, they found, at the gate, a distinguished gentleman who greeted the invaders with smiles and bows. Neither officers nor soldiers deigned to look at him. In the eyes of the new garrison he meant no more than the ragamuffins and donkeys in the gateway.

"Wang Lung" did not lose courage. He hurried in advance to his palatial house in the high street and took his stand at the entrance. The leader of the troop, a captain, threw a glance at the splendid house, ordered halt, and shouted:

"This house will be our headquarters!"

"Wang Lung" came up, bowed, and said in a humble voice: "This is my house. I bid you welcome as my honored guests."

The captain gave him a withering look, slapped his face, and roared:

"Get out of the way, you dog! We ask no permission. We are the masters of this house."

The beautiful house was decorated and prepared to receive the honored guests, but the captain turned to "Wang Lung" and shouted:

"The house is full of dust and rubbish. Sweep it!"

"Wang Lung" stammered, "I shall get my servants at once."

The captain thundered, "Shut up, you cur! Find the broom yourself if life is dear to you."

Kicked and beaten, the poor merchant had to work like a coolie with his broom, while the soldiers dirtied his rooms, made a fire in the middle of the floor and boiled their rice. After a few days there was not a whole piece of furniture in the house. Everything was ruined.

But one day the Eighth Army came from the northwest, recruited with former communists from the neighborhood of Sian, where they had witnessed the imprisonment of the Marshal. They stormed the city, which was deserted by the Japanese.

Once more "Wang Lung" stood bidding welcome at the entrance of his house. He blessed and thanked his new guests for having driven away the human devils who had beaten and tortured him and destroyed his property. And now he preached a new doctrine: Fight the Japanese to the bitter end! Drive out the beasts, the barbarians! And then he took the commissariat of the Eighth Army to his watchtowers and showed them that they were full of grain which he was only too happy to place at the disposal of the blessed troops.

In this and similar ways the Japanese invaders have behaved everywhere in the occupied provinces. They have tortured, beaten, outraged, and in every conceivable manner insulted the Chinese, thus everywhere kindling eternal hatred. When the Chinese peasant sees the Japanese soldiers take his grain in order to feed their horses, while his own children are starving to death, the savage within him is aroused, and he swears a solemn oath that he will take revenge. And there are plenty of peasants in China! By their cruel and ruthless ways the Japanese have made the accomplishment of their aim impossible. It would perhaps be possible to subjugate 450 million people if the conqueror fared gently and created order, prosperity, and justice in a human manner. But it is absolutely impossible when he kindles a hatred in these millions which will never die.

A person who probably has more personal experience of Inner and Outer Mongolia and the northernmost provinces of

China than any other European of today is my old friend
and caravaneer, F. A. Larson, "Duke of Mongolia," who arrived in Kalgan as early as 1893. When Larson left his old
hunting grounds, he had lived forty-six years almost like an
uncrowned monarch in one of the most interesting parts of
the world, and had experienced all the great political re-
adjustments that have taken place there. He had thus seen at
close range the Boxer Rebellion in 1900, the Russo-Japanese
War, the Chinese Revolution in 1911, the Mongolian Revolution in 1913, Russia's peaceful advance, the fall of the
Manchu Dynasty, the visit of the Dalai Lama to Urga and
Peking, the Yüan Shih-k'ai rule, the Japanese conquest of
Manchuria, Jehol, Chahar, and the five Northern Provinces,
and finally the outbreak of the Sino-Japanese War. The violent intolerance of foreigners expressed during the present
war made life in his old beloved districts impossible and
caused him to turn his back on Asia. When he visited me in
Stockholm on Whitsun Eve, May 27, 1939, it was his intention to stay in his native country for a couple of months
and then in the autumn go to his children in America and to
procure and manage a farm in Nevada. In spite of his seventy
years he does not like a sedentary life.

It was not difficult to guess the side that Larson took in the
present war. He was absolutely convinced that China would
win the game. Time is one of Chiang Kai-shek's very best
allies—the more time he gains, the stronger the Marshal's
position. The Japanese were mistaken when they thought
that they could effect the conquest in three months. To stop
fighting would be to lose face. In case of collapse the military
party would have no more to say—that is why the war
continues.

In 1936 Chiang Kai-shek telegraphed to Larson to come
down to Nanchang where the Marshal was staying at the
time. Larson immediately obeyed. The Marshal, Madame
Chiang, and Larson had held private conferences. It was not

the first time that Larson served as adviser to a Chinese Government concerning Mongolian affairs.

The Marshal had contrived a plan to form a military police corps which should be stationed chainlike from the district north of Kalgan over Kuku-irgen and down to Alakshan, Ninghsia, and Kansu, this corps to protect northern China against bandits and Japanese partisan corps. The command was to be in the hands of four Swedish officers and twelve Swedish N.C.O.'s, while the privates, five thousand able, young Mongols were to be trained and instructed by the Swedes. Larson offered to go home to Sweden at once to arrange the matter. But the realization of the plan was postponed on account of the political events that year, and of course had to be abandoned entirely when the war broke out. In spite of all precautions the news of this plan leaked out in the press.

Larson also related that the Japanese soldiers cannot live on Chinese food but want salt and raw fish as in Japan. Fish is thus an important article in the military commissariat, and it is easy to understand the fairly frequent trouble between Japanese fishing fleets and Russian patrol boats at Sakhalin.

According to Larson the occupation troops in northern China lead a rather precarious life. Small troops consisting of say twenty men are placed at the various railway stations. One station after the other is attacked at night by guerilla bands of a thousand men or more, who surround the station and kill the guard. No one is safe two or three kilometers from the railway. A Swedish missionary who had been called to a sick person outside Peking was captured by a guerilla patrol and taken to their well-concealed headquarters. Fortunately he had the patient's summons with him and was escorted back to Peking.

Similar episodes, though unimportant in themselves, spread a strange light over the efficiency of the Japanese occupation. In the cities where strong garrisons are stationed, the Japanese have the power, but in the country outside the city walls the guerilla bands, or the "flying divisions" as the Chinese call them, reign supreme. War is still going on even right outside Peking. There are no fronts; no methodical operations take place, but enemies of the invaders crop up everywhere like shadows in the night and do away with them, one by one or in small contingents. Some time ago it was stated in the press that the Japanese military command had decided to free the occupied areas from the guerilla bands. Such an enterprise is impossible. For it is not possible to extinguish the entire male population.

Since Peking came under Japanese sovereignty, 30,000 Japanese, men, women, and children from the very poorest and most worthless strata of the population, have been taken there, as Japan wanted to get rid of them. Six thousand proletarians had been transported to Kalgan. Neither Japan nor China can derive any advantage from this artificial transmigration and compulsory emigration. This rabble is said to behave in Peking as if they were the masters of the town. They drive honest Chinese from their homes and settle down there themselves. They grab what they want in shops and stores without paying, and if payment is demanded they complain to the military authorities, and are apparently always on the right side of justice. They receive no pecuniary support and must therefore steal.

As told above, Teh Wang, our friend Sunit Wang, was now President of the Government at Kweihwa (Suiyuan) installed by the Japanese. Larson had been his adviser in 1933.

Larson felt the same admiration for Chiang Kai-shek as all others who have had the advantage of having learned to know the Marshal. He compares him to Gustavus Vasa and rightly states that he is the man who will save China. Evidently the Japanese are of the same opinion, for when there is talk of peace negotiations their first demand is always that the Marshal is to be removed, and when a settlement of the disputes between Japan and England about Shanghai and Tientsin was discussed, the Japanese first of all demanded that the English stop supporting the Marshal.

The "Duke of Mongolia" is an optimist. He told us in confidence that as soon as the old order had been restored, he would return to Mongolia, put on his old fiery red wolfskin fur coat and his yellow foxskin cap, jump into the saddle, and race after his horses across the endless steppes.

XXIV

The Degeneration of the War

AS THE WAR CONTINUED AND SPREAD, THE CHINESE HAD AN opportunity of reorganizing their defense and making other changes. They moved their arsenals westward and concentrated their troops toward Szechwan and Yünnan. They thus proved that they were going to prepare for a very long war. The coal and ore mines were exploited to the utmost. The best men and most determined youths of the country retired to Chungking, Kunming (Yünnanfu), and Chengtu. The Japanese anticipation that the occupation of China proper would be just as simple a matter as the conquest of Manchuria in 1931 and 1932 was not realized. In certain places, particularly in the north, the Chinese certainly did retreat, but in others they offered unexpectedly strong resistance and then judiciously withdrew, decoying the Japanese, often using the Russian tactics that led to Napoleon's defeat in 1812.

After England's failure at Munich the Japanese considered that there would be no risk in striking a blow at Canton close by Hong Kong, which for a hundred years had been a British possession and is a Crown Colony as well as one of the largest transit harbors in the world. Shipping to and from China largely took place via Hong Kong. Shanghai is the other large door into China, and there England has greater interests than any other power. Large quantities of war material had passed via Hong Kong to Hankow. The Japanese know that if they realize their plans, Hong Kong will fall like a ripe fruit into their hands, even without any attack. Japan's winning the war will probably mean the end of England's power not only in Hong Kong and Shanghai but also in the whole of East Asia. Not even with France as an ally had England at her disposal sufficiently strong military forces to venture a war with Japan. Only this knowledge and the threat of a war in Europe can explain the apparent indifference and passivity of the two Western powers.

At the beginning of 1939 the war found other expressions. The Japanese military command was faced with the problem of what should be done to bring the war to a conclusion with results as far as possible corresponding to the promises given the Japanese people.

Chiang Kai-shek was still saving his best troops for the final settlement. During the intervals when the world heard nothing of him, he was working day and night to save his country. He led the defense and enlarged his best cadres to enormous armies. These troops are far superior to those that have already fallen at the fronts or have been split into guerilla groups. The more the war is prolonged, the better will the troops be that the Marshal throws against the Japanese fire, while the Japanese troops will be growing tired and demoralized as a result of the increased difficulties.

The war has not developed along the lines sketched and anticipated by the powerful military party in Japan. The predicted two or three months has become more than three years. When the prediction turned out to be wrong, Japanese propaganda announced that the fall of Shanghai would decide the war. But that prophecy proved equally incorrect, and it was said that at Nanking, the heart of China, the Chinese were to receive the death blow.

The Chinese troops retired in good order and without trouble. Hsüchow then became the key to China and thus to the final victory. When that was also found to be a miscalculation, it was stated that the fall of Hankow and Canton would be the final blow. But nothing decisive happened there either. It turned out to be more difficult than imagined by the

invaders to reach Nanchang and to advance to Changsha from
Hankow. Chinese people that I have met openly admit that
the resistance offered by their troops is just as great a surprise
to them as to the Japanese officers.

The Japanese considered that the conquest of Hankow
would mean the possession of the Yangtse valley. But it was
only five months after the fall of Hankow that they could
reach Nanchang, the capital of Kiangsi, which is connected
by rail with Kiukiang on the Yangtse. All they found on this
triumphal march was a destroyed railway, a city in ruins, innumerable homeless Chinese, devastated fields, and corpses.
The Chinese burned Changsha, and many of the inhabitants
perished in the flames. This was done in order to deprive the
Japanese of their prey. But the invaders did not reach
Changsha. The destruction of that city was rash and deplorable. In spite of the tragedy of having to destroy their property and burn their homes, towns and villages, the Chinese
preferred this to letting them fall into the hands of the Japanese.

The enemy makes concentrated attacks in areas where the
Chinese development has made the best progress and where
the foreign interests are greatest. For that reason the Kowloon
area was bombed, i.e., the part of the mainland opposite Hong
Kong that is British, although under normal conditions such
an action would probably have been looked upon by England
as *casus belli.*

The sweeping and strategic lines were becoming indistinct,
and the final crushing advance was postponed. Chiang Kai-
shek considered it bad business to waste his best troops on
Hankow and Canton. After Hankow the Chinese took the
initiative more and more and Chiang retained full freedom
of movement and action. No extensive operations took place,
and the Japanese hope of forcing the Chinese into a final huge
battle or driving them into a blind alley was frustrated. As
the Chinese withdrew farther west, the Japanese lost contact

with the Yangtse and the support the navy had been giving the army.

The invading armies now have before them a hilly landscape with forests, valleys, and passes, easy to defend, where the Chinese have built and are still strengthening their positions. They are building new roads, their arsenals and factories are working at high pressure, and they have transported rails and rolling stock there from lines in the occupied parts of the country, using them for new railways in the western provinces.

The highest leader of a great people could not have been faced by a greater task than to build up, recruit, train, and organize new armies in the west while his armies in the east were fighting for their lives against a ruthless and mighty foe. At the beginning of the war only the elite troops did good work, while the troops from the provinces and the great levies were below the standard. It is the war itself that has forced the Chinese leaders to produce enormous capable armies. If the Chinese succeed in creating new armies while the war is raging, and if those armies can make just as ruthless and powerful offensives as the Japanese, it is merely a question of time until the Chinese have got so far that they are superior to their enemies in the field, for their human material is inexhaustible and their lines of communication are short, whereas those of the enemies become longer.

To the Japanese China is only a geographical conception. Mr. Hiranuma, when Prime Minister, declared that in the future China would be used as a training ground for Japanese troops. However, April 1939 rendered them nothing but Kuling on the Yangtse, where there were sanatoria for aged and sick Europeans. Here, too, is an example of the Japanese fondness for places that are of interest to the foreigners.

Both Hankow and Canton were in the hands of the Japanese, but the railway between these two towns had not been taken by them. After the Japanese occupation of the Kulangsu concession a number of British, American, and French marines were landed at the end of May, a protest which made a deep impression in Tokyo and showed that there was a limit to the kind of treatment the Western powers would stand. No energetic British protests were made when the Japanese fleet sank or destroyed 216 fishing vessels in British territorial waters near Hong Kong from June first to November 30th, 1938.

The fronts were comparatively quiet during the winter 1938-39, although according to Japanese calculations about one thousand Chinese fell daily during the quiet periods. The Chinese, on the other hand, told of a very effective Chinese offensive in Hunan at that time. Kweiyang, the capital of Kweichow, was bombed in February. Professors and students had taken refuge there.

Kunming, formerly Yünnanfu, is also one of the newly founded centers of Chinese scientific research. At the end of May, 1939, I received a letter from the chief librarian Tung-li Yuan, an old friend of mine and also of the Swedish expeditions, requesting me to send our latest works to Kunming where The National Library of Peiping was stationed. The fact that Chinese research is continuing its work under the present conditions in China speaks very well of Chinese fortitude. According to a letter received, the brother of Dr. Tung-li Yuan, Professor P. L. Yuan, who took part in our expeditions in Sinkiang 1927-1933, is now on a geological expedition in western Szechwan.

It is a point of honor with the Chinese to save their old and new culture from the whirlwind that is threatening to lay waste so much of value. With deliberate cruelty the Japanese destroy all seats of learning, down to the smallest schools. The fact that Chiang Kai-shek himself has acted as chairman of the meetings in Chungking when the new organization of the educational system has been discussed, shows how clearly conscious he is of the importance of education and also that he is preparing for a long war. Colonel Carl Taube states that the determined destruction of all kinds of schools and colleges is due to the fact that the Japanese look upon them, and particularly the universities, as centers of anti-Japanese propaganda. He adds that the value of the universities, libraries, scientific institutions, instruments, etc., destroyed during the war was estimated at 217 million silver dollars in the spring of 1939. The number of students at the new universities in Szechwan and Yünnan is said to be not less than at the old ones in Peking, Tientsin, Nanking, Shanghai, Canton, and other cities. The work is pursued with greater intensity and ardor than ever, for now the students have a tangible aim, the salvation of their civilization, the future of their country. Great honor is due a nation that in the extreme hour of its affliction holds high the torch of human knowledge! Such a people is not doomed.

The aim of the intensified Japanese air raids was to demoralize the people and to scare Chinese capital from the new industries in western China. But this plan did not work. The more bombing, the stronger the unity of the civilians and the greater their readiness to make sacrifices. After a Chinese victory, hatred of the Japanese military will survive due to the cruelty exercised by their bombers.

Should Japan be defeated by China, she will no doubt go in for compensation at the expense of Great Britain, France, the United States, and Holland. She has long been flirting with Siam. Japan is playing for grandiose stakes. It is believed that she has a million men in China. But they will not go far in terrorizing and forcibly checking 450 millions! No facts are available regarding the number of troops stationed on the northern boundary of Manchuria. Statements vary between 30,000 and 300,000. It is said that Japanese who have been killed in Manchuria are burned and their ashes sent home in small urns. But the number of urns is said to be so great that they are retained on the continent for the time being, in order not to frighten the people at home. From April to November, 1938, the number of relatives at home of the Japanese soldiers fighting on the mainland had grown from 1,125,000 to 1,558,000. And still the Japanese do not call the war with China a war, but an incident!

The Japanese hope had been that they might appease and win Chinese of a high position and then dictate advantageous peace terms. When the determined resistance of the Kuomintang, the army, and the guerilla bands had put such hopes to shame, the invader had to increase his efforts and his violence. The energetic warlord Wu P'ei-fu, famous from innumerable battles, had not yielded to the Japanese attempts to persuade him to accept the position as chief of the administration of Northern China under Japanese sovereignty.

The former prime minister, Wang Ching-wei, who wished to put an end to the suffering of the people and who coveted peace—even on hard terms—was finally expelled from the Kuomintang. Only one of his friends accompanied him when he withdrew to Hanoi, the former Vice Minister for Railways, Tseng Chung-ming, the man who very courteously had received our automobile expedition in February, 1935, upon its return to Nanking. I have been told by Chinese that the people in Hanoi were so furious about Wang Ching-wei's action for peace that they decided to murder the minister. When the attack was to be carried out, however, they made a mistake and shot Tseng Chung-ming instead of Wang Ching-wei.

At the beginning of July, 1939, it was announced that Wang Ching-wei had formed a new Kuomintang party at Tsingtao (Kiachow), which was to open peace negotiations with Japan on the basis of the terms presented by Prince Konoye in December, 1938. One of the demands was that China should accept the "New Order in East Asia" introduced by Japan, or in other words, that the Chinese should voluntarily become slaves under Japan. After this last action of Wang's the Central Government issued a warrant for his arrest.

Great political events in East Asia may interrupt the war or alter its character. The Russians have a free hand in the north and are the immediate neighbors of the Japanese Empire. Mr. George Sale estimated that considering the war expenditure of Japan, compared with those of the great powers during the Great War, and on the supposition that it remains the same as in the spring of 1939, the Japanese would be able to continue the war for another two or three years. Japan would be able to keep on for four years or even longer if the expenditure is curtailed.

Meanwhile China is impoverished, but her people are sustained by determination, pride, and patriotism, more valuable in the long run than the very greatest credits. The Chinese are inferior in the air, but on the ground and fighting man to man they are at least equal to the Japanese. China's human resources are inexhaustible, the Japanese limited. To this is added the nearness to Russia which is an advantage for China but a disadvantage for Japan. Morgan Young rightfully expresses surprise at the Japanese belief that they can conquer a country of five million square kilometers in one sweep. Ever since Japan started to "secure the peace of the Far East" in 1894, peace and quiet have deserted East Asia.

It is sometimes reported that the inhabitants in the occupied areas are satisfied with the Japanese rule. No doubt there are great numbers of deserters who derive personal advantages from serving the conqueror. But their numbers are infinitesimal compared with the whole great nation, who despise their treachery to the Middle Kingdom. In the areas that are effectively occupied by the Japanese the people must do their bidding.

Air force has never before been used in a war in the manner adopted by the Japanese. Ancient monuments of

The Modernization of Chinese Industry Is Exemplified
in This Weaving Factory in Kunming.

Photograph by Bosshard

Air Raid.

various kinds, created throughout thousands of years, are obliterated for no good whatever, causing archaeological research irretrievable losses. Bombing is justified only when attacking military objects. The Canton-Hankow railway, for instance, was bombed 171 times from September, 1937, to February, 1938, 1,994 bombs having been dropped. During those five months only 17 persons were killed and 25 wounded. The damage caused was immediately repaired and the longest stop in the traffic was three days.

The Japanese feel no compunction about dropping highly explosive bombs in the most densely populated quarters. Chungking has been bombed many times and terribly ravaged. Thousands of civilians became the victims of those air raids and many foreign consulates were destroyed. Chungking was Chiang Kai-shek's headquarters, but in reality nobody knows where he is at any time. Even if it is known that he is in Chungking or some other city, only a few know in which house he is staying. With each day his life becomes more precious to China. He and he alone can save his people and he is always sought by spies, traitors, and assassins.

Despite their enormous sacrifices the Chinese are still making resistance. Their direct sufferings are dreadful, and indirectly they suffer just as much by the throttling of the foreign trade. Hiranuma declared that Japan, above all, wished to annihilate foreign trade—first of all the British. Some years ago the Chinese Republic wished to nullify the concessions and the so-called unequal treaties. The concessions originated in the days of the Opium War and the Taiping revolt. In the Versailles Treaty China wished to be freed from the capitulations, but was successful only so far as the German and Austrian concessions were concerned. After the Japanese occupation of Shanghai, Tientsin, and Hankow, the foreign concessions became an eyesore to the conqueror, who daily exerted increased pressure upon them. The abolition of the concessions would mean a severe blow to Europe's in-

fluence in China and to the world trade in the Middle Kingdom. Not only would the trade be stopped, but the enormous
capital invested in China would also be lost. It is thanks to the
concession system that Shanghai is a great city and the fifth
in the world. Had China been a free, open, and supreme
country, the concessions might have been abolished. The fate
of Manchuria has shown that a Japanese occupation means
Japanese monopoly and closed doors to all other countries.
The abolition of the concessions will mean the end of European and American interests in China and a complete loss of
prestige for the white race throughout East Asia.

The Japanese had now (1939) continued their occupation
of Chinese territory for more than two years without effective
protests from the Western powers. The Japanese action at
Kulangsu, the island with the international settlements at
Amoy, was too much for Great Britain, France, and the
United States, and they sent warships there and landed troops.
The Japanese then found it best to withdraw the greater part
of the forces. Had they succeeded in taking this international
settlement, they would probably have tried to treat Shanghai's
settlement in the same manner.

Distinct fronts were hardly found anywhere except around
walled cities; otherwise the war was mobile. West of Hankow
the Japanese had got as far as the Hankiang, but no great
numbers had succeeded in crossing that river in the direction
of Loyang. Chinese forces had entered Chengchow and Kaifeng, both these cities being occupied by the Japanese. In
Kaifeng, as well as in other occupied areas, the Japanese had
installed local puppet governments consisting of bought or
frightened Chinese, willing tools in their hands, large numbers
of which have been shot by Chinese patriots. The puppet government in Kaifeng consisted of six men. On one occasion
when five of them had gathered to a meeting, Chinese soldiers
broke into the room and shot them all. A successful coup in

the middle of a large city occupied by Japanese troops! The perpetrators were patriots who wanted to liberate their country from traitors. They all escaped. Their action aroused admiration all over China.

Colonel Carl Taube, who was able to follow the development on the spot, said that the parts of China that were not occupied were being consolidated and were growing stronger from day to day. In the eyes of the world the Chinese are a splendid example of a nation having courage and willingness to make sacrifices in the defense of their country and its liberty. They have shown that it is not the modern war machines and the organization that decide the battle, but patriotism and an unwavering determination to win or die.

A touching news release from Chungking shows how far the love of the country and veneration for the great leader have penetrated into the Chinese soul. It is of a wandering group of children who on their own initiative were making propaganda with the following battle cry:

"We have gathered to protect our country. With song and music we have spread the message 'To arms!' among the masses in nine provinces, in order that nobody may slumber at a time when the peace of our homes is in danger. We are far too young and much too weak to carry guns, but we have done our duty. Go and do yours."

They stood at street corners in Chungking, and large numbers of other children gathered around them. They sang about their own feats, the exploits of others, and of wonderful adventures.

There are sixty of these small representatives of the China of tomorrow, recruited from the refugees' camps, and calling themselves "The singing and dramatic corps of young fugitives." There are forty boys and twenty girls. They have often traveled on lorries, trains, or boats, but they have also tramped thousands of kilometers through the provinces of Kiangsu, Chekiang, Anhwei, Honan, Hupei, Hunan, Kwangsi,

Kweichow, and Szechwan, in whose towns and villages they have sung and enacted plays, making many a patriotic spark burst into full flame. And finally they landed in Chungking, the temporary capital of China.

In Kweilin, the capital of Kwangsi, which had often been exposed to bomb raids, they were allowed to live in a schoolhouse. In groups of seven or eight they went out in the city, singing and playing at the street corners, attracting all the playing children of the neighborhood, and often their parents and others. These little singers and actors also act as teachers in backward districts.

After a few weeks in Chungking the wandering Liliputians had acquired enormous popularity. They were invited to all patriotic celebrations and gatherings and to the public schools in the city, and their plays, songs, and fairy tales were met with great enthusiasm everywhere. Three of the most popular plays were called: "Arrest the Traitors," "Help our Guerillas," and "The Blood of the Children." The plays, written by the children themselves, told of their own experiences. They had actually organized the peasants of many villages into new guerilla bands, and in others they had taken part in the search for traitors.

Once when a Japanese fleet of airplanes flew over Kweilin, sending death and destruction over the city, the children sought shelter in "The cave of the seven stars" in the outskirts of the city. They then observed two men in a sugar plantation, and found their actions suspicious. They surrounded and captured them. They then took them to the military authorities, who found that they had been signaling information to the planes.

They had lost their homes and often also their parents in the stricken parts of Shanghai and in Chapei. In a crowd of irresolute and homeless children a youth stood up and cried, "Let us do something, let us go forth and help our country." His name was Wu and he became their leader. They followed him and set out for great adventures. On the way their number grew, other children being hypnotized by the song "Arise, ye children of China!"

In Hankow, they caused a great sensation and were taken care of by "The Political Training Corps of the Military National Council."

They finally reached the goal of their desires and were allowed to appear at a children's party in Chungking under the personal patronage of the Marshal. If the new generation growing up in China is of such material, then the Middle Kingdom need harbor no fears for its future.

XXV

The Chinese Resistance Hardens

WHEN JAPAN BEGAN HER ATTACK ON NORTHERN CHINA
and then broke in upon the five provinces with motorized
troops, and the fleet made its violent attack on Shanghai,
resulting in the retreat of the Chinese and the fall of Nanking,
the Japanese staff felt convinced that the collapse would come
at the beginning of 1938, and that China would be split as
it was when the warlords were fighting each other. The
optimistic view of the Japanese was quite natural, for neither
Japan nor the rest of the world was unaware of China's
weakness and insufficient military preparation. Then came one
surprise after another. The Chinese army certainly was poorly
equipped and badly trained, and also demoralized by the numerous civil wars. Faced with Japanese fire and steel and
bombs there was nothing else for Chiang Kai-shek to do but
to retreat. The retreats were cleverly accomplished and there
were no great losses of prisoners. In the east the land was
given up to the enemy; in the west, where the Japanese no
longer had the support of the Yangtse River and where the
terrain became more and more difficult for motorized equipment, the advance grew slower and slower and finally stopped
entirely.

The position of the Japanese armies in the middle of China
does not seem enviable. Their advances miss the mark as the
Chinese always escape. About one third of the Chinese forces
consist of guerilla formations, which are inaccessible. The
Japanese build up repair shops, temples, and brothels in the
occupied areas, which are continually disturbed and do not
contribute to safety. The Japanese forces are not believed to

suffice for the defense of all these different establishments and for the transport of war material, troops, and food. The occupation troops are described as being cruel and ruthless, and the civil population is fleeing in large numbers from the occupied areas. Hangchow, for instance, formerly had a population of 600,000, of which only 100,000 are left; Nanking had 1,000,000, now 300,000; Wusih, the silk city, had 300,-000, now only 10,000. It is estimated that 16 millions have fled from the triangle Shanghai—Nanking—Hangchow. In northern China the population has been reduced by 25 per cent. Many of the fugitives die of starvation and suffering, others are saved by white men, others succeed in making their way to the large provinces in the west, where a new country is coming into being. It is easier to effect such absolutely fantastic migrations in China than in other highly civilized countries.

Anyone attempting to follow the course of the war in China from a distance receives the impression that its character and aim are rapidly changing as time goes on. The important initiatives seem more and more to be transferred from the army to the navy, and the statements made by responsible Japanese statesmen that the war is waged less on China than on England, becomes more and more significant. Shanghai, Canton, Hainan, Tientsin, and a number of other coastal places are links in a complete blockade of the whole Chinese coast and a gradual paralyzation of all foreign trade.

Dr. Wang Ch'ung-hui, China's minister for foreign affairs, touched upon this question, so vital to Europe, in a message stating that the powers are today faced with the vital choice of retaining or abandoning the rights assured them by agreements in Asia. No compromises will be tolerated; Japan's aim is the monopoly of the continent. Every demand conceded will be followed by new demands. "The war has acquired a new aspect." In order to rid themselves of the foreigners and their interests the Japanese have started a new antiforeign movement. So far they are concentrating on England, but the others' turn will come. They speak of creating "a new order in East Asia," says Dr. Wang Ch'ung-hui, but disorder is following in their tracks. As stated many times by authorities in Tokyo, they want to seize all the foreign concessions in China. By blockade they have stopped all trade on the coast and have closed the Yangtse to foreign shipping. Dr. Wang expresses his and all China's disgust at Japan's scandalous treatment of Englishmen in Tientsin and in other places. He has no worries for the future of China.

In the summer of 1939 the blockade was continued and made still more effective. Fuchow and Wenchow were threatened by troops attempting to land, which, however, could be turned off for the time being. Twenty-six men-of-war lay outside Fuchow for several weeks, and the town was bombarded. Japan's ultimatum to England and the United States to remove their ships from Fuchow was turned down, and the consuls of the two countries remained at their posts. The British landed 36 marines to protect the English subjects and their property. The Japanese landed 200 marines and as many Formosans on the island of Sharp Peak near Fuchow. They looted foreign bungalows and one sanatorium. The whole coast around Fuchow was bombed. All trade between Hong Kong and Fuchow and Wenchow was stopped. If British ships came there they were prevented from unloading their cargoes.

After the occupation of Swatow, the navy continued its operations on the southeastern coast of China. Islands at strategic points were occupied in order to control the channels.

At about the same time, Sun Fo and Anastasy Ivanovich Mikoyan, the commissar for foreign trade of the Soviets, signed a Sino-Russian commercial treaty in Moscow. The Chinese managed the difficult game very skillfully. As the Japanese close all doors from the seas, the Chinese, assisted by the Russians, open new routes for trade through Inner Asia.

The Japanese endeavors are hopeless, and it is safe to say that they will never win the game, no matter how they try. They can possibly block the entire coast by employing their whole fleet, but the inland roads cannot be closed and the trade through Inner Asia cannot be stopped. In spite of all her excellent military machinery, Japan is too small to conquer the whole of China. Erik Nyström was right in the following statement made late in the autumn of 1936, nine months prior to the outbreak of the war: "One would like to whisper in Japan's ear: 'Stick to your colony, Manchukuo, that glorious country of the future, but hands off China proper! The great powers have too many interests at stake there, and chances are that victory would cost you your life!' "

Japan's military command and government used the Tientsin blockade in an endeavor to force England to acknowledge Japanese sovereignty over the five northern provinces and to cease supporting the Chinese government. Japan demanded complete control of the British concession and that Japanese banknotes and no others be current in the district. England would thus have to acknowledge Japanese monopoly and sovereignty in a country occupied in a war which had not even been declared and which the Japanese themselves called an "incident." England would have to betray China and waive her own interests! The British investments in China amount to 300 million pounds.

The scandalous undressing incident at the barricades in Tientsin was looked upon by the whole of Asia as a symbol of the subjugation and enslavement of the vanquished. That is what happened in the days of Chinghiz Khan when thousands of women were forced to parade naked after the fall of Peking. The undressing incident is but a premonition of what may be in store.

In the war with China, Japan has introduced methods—for instance at Nanking and in the bombing of nonprotected, densely populated cities—which have aroused indignation and horror in the West. It has a new expression of contempt, never before heard of, to tear the clothes from white men and women and leave them naked to be viewed by people of a different race. The real, symbolic ulterior motive was no doubt that just as these respectable men and women were undressed by the brutal sentries guarding the barricades, so will in time the white robe be torn from Japan as well as the rest of Asia. One could not but pity the ambassador, Sir Robert Craigie, who had to retain his dignity when talking to the Japanese minister for foreign affairs about insults that were destroying Great Britain's prestige, and which, if England's hands had been free, would not have been discussed in words and protests, but with battleships and cruisers.

Xenophobia, the hatred of foreigners, appears in many forms in East Asia today. In areas inhabited by Englishmen, the Chinese mob is inpired with hatred and rebelliousness toward the whites, with the single purpose of causing some Englishman to lose his self-control and shoot the offender. That would be a welcome excuse to accuse the whites of cruelty toward the Chinese and to tear up heaven and earth. But the Englishmen swallow the insults with stoical calm.

Economic war was also raging between Japan and China, and the Japanese were furious about the credits placed at the disposal of the Chinese government by the United States, England, and France, in order to strengthen the Chinese currency. But this assistance could not prevent the Chinese dollar from falling rapidly.

A readjustment of China's foreign trade was made at the initiative of the minister of finance, Chiang Kai-shek's brother-in-law, Dr. H. H. Kung, in order to strengthen the economic position of the country. He abolished the silver standard and tied the Chinese dollar to the pound, making it possible for China to send her silver to England and America, so that she now had metal reserves in foreign countries. Dr. Kung prohibited the import of articles of luxury and everything that could be dispensed with. Exports were stimulated, particularly of wood oil, tea, bristles, and minerals, and transport facilities were improved. Through the import prohibition Japanese wares were shut out. This meant a saving of 68 million gold dollars, which was used for the work of restoration and for the strengthening of the armed resistance. Dr. Kung said, "Although the burdensome military operations have been going on for two years, China's financial structure is still intact and developments show that our country is able to carry its present burdens."

He considered that China had endured the strains of the war better than Japan, for the following reasons:

1. The improvement in the finances of the country during the years immediately prior to the war.

2. The political unification and national development of the people.

3. China's simple economic life—an agricultural people being less vulnerable than an industrialized one such as Japan.

4. The vast hinterland, the endurance, the tough resistance, and the tactics of exhausting the enemy adopted in this war.

5. The entire world is in sympathy with China and disapproves of Japan's methods, which have resulted in disorder and economic insecurity also for other powers, at the same time as it threatens China's liberty and independence.

Occidental sympathies for China found expression in the financial support given by England, the United States, France, Russia, and other countries, while foreign money markets were closed to Japan. China's satisfactory financial position rested above all upon the solid foundation laid by the currency reform in November, 1935. During the first two years of the war China had a currency that won the confidence of the people, which could not be said of the currencies of Japan and her puppet governments. In the course of twenty-one months China paid 530 million dollars on her debts to foreign countries in spite of the fact that Japan had appropriated the salt tax and the customs revenues. In some cases China asked for a postponement of certain payments abroad and this was granted.

Behind the war zones there has been developed great economic activity to promote restoration and to keep the pulse of the country beating. With reference to Japan's treatment of the whites in East Asia, Dr. Kung asks if Occidental interests in this part of the world will profit by Japan controlling the enormous wealth of China and the labor represented by her millions of people. No, he rightly states that an orderly, peaceful, and friendly China is more advantageous also for the Occident.

Colonel Taube wrote from Chungking in June, 1939, on the same subject. He emphasized the fundamental difference between the two countries, which is that Japan possesses industry but no raw materials, while China possesses raw materials but no industry. Both must thus finance the war with foreign money, and when this is no longer available the collapse will come. In the race between yen and dollars, the latter had up to that time made the best showing.

The finances of Japan are based upon industry and export, above all of textiles of cotton, wool, and silk. The requirements of these raw materials cannot by far be filled in the country, but China can do it. That is why China must be conquered. The productive resources were to be exploited in the occupied provinces—with the assistance of Japanese banknotes, lacking covering. These notes were printed by the Federal Reserve Bank and were forced upon the people under threats, but they, as well as the foreign commercial houses in Tientsin, received them with suspicion.

After the fall of Hankow the Japanese established a new

bank also in the Yangtse valley in order to stamp out the Chinese dollar. The new currency was not accepted in Shanghai and dropped still more than in northern China. According to Taube, China will win the financial struggle, for the crisis has already commenced in Japan, "and no one in the world can outwit a Chinese bill-broker."

In the summer of 1937, Dr. Wong Wen-hao, Director of the Geological Survey of China, paid a few days' visit to Stockholm, and we spoke frankly about the dangers then threatening China. He had more than once refused the offer of becoming Minister of Education in the Nanking Government, but when his native country was drawn into war, he accepted the Marshal's offer without hesitation, and took charge of the newly founded Ministry of Economy. The creation of a positive trade balance is one of its very special tasks. The goods which more than any other yield foreign currencies are wood oil, tea, bristles, and minerals. According to Colonel Taube about sixty cotton mills were destroyed by the Japanese, representing a loss of a hundred million dollars. The mills at Hankow were transported to Szechwan and Yünnan in time. They are now running at full speed and as they have not time to manufacture all the cotton cloth required by the people, some weaving is done in the homes.

The province of Szechwan produces rice, wheat, potatoes, Indian corn, sugar cane, beans, cotton and other crops. Wood oil, silk, tea, bristles, hides, goat skins, squirrel skins, wool, medicinal herbs, iron, petroleum, gold, sulphur, and salt are important export goods.

There are enormous supplies of coal in China and the iron-ore supplies are not negligible although the best fields are in the hands of the Japanese. In 1938 the ironworks of Hanyang were moved to Szechwan. Blast and Martin furnaces are being erected, and Colonel Taube relates that one of my countrymen, Matts Liljefors, a nephew of the great painter, has installed a steel works at Chungking which is growing rapidly.

Is it possible anywhere in the history of war to find an example that can even be compared with the re-location of a great people that is now taking place in China? Certainly not! The drama now being enacted in the Middle Kingdom beats all records. During the Olympic Games in Berlin in 1936 the Japanese runners won the Marathon race, but during the war with China they have given proof of no remarkable accomplishments as far as marching is concerned. They have got so far that they dare continue no farther in among forests and mountains. As Professor Erik Nyström says, their invading army is like a fly caught on flypaper, trying to free one leg after another, and meanwhile sinking deeper and deeper into the glue.

The Chinese on the other hand have given proof of superhuman endurance over the long stretches and in the most exhausting marches. We recall the fantastic march of the communists after their defeat by the Marshal, through practically the whole of China, until they finally reached Shensi and Kansu. The whole war has shown how cleverly the Chinese armies have withdrawn when threatened by the first-class equipment and war machines of the Japanese. In this manner the Marshal has saved his best troops for a final battle —if necessary.

A general migration from east to west and southwest has been going on for three years in China. Not only the troops march; a large part of the civil population is also on the roads to save their lives and to escape the "New Order" the Japanese are introducing. An idea of how enormous is the transmigration is afforded by the fact already mentioned, that 16 million people have left the triangle Shanghai—Nanking—Hangchow—as many as the entire population of Sweden, Norway, Denmark, and Finland.

Naturally not all of these emigrants reach the new land in the far west. Most of them stop fairly soon and manage as well as they can in the hope of returning to their devastated homes when the Japanese have evacuated China. But there are millions who for the first time in their lives see Szechwan's mighty mountains and endless rice fields in the valleys and the open, flat regions of the province. True to their inherited endurance, capacity for work and contentment, the Chinese immediately begin to break up the ground, plow it with primitive implements, dig irrigation canals for new fields, build roads, houses, and bridges, or find employment in new mills, mines, or ironworks.

In our time so filled with events, revolutions, and surging unrest, a new China is being built up, a new Middle Kingdom, a new realm crowded with people and life, an anthill of humming work. The Chinese who have lived there for centuries, one generation after the other, must have gasped when they saw the impoverished and starving throngs coming from the east and settling down around their farms and fields. They, too, are faced with hard times. The rice, grain, fruit, and other foodstuffs must now suffice for the rapidly growing population. The supplies become smaller and smaller and the prices higher.

But the great Marshal lives in their midst and his voice resounds over hills and valleys. He speaks of unity, willingness to make sacrifices, relationship, patriotism, and reminds them that all of them—the old inhabitants and the newcomers —have a common enemy, the hordes of soldiers from the Land of the Rising Sun. Then no one complains. They all do their utmost. The old fields are enlarged, new fields are cultivated. Grounds never before touched by a share are now tramped by the gray, phlegmatic buffaloes, dragging plows, preparing the good earth that is to give the people new harvests of rice and bread.

While the occupied parts of the lowlands are deserted, devastated, laid waste, looted, the western provinces are changed into a highly cultivated and in all respects thoroughly utilized land. Among the millions who start for the west, there is an automatic thinning out, a natural selection, the fittest surviving while the weaker elements are left behind. The population of the western provinces will thus be mixed with people hardened by the war and by the march westward. The factors forcing them to work sedulously for the necessities of life will harden them still more, and a new Chinese race will emerge in western China; and, remembering their sufferings during the Japanese war, they will demand revenge and resolve to reconquer the provinces and coasts that have wrongly been taken from them.

Whatever the outcome of this war which already now is beginning to degenerate, the events in the Middle Kingdom offer the world one of the most magnificent spectacles in history. We see a people, attacked without declaration of war by an enemy far superior in technical equipment, in the midst of raging war improving its defenses to such a degree that the enemy is offered effective resistance; it cedes part of its country to the invading armies, and fortifies itself in districts that cannot be reached by the enemy. The western provinces are thus changed into fortified regions, manned by well-trained armies, and their strength is ever growing.

No very large numbers of Japanese will emigrate to China, just as little as they have done to Formosa, Korea, and Manchuria. But if the Japanese want to remain in the present occupied areas, they must, in order to manage them, hold strong garrisons in every city and along all railway lines. No matter how well equipped these garrisons may be with men and material, they will certainly have trouble with the new country in the west as their next-door neighbor.

Japan's desire for supremacy in China precludes every thought of a just and sensible peace. And a peace satisfactory to both peoples is the only solution that would do East Asia and humanity as a whole any good. Let us hope that Japan's moderate statesmen and China's growing strength will find a formula that will put an end to the triumph of the God of War, check the bloodshed, stop the flowing tears, and quell the hatred, bitterness, and sorrow in millions of homes in the Middle Kingdom and the Land of the Rising Sun.

XXVI

China Endures the War

THE WAR BETWEEN JAPAN AND CHINA CAN BE DIVIDED into four phases, each of the first three, strangely enough, having embraced five months and six days, while the fourth, still going on, has lasted much longer. Nobody knows how long this last phase will be, how many months and years will pass before peace is finally made. Opinions differ considerably. General Itagaki, formerly War Minister of Japan, stated that Japan was prepared to continue the war fifteen or twenty years. When the military party believed that the victory over China would be won in a couple of months, they calculated upon a schism within the Chinese Government, which never came. When the fall of Chiang Kai-shek was believed to be imminent, it was found instead that his power grew, that the people's faith in him was not to be shaken, and that he was becoming a symbol of united resistance. The theory regarding China's expected politico-economic collapse proved equally wrong, as China has proved to be economically far stronger than Japan. It was believed that China could be bought and demoralized. But the truth is that when the Chinese once have decided on war, they will hold out to the end, especially when they know that surrender means slavery.

Dr. Zotora Kimura, the head of the Chamber of Commerce in Tokyo, considers it impossible to subjugate China in one generation. That will require three generations, or a hundred years. And that prophet is a Japanese! He is both right and wrong. He is right in that it will take a very long time to crush China. Personally I believe he is wrong in fixing one century as the time necessary. If I know the Chinese right, they cannot be crushed in a century. They have carried on for four thousand years and in times gone by they have sunk as low as today, even lower, but they have always come up to the surface. It is impossible to subjugate a people of 450 millions with an army, no matter how modern it is. It is just as impossible as to introduce Japanese military laws to replace the natural laws ruling in China, which have helped to give the Chinese race its amazing power of resistance to all outside influences.

I say this, that those who love and admire China's wonderful people shall not think that its last hour has come.

It goes without saying that political regroupings of the great powers, about which we know nothing at all at present, may at any time overthrow all prophecies as to the duration of the war. The treaty between Germany and Russia is one factor; co-operation between Japan and Great Britain another. It is best not to prophecy about the duration of this war. Probably its course will be crossed by happenings of far greater import, and it will be swallowed up by revolutionary events.

The great war of conquest that Japan started in China will, no matter how it ends, represent the climax of Chiang Kai-shek's career. He had liberated the country from the warlords and had assured the Kuomintang Government supremacy over the whole country, with the exception of the peripheral possessions, particularly Manchuria. Through the New Life Movement and the politico-economic restoration movement he had begun his great work of unification, which already was well on the way to becoming a success. With composure and confidence he looked toward a brighter future with a strong and united China. Like a bolt from the blue sky—not very blue, to be sure, but still not hopelessly cloudy—the war struck China, Chiang Kai-shek, and his work. Like devastating tempests the Japanese armies swept forth over the yellow earth and her people, leaving chaos in their wake, burned farms and villages, ruined cities, ravaged fields and gardens, and innumerable dead.

It must have been distressing for the great reformer, the leader of the Chinese people, to see the fruits of his work wither away and disperse before the storm. But he was calm and unshaken and did not for a moment relinquish the hope of finally attaining his goal. Other feelings than grief and mortification at the violence of the invaders soon struck root in his soul. The more the bombers of the Japanese extended their murderous raids, the more their fleets grasped for China's coastal cites in the south, and the farther their armies penetrated toward the heart of the Middle Kingdom, the more thorough was the awakening of the people from their carefree ease. Their patriotism and national feeling grew stronger, and their different elements were welded into a unity never heard of before, as are metals melted together into a single, homogeneous alloy in a crucible. The unity of which the leader had dreamed and of which he had spoken, preached, and written manifestoes and books, and which had already started to grow, suddenly became a reality, as if produced by a magic wand, from the areas bounding on Siberia and Mongolia, from the coasts of the Yellow Sea and the East and South China Seas to the areas in the far west, bordering on the deserts of Central Asia and the snow-clad Tibetan mountains. The croakers in Japan and other countries who believed that the Chinese masses would rather sacrifice Chiang Kai-shek and their patriotism than allow themselves and their families to be killed by the bombs, tanks, and machine guns of the intruder, were put to shame. With a blindness and absence of psychological judgment that astonishes the Westerner who is at all familiar with Chinese mentality, the Japanese soldiers sullied their march to victory with repeated acts of cruelty, ruthlessness, and bloodshed upon innocent people, actions unparalleled in modern times and perpetrated by no civilized nation. The intention must have been to frighten the attacked people by unheard of cruelty and terror into agreeing to any foreign yoke in order to put an end to the massacres and to save their own lives and those of their wives and children. The Japanese wanted to make a number of terrifying examples in order to make the Chinese compliant, force them to desert Chiang Kai-shek, and gradually surrender. But their calculations went amiss. They had judged the Chinese mentality wrongly. The peasants of China were hardened through thousands of years of injustice, tribulations, and misrule. They could suffer without complaining and they were not afraid to die. Powers that had lain dormant since time immemorial were aroused—not sporadically here and there, but consistently and throughout the whole of this world of humans. The thought that inspired these poor, simple peasants, and which has been observed by many writers, is both true and logical: "As we are to be killed by the bullets and bayonets of our enemies, as our wives and daughters are to be outraged, our fields trampled, our homes burned and our graves fouled, we may just as well die with swords in hand, and while we await the summons of the Reaper we may have the satisfaction of running our daggers into an invader or setting fire to one of his warehouses or transport trains."

Chiang Kai-shek knew the power that slumbered in the soul of the Chinese people. When he decided to defend China's liberty and independence to the bitter end, he knew that he had the whole people with him and that a government that would have surrendered to Japan's demands would have been hopelessly lost.

The Japanese invaders have thus been surprised and disappointed to meet a resistance such as they had never dreamed of. If the invasion had taken place while rival generals were still waging their harassing civil wars, it is possible that the people would have hailed the Japanese as liberators, if they had fared mildly and mercifully, promised order and safety, and kept their promises.

But now the warlords had been crushed by a man who was stronger than they, a man of whom all China knew that his aim was order, safety, and justice for every Chinese, a man who had devoted his life to the welfare and happiness of the people and who had shown that his one desire was the salvation of the country, a man for whom it would be an honor and a joy to die. If the Marshal's spirit had not hovered like a guardian angel over the yellow earth, it is possible that this great, maltreated, deserted, and tortured people would have given up, and would have received the Japanese as deliverers—if they had refrained from bloodshed and torture.

XXVII

The Marshal Speaks

LIKE A FIRM ROCK IN TURBULENT WATERS THE GREAT
Marshal stands in the midst of this endless ocean of struggling humans. All eyes are turned on him. The Chinese regard him with devotion, loyalty, and confidence; the Japanese with hatred, envy, and fear, and the rest of the world
is filled with astonishment and admiration.

He himself is imperturbably calm and determined. He
knows his duty and will not fail it. He knows that the
fate of his country is now to be determined, that the salvation of the people is primarily dependent upon his own
firmness and that victory mainly depends upon his will
power. If he did not know that his people possesses endless
patience and superhuman endurance, he would not be able
to aim so high.

He does not stand out among the greatest warriors in
history as a conqueror of other countries, a Chinghiz Khan
or a Tamerlain. His only aim is to defend the provinces that
since time immemorial have belonged to China and are now
invaded by a foreign people. When appealing to the millions who follow and obey him, he uses no harsh words;
he does not frighten them, he promises nothing, and he does
not give vent to his hatred of the enemy. Calmly and soberly
he keeps to the naked truth, does not make the position
better than it is, and conceals none of the triumphs of suffering and death among his own people.

On the anniversary of the revolution, now a national holiday, October 10, 1937, after three months of war, he said
in an appeal to the sons and daughters of China:

"The whole country is fighting an heroic battle for its existence, a struggle for life against a foreign invasion. This hour is no doubt the most difficult and grievous one in the history of our national liberation. . . . It is necessary that all our citizens fully realize that still greater sacrifices will be demanded than those already made if we are to succeed. We must be fully aware that there is not the slightest hope of concluding the hostilities in a few months. We must familiarize ourselves with the thought of ever growing hardships just as long as this bitter struggle goes on and be prepared bravely to face situations and dangers ten times as difficult and horrible as those we are now encountering."

More than eighteen months later, on the sixteenth day of May, 1939, the Marshal made a speech in Chungking about the air raids that just then were ruining large parts of the new capital and killing people by the thousands. His speech was reported as follows:

"Generalissimo Chiang Kai-shek declared that . . . far from accomplishing their aims, the Japanese air raids have only had the result that the firm determination of the Chinese people has been strengthened in the face of the horrible sufferings to which they have been exposed." The Generalissimo added that during the past month the Japanese flyers have bombed inhabited quarters throughout the whole country more than fifty times, and that thousands of civilians have been killed in Chungking.

"The enemy fully realizes that China's national welfare rests with the masses of the people and that the most vital step toward the annihilation of the Chinese race is the destruction of the means of subsistence of the people. That is the reason for the massacres at Chungking and other places.

"The Generalissimo warned the Chinese people that the Japanese flyers will in the future not be satisfied with bombing a city; their aim is to annihilate the entire Chinese race. The fact that some unfortunate place is attacked from the air repeatedly and without mercy shows that unless China's people provides for a strong defense and is determined to make resistance to the very end, the whole people will be disarmed and massacred.

"In order to defeat the three Japanese aims the Generalissimo has recommended (1) calm; (2) cultivation of the rural districts, since agriculture is the foundation of China's finances; (3) suitable preparations, such as the digging of trenches, procuring sand bags and water for extinguishing fires.

"The attack, defense, occupation, and evacuation of the important cities in the occupied area," said the Generalissimo, "are always in our hands. On the other hand, the Japanese are sinking deeper and deeper into the ruts and are not only exposed to our incessant attacks, but are also surrounded by us. The position of the enemy is more serious than the world realizes.

"Japan has always bluffed the world about the zeal of her army, but now that we have begun to make resistance, the world knows what to believe. Japan has but 2,000 airplanes. Granted that they could be utilized to their utmost capacity, they could not destroy more than 2,000 cities, and not our millions of villages. They could massacre large numbers, but never destroy our will to resist."

On July 24, 1939, the Marshal spoke about the British-Japanese negotiations, and explained that the Japanese were mistaken if they thought that they could subjugate the Chinese by making a compromise with the powers or by encouraging traitors in their attempts to strangle China financially. He said that no Munich is possible in East Asia. The situation there cannot be compared with that in Europe. "In all fields, the military, the financial, and the diplomatic, we can calculate only with our own strength. We feel confident that none of our friends will desert or fail us so long as we ourselves stand firm. The enemy will not be able to persuade any nation to alter the political course it has always pursued vis-à-vis China.

"The military situation and our relations to foreign powers have been greatly stabilized since the desertion of Wang Ching-wei. China's defensive war is a fight for the realization of the revolution, and no accidents can alter its course. China will not allow herself to be frightened by Japan's attempts to make use of traitors, or to try to isolate her from friendly powers who are too well informed to waive their rights and their juridical positions. Moreover, China is not a Czechoslovakia, since the Chinese revolution is a product of our own efforts, while the Czechoslovakian state came into existence as a result of the Great War and the subsequent peace treaties. Our Government is unanimous and the will of our people is firm. Nothing can persuade us to neglect our sacred duty. And the world knows this.

"A nation attacked from without and lacking the courage to defend itself cannot hope for help from others. We consider it out of the question that England will make a compromise with Japan. England knows better than we what is happening in Japan. England knows that Japan is not the same country as twenty years ago, when it served as England's watchdog in the Far East, where it is now behaving like a mad dog toward its benefactor. Great Britain can only make such concessions as are not in opposition to Chinese interests and to the Nine-Power Treaty. Great Britain signed that treaty and the United States has upheld it. It is unthinkable that Great Britain might join in the Japanese attack and sacrifice her old connections with China. We rely on public opinion and on justice.

"Our courage is indomitable and will never desert us. This is a decisive factor. We shall never become foreign subjects."

Finally the Marshal once more emphasized that help would come from without if the Chinese first helped themselves.

In an important interview granted to the Manager of the Far East Branch of the Transocean Agency when that gentleman visited Chungking, the Marshal said that there is not the least hope of peace as long as Japanese troops remain in China, the aim of the Chinese resistance being to drive out the invaders. The Chinese Government will not think of peace until that aim is reached. Mediation by a third power would hardly be accepted by China unless it were based on this fundamental condition.

China, the Marshal said, is able to defend herself for an unlimited length of time and without help from abroad. Generally speaking "independent" China is supporting herself. As this part of China has been cut off from Shanghai and Hong Kong, its financial position is strengthened, for the import of such foreign merchandise as is not necessary has become impossible.

China's finances are still mainly based on agriculture, and the material life of the peasants has not been very greatly disturbed by the air raids. The Government is therefore emphatically adhering to its program, which consists of developing "independent" China, including among other provinces, Szechwan, which alone is as large as Germany.

Thus the Marshal of China speaks to his people and to Japan and the rest of the world. The tone of the messages issued at different times is the same, and there are no signs that his courage and determination are flagging. On the contrary, he feels more secure and convinced as time goes on that victory will be China's. He does not get lost in details from various battlefields. He does not boast about the bravery of his soldiers. He makes no statements at all about events on and off the coasts. He is not worrying about the loss of old Chinese land, harbors, and coasts, nor does he lament the fact that the enemy is trying by blockade to starve the Chinese and make them into a nation of hungry ragamuffins. He may be thinking that the trials to which his country is now subjected will make it fit for heroic deeds, unknown in its past history. The future will show whether or not the Chinese needed the shock given them by the Japanese invasion in order to awaken from their coma and to grow in greatness and power.

The drama being enacted in the Far East will have the same significance for the future of Asia as the Great War had in regard to the distribution of power and the historical development in Europe. In the war with Germany the colored races, among them Japanese, Chinese, Indians, Arabs, and Senegal Negroes, learned that the great colonial powers of the Allies required their help. They learned that they themselves represented considerable factors of power and that the whites were not unconquerable. We have seen in Shanghai and Tientsin what the strongest military people of the colored races thinks about the most expansive white power.

But everything may change, and the past fifty years have demonstrated that alliances and treaties between great powers usually have but short duration. Paroxysms of nervousness and unrest are shaking the human race in our day. We are witnessing the travail of a new era. The division of the earth, the power over its lands and seas, will be different from what it is now. When China, wounded and fleeced, has gone through the fires, she will be reborn and rise to a new and truer glory.

XXVIII

China's Last Routes to the Outside World

EXCLUDING TIBET, OUTER MONGOLIA, AND MANCHURIA, China has a boundary 13,750 miles long, 3,400 of which are coastline. All the termini of the Chinese railways on the coast and the mouths of all rivers are in the hands of the Japanese. There were seven such commercial centers, connecting China with the outside world.

The first aim of the Japanese blockade of the entire Chinese coast has been to break off all connections with other countries, to stop the import of arms, and to seize all customs revenues. The only railway line from China to Europe, the one from Peking to Siberia and Russia via Shanhaikwan, Mukden, Harbin, and Manchuli, was lost by China in 1931 when Manchuria was taken. The important railway from Hong Kong via Canton to Hankow, on which most of the arms imported were transported, was blocked after the conquest of Canton and Hankow, although the railway is in Chinese hands and stretches of it are used by them.

At last there was left but one route to the outside world, the railway from Kunming in Yünnan to Hanoi in French Indo-China and the harbor outside, Haiphong. The French import of arms to China along this route greatly annoyed the Japanese, and they threatened to occupy the large island of Hainan and to bomb the railway unless the transports of arms were discontinued. The French accordingly stopped exporting arms to China. None the less the Japanese occupied Hainan in the Gulf of Tonking and some smaller islands.[1]

[1] After the defeat of France by Germany, Japanese pressure resulted in the complete closure of the route through Indo-China to the transport of military supplies into China. [Ed.]

On account of the risks to which the French railway was exposed, the importance of the road through Burma very soon increased. China, having always had her connections with the outside world directed eastward toward the harbors on the coast, now had no choice but to do a right-about turn from east to west and south and try to find a new outlet for her exports and a fresh inlet for her imports, above all of arms. The three European powers whose possessions bound on China, viz. England, France, and Russia, gladly helped to liberate China from the absolute isolation that is Japan's aim. And above all England assisted her great neighbor by opening the all-important road through Burma, which became the most important route to foreign countries.

This artery begins as a railway at Rangoon in British Burma on the coast of the Indian Ocean, and runs via Mandalay to Lashio in northern Burma near the Chinese border. From there it continues as a newly built automobile highway to Kunming and Chungking. A railway from Lashio to Kunming and Chungking is being built alongside the highway. This route is also very important to England, particularly since all Chinese harbors and the whole of the Yangtse River are closed. Kunming will be one of the most important cities in independent China, as it will become a center in the new railway system of western China and it will shortly be in direct connection with the Yangtse River through railway lines and highways. Kunming will also be an important administrative, military, and scientific center. With foresight and in good time the Chinese transported as much rail and rolling stock as possible from areas that could not be defended to Chungking, Chengtu, and other places in the west. This change in the front was carried out with admirable speed and precision. Again the Chinese demonstrated that they are able to concentrate on what is really important and for the time being leave aside what is of secondary importance.

Photograph by G. L. G. Samson-Pix

Construction Work on the Five-Hundred-Mile Burma-
Yunnan Railroad, Which Is Being Built to Parallel
the Famous Highway from Burma.

A Camel Caravan Passes Typical Chinese City Walls.

The Burma route runs through tropical forests, across meridional mountain ranges and passes, and reaches a height of 2,700 meters above sea level, crossing roaring rivers and smaller streams on 290 bridges. The two largest rivers bear the classical names Salween and Mekong. The work on the automobile road, which is 900 kilometers long, began in the autumn of 1937 and was concluded at the beginning of 1939. A couple of hundred thousand workmen were busy on this gigantic enterprise. They were mobilized on the spot and were drafted, so that the total expenditure did not exceed five million U. S. dollars. An Englishman who visited the place told me that the workmen were crowded like ants in the various sections, curves, and slopes of the road. The enormous intensity brought to the spectator's mind a person drowning and struggling for air. Every man knew that China's life was at stake and that they were not doing ordinary paid work.

The route through Burma cannot be utilized to its full capacity the year round, as the traffic is greatly reduced or stops entirely during the rainy season in the summer. Thanks to these revolutions in commercial geography, however, British Burma has suddenly and unexpectedly found a new market of 200 million people, which is a great deal for a country of 15 million inhabitants! [2]

Special steps must be taken if the Empire is to make full use of this promising opportunity. Rangoon, the only harbor that can be used, is situated 21 miles up a river, or rather up a delta branch of the Irrawaddi, which runs the risk of being choked up by detritus. Vessels drawing more than 26 feet cannot go up to Rangoon, and if they measure more than 10,000 tons they must discharge their cargo into lighters.

[2] After Dr. Hedin wrote, the British Government agreed under pressure from Japan to close the Burma route to war supplies during the three months' rainy season of 1940, but it was reopened at the end of that period. [Ed.]

Everything required for the transshipment is available. Docks, cranes, and warehouses have been erected and the supply of labor is inexhaustible. The gauge of the Burma railway is only one meter and the capacity of the trucks only 12 tons. The rolling stock is excellent, and the 100 miles of railway bank are solid. The railway now runs to Lashio, not far from the boundary between Burma and Yünnan. The freight charges are higher than in China and Japan, but thanks to the Chinese exports, the trucks run with full loads in both directions. Heavy goods can be shipped up the Irrawaddi to Bhamo, which is nearer China than Lashio. A complete revision of the entire trade and everything pertaining to it, for instance customs tariffs, is necessary. China, which is meeting England halfway, opened a branch office of the Bank of China at Rangoon, and started a South-Western Transport Company. With all other entrances closed, the Chinese were trying to save their lives through this back-door route, along which there passed an almost continuous stream of foodstuffs and war materials.

The road through Burma is the last artery that connects the new, growing country of western China with a port on the coast. The future will show whether this route, replacing all China's former lines of connection with the sea and foreign countries, will be left in peace, or whether Japan, having carefully blocked all other routes, will attack it also and stop its incessant traffic of lorries transporting war material and other necessities.

Commenting on China's last lines of connection with the outside world, Miss Freda Utley said in 1938, "If Britain and France should desert China completely and accede to the Japanese demand that they should put a ban on munitions shipped to Hong Kong or Haiphong, China would be left with only the difficult land route from the U.S.S.R. to Sinkiang, since the somewhat easier land route from Outer

Mongolia has been cut off by the Japanese occupation of Kalgan and Eastern Suiyuan." [3]

The two roads running south which she mentions are already practically closed. The old Russian caravan route Kalgan-Urga, along which the Chinese tea was formerly transported to Russia, is also cut off, as she points out. There is another desert route in the northeast, the one running from Ninghsia to Urga (Ulan Batur khoto). However, this is no real road, but a haphazard route of the kind that can be chosen anywhere where the terrain is smooth and the ground sufficiently solid. At the time when Miss Utley wrote, the Burma road was not yet of current interest. But she is quite right in saying that when all arteries running east and south have been cut off, there is always one way out, the overland route to Sinkiang and Russia.

As I have traveled this route both in the old manner, on the backs of camels, and in the new one, by car, and as it may become China's only and last line of connection with the outside world I shall summarize in another chapter what is known of its present function and the part it is already playing.

[3] *Japan's Gamble in China*, p. 249.

XXIX

China's Imperial Highway through Asia

EVEN IF JAPAN SHOULD SUCCEED IN CLOSING THE LAST route to Inner China from the Pacific, and the first route from the Indian Ocean, there always remains the classical "Imperial Highway." Count von Richthofen called it "The Silk Road," because two thousand years ago, in the Han Dynasty, the precious Chinese silk was transported on carts and camels from Sian in the extreme east through innermost Asia, along the Great Wall, to Lop-nor and Lou-lan, to Kashgar, over Pamir, and through the Near East to the coast of the Mediterranean, finally to be sold to the patricians in the cities of the Roman Empire.

In my book *The Silk Road* I have described this artery, the longest, oldest, and most famous of all caravan routes, and have told the strange circumstances that intimately connected my destiny with the old route of the silent desert waste, where the footprints of thousands of camels and the ruts made by innumerable cartwheels have long since been erased by the winds.

During my subsequent travels in Sinkiang and my camel ride from the northern part of China proper to this province, it struck me that the trade of Sinkiang which of old was mainly a Chinese concern, but in latter times has fallen into Russian hands—and to a certain extent also into British-Indian—with the aid of improved communications might be restored to Chinese merchants.

I spoke about this to Liu Chung-chieh, the Chinese Vice Minister for Foreign Affairs, in Peking on June 28, 1933. He immediately realized the importance of the matter and asked me to write a memorandum, accompanied by a map, stating what I considered should be done. This idea, and its results, being closely connected with China's perhaps last line of connection with the outside world and also constituting an historical prelude to the present communication between China and Russia, I believe it to be my right and my duty to recall in this connection a dream that became reality —even though the reality proved to be far greater than anything I had ever dreamed of. For it will be readily realized that I was not contemplating the possibility of a war between Japan and China, but above all the commercial aspects of the matter, the administrative control of the province, and the possibility of quelling revolts at an early stage by the rapid transportation of troops.

In my first communication to Liu Chung-chieh I discussed mainly the route that I considered to be most urgent, the one running across the desert and uniting Kweihwa in Suiyuan with Hami, along which route most of the caravans passed prior to the revolt in Sinkiang, and which in the main runs north of the "Imperial Highway."

My memorandum is dated Peking, July 2, 1933. After a short geographical survey I mention the fact that the distance from Kweihwa to Urumchi is 2,100 kilometers as the crow flies, which distance is covered by the caravans in three months. From Kweihwa to Kashgar the distance is 3,400 kilometers as the crow flies. The trade of Sinkiang is controlled by Russia in the north and by India in the south. It would be far too expensive to build a railway, and the German-Chinese air line, Eurasia, which with certain interruptions has trafficked the stretch Shanghai-Urumchi, or parts of it, takes only mail and passengers.

It would be simpler and cheaper than anything else to build an automobile road from Kweihwa to Urumchi and Kashgar. The direct desert route is much easier to transform into an automobile road than the "Imperial Highway." The former needs but a few bridges across rivers and brooks; the latter several hundred. For many years it has been possible to go by motor car from Hami to Urumchi. Hundreds of motor cars might be put in service in both directions through the desert between Sinkiang and the coast. Three petrol stations and some inns would have to be built. Officers, merchants, and merchandise would be able to travel the distance in two weeks; now it takes three months. The Siberian railway need thus not be used in making the trip from China proper to Sinkiang. Side roads should be built to Chuguchak, Kashgar, Khotan, Suchow, and other places. The trade would flourish to the benefit of China.

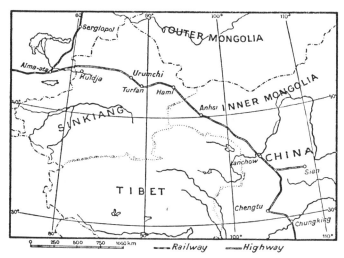

Sketch Map of the Main Road between China and Russia.

Since 1911 the governor generals of Sinkiang had acted like independent kings. An automobile road would bring the distant province much closer to China proper and facilitate administration.

The Sino-Swedish expedition had operated for six years in the very areas through which the great road would run. With three or four companions I could carry out the preliminary investigations, after which the building of the road could commence. I suggested that the expedition start before the end of the summer of 1933. "One thing is certain, and that is that if China intends to keep Sinkiang as a Chinese province in the future, there is no time to lose, and if the large and rich province is to be developed and defended, preparations in the right direction must be started at once. Personally I ask for no other compensation but the knowledge that I have started an important enterprise, which may prove of value to China, this great and wonderful country, where I have ever been received with kindness and hospitality, and in whose future greatness and growth I have the deepest faith."

That is the end of my first memorandum. I handed the communication to Minister Liu, who had it translated into Chinese and sent to Chiang Kai-shek, Wang Ching-wei, and Kuo Meng-yü, the Minister of Railways.

In a supplement dated July 18, I emphasized that particular attention should be afforded the old Silk Road over Suchow, Tunhwang, Lop-nor, and Lou-lan. The *Peking Chronicle* of the same day published a statement by President Wang, which on vital points differed from my suggestion, but in which he, like myself, first of all had in mind the salvation of the neglected province. He said, "Due to the lack of convenient means of communication it has not been possible fully to develop this large area to any considerable extent. This shows the urgent need of completing the Kansu-Sinkiang railway as soon as possible and of building motorcar roads in the province."

On the third of August I received the following telegram:

"President Wang Ching-wei of the Executive Yuan wishes to see you in Nanking as soon as possible. Please reply to Liu Chung-chieh."

So I went to Nanking and immediately had an exhaustive discussion with the President of the Council. As the building of a railway 3,500 or 4,000 kilometers long would take years and cost hundreds of millions, it was decided after long discussions with road experts and engineers and after I had submitted three new memoranda that first of all two motorcar roads should be built, the northern one between Kweihwa and Hami, the southern one along the "Imperial Highway" from Sian over Lanchow, Suchow, and Anhsi to Hami. The task entrusted to me and my companions by the Government also included the road from Hami over Turfan to Urumchi and one of the following three roads: Urumchi—Chuguchak, Urumchi—Kuldja, Urumchi—Kashgar. My suggestion to make the activities of the expedition include an investigation as to whether the new lower course of the Tarim, Kumdarya, might be used to irrigate the areas of the old kingdom of Luo-lan, which could then be made fertile and suitable for settlement, was accepted by the Government.

I have told of the preparations for the expedition, the equipment, the participants, the organization, and the trip in my three books, *The Flight of Big Horse, The Silk Road,* and *The Wandering Lake.*[1] The expedition consisted of one passenger car and four trucks, all Fords; one of the trucks was a gift to the expedition by Mr. Edsel Ford. We left Peking on October 22, 1933, traveled via Beli-miao (Peilingmiao) through the desert to Etsin-gol and westward to Hami. We continued over Turfan to Karashahr, Korla, and Kucha, visited and mapped the Kum-darya and the northern part of the new lake Lop-nor, returned over Karashahr to Urumchi, and then traveled via Turfan and Hami along the "Imperial Highway" to Anhsi, Suchow, Kanchow, Liangchow, Lanchow to Sian, taking the railway from there to Nanking, which city we reached the night between the fourteenth and fifteenth of February, 1935. The distance traveled was 17,000 kilometers.

The two road experts, Irving C. Yew and C. C. Kung, submitted to the Minister of Railways a technical report on

[1] E. P. Dutton & Company. New York.

the roads traveled and on the preliminary work in connection with the building of the two motor-car roads. Yew, Kung, Bergman, and Chen made a road map of the routes suggested by us. In certain parts of Sinkiang, only, this work was hampered by the revolution.

In an earlier chapter I have described my visit to Marshal Chiang Kai-shek when I had the opportunity of giving him an oral report on the trip. I also discussed the results with Wang Ching-wei, the President of the Council, Kuo Meng-yü, the Minister of Railways, and many others.

After my return home to Stockholm on April 15, 1935, I did not hear a word about any roadbuilding in Inner Asia for almost three years. But in December, 1937, a telegram from Shanghai reported that the Chinese Government had decided to build a motor-car road from the Russian boundary at Chuguchak through Inner Asia over Urumchi, Hami, Anhsi, Suchow, to Lanchow. This road is 1,800 miles long from Sergiopol on the Turksib line (between Tashkent and Novo Sibirsk) to Lanchow. According to the telegram the road from Lanchow curved southward to Szechwan, where it meets the road from Rangoon earlier mentioned. The Shanghai telegram said that the work on the new road already was under way and that 700,000 laborers had been mobilized from towns and villages in the neighborhood.

A letter received a little later from one of my fellow travelers, Mr. Irving C. Yew, was dated December 25, 1937. He said that he had followed the Silk Road from Sian to Urumchi and returned by plane to Sian.

A telegram from Delhi to *The Times* dated February 10, 1938, reported that General Ma Chung-yin, "Big Horse," had arrived in Sinkiang from Moscow en route for Kansu, where he was to help the Chinese fight the Japanese. It was said that his cavalry general, Ma Ho-san, who had been badly wounded by a fragment of a Russian shell near Urumchi at the begining of 1934, but who was treated and cured by the doctor of our expedition, Dr. Hummel, had also gone to Kansu—from India, where he had spent some time as a fugitive.

The Russians in Moscow as well as the Englishmen in Delhi surely knew what they were doing when they released the two imprisoned generals and helped them to go to Kansu. Ma Chung-yin is among the Tungans what Lawrence was among the Arabs and Doihara in Manchuria, and Ma Ho-san is a close relative of his. There were people in Russia as well as in England who understood that the two Mohammedan generals would be excellent men in the huge game of chess played on a board consisting of Inner and East Asia. There are millions of Tungans, Mohammedan Chinese, in Central Asia. They are excellent soldiers, enterprising, unafraid, enduring. I speak of them with a certain amount of experience, for they have fired at me and kept me imprisoned, and I witnessed their war in Sinkiang in 1934, when they no doubt would have beaten the troops of the province unless Sheng Shih-ts'ai had received help, men, airplanes, and other material, from Russia.

The information received from Central Asia is very meager. But occasionally a rumor does leak out, and the information I have received bears out the above-mentioned telegrams and the letter. On June 1, 1938, I was honored by a visit in Stockholm by Minister Sun Fo, the son of Sun Yat-sen, who told me that the desert road from the Russian border to Lanchow and Szechwan, i.e., the Central-Asiatic part of the Silk Road, had been enlarged and was being heavily used, and that about a thousand lorries were transporting war material from Russia to Szechwan. There had been much snow during the winter 1937-1938, but the road was kept clear by enormous numbers of workmen.

In his book *Under brinnande krig*, published late in the autumn of 1938, Professor J. G. Andersson tells of "a man who until quite recently had lived in the center of the happenings in China," who had informed him that the traffic capacity of the road from Siberia over Urumchi and Lanchow was not at all negligible. "He says that he himself saw enormous caravans of lorries in Sian, which had come from Siberia with war material, and Chinese tradesmen, coming from Urumchi, report that a railway is being built through the desert."

According to Professor Erik Nyström the traffic along the old Silk Road was already in full swing in June, 1938.

Mr. John Andersson, a Swedish missionary from Kashgar, is also one of my sources of information. He returned to Stockholm in January, 1939, coming straight from his missionary field, and told me that thousands of lorries were running on the new road from Chuguchak over Urumchi and Turfan to Hami, and from there farther to the east through Kansu.

Two new sources of strength have thus arisen in Inner Asia as a consequence of the Japanese invasion in China, first a route from the Russian border through the oases and deserts of Dzungaria, the Turfan basin, and Kansu, to Lanchow, and, second, according to rumors, a levy of 400,000 Tungans under the leadership of the two generals Ma Chung-yin and Ma Ho-san. It does not seem impossible that these two generals will co-operate closely with the Chinese communists in Shensi.

It remains to be seen whether matters will ever develop so far that the theater of war penetrates to the heart of the continent. It is certain, however, that great preparations are being made there, and the news indicates that Chiang Kai-shek and his people are prepared for a long war over extensive fronts. It then also remains to be seen how the Japanese, coming from their islands surrounded by surging breakers and blessed by abundant rain, will like these arid, endless deserts, without vegetation and without inhabitation. There are even some Chinese who fear the desert—how much more sensitive the

Japanese must be to the aridness, solitude, and barrenness!

Even if it should be possible to check the import of arms through Rangoon, it is impossible to stop the import of war material from the Russian side. On the ground Ma Chung-yin will protect the Silk Road and its continuation north-ward, and it would hardly be worth while to attack the road from the air, considering the enormous distances.

The new Chinese road runs from Lanchow, which in the south is in connection with Chengtu and Chungking. Toward west-north-west it follows closely the Silk Road, the new motor-car road that we planned via Liangchow, Kanchow, Suchow, Anhsi, and Hami to Turfan, where it leaves the Silk Road on the left and runs north over Tienshan to Urumchi, the capital of Sinkiang. Anyone familiar with these districts would naturally presume that the last stretch of this endless road to the Russian border, resuscitated from nearly two thousand years of sleep, follows the main road from Urumchi over Manas and Chunguchak to Bakhty and Sergio-pol on the railway between Turkistan and Siberia. But actually it is said to run through the Ili valley to Alma-ata.

It is not easy to obtain any definite information about what is happening on this road. Nothing is disclosed by Russia, and it seems as if Moscow wishes to conceal the invaluable sup-port she is giving China. And Chinese living outside China know just as little as anybody else.

However, an interesting contribution to the knowledge of our road and its significance reached Stockholm, in a valuable article by Colonel Carl Taube, published in the *Svenska Dagbladet*. It bore the significant title, "China Opens her Back Doors," and the subheadings, "Gigantic Chinese Road Con-structions," and "New Lines of Communication Westward."

Having described the southern roads from the sea, Taube began his description of the road to Siberia with the words: "The new connections with French Indo-China and Burma appear insignificant, however, when compared with the gigantic enterprise now completed, the new road from Lanchow to Siberia." He said that Japanese propaganda stamps this road as a proof that China is intimately mixed up with Russian Bolshevism.

Colonel Taube believed that the strategical importance of the new road was as yet small, "but nevertheless its existence is striking evidence of the will and ability of modern China to carry out magnificent enterprises." He said that the road from Urumchi ran to Kuldja (Ili) and from there to Djarkent on the Russian side, "from where there is a line of communication with a station called Alma-ata on the railway line between Tashkent and Semipalatinsk." Lanchow is in communication via Sian with the Yangtse Valley. He figured the distance from Lanchow to Ili to be 5,000 kilometers, and pointed out that the road was completed in only two years. He concluded his article with the words: "In this way China has now thrown her doors wide open toward the west. It has been done under the pressure of war and mainly with a view to serving its ends. But all the roads have been built with a clear realization of their future commercial purposes, and the enormous work will then bear plenty of fruit. Perhaps it is becoming more and more evident that that day is not far off."

Five years and a half have soon elapsed since I left the old Imperial Route, and nothing but rumors and assumptions have reached me since then. Thanks to the war this road is once more of current interest, and thanks to the road China is receiving assistance from Russia, the value of which cannot be overestimated. It is indeed possible that this road may become far more important to China now than it was in the old days when it saw bales of silk carried westward.

On the twenty-ninth of July, 1939, however, I received a greeting from the old road, the truth and reliability of which surpassed all records. For on that day I received a visit from a Chinese gentleman who a few months earlier had traveled the new road all the way from Lanchow to Alma-ata. He had flown from Lanchow to Urumchi, closely following the Silk Road over Liangchow, Suchow, Anhsi, and Hami. They had then left Turfan on the left and flown over Kuchengtze to Urumchi. From there he had traveled by motor car.

He said that the transports from Siberia to the Silk Road and Lanchow were in full swing and steadily increasing. The year before Sheng Shih-ts'ai had visited Stalin, who advised him to join Chiang Kai-shek and the Nanking Government, thereby contributing to the national unity and strength of China. A strong China, counterbalancing Japan, is an advantage to Russia.

Already before the war there was a road between Lanchow and Chengtu, the capacity of which has now been increased. The flight from Lanchow to Urumchi had taken seven and a half hours, for which distance the caravans need almost three months. The whole time, except for a short half hour at Suchow, the air was hazy on account of dust storms. It had thus been impossible for him to form an opinion of the appearance of the landscape, nor had he been able to make out whether railways were being built along any part of the road. He did not think that was the case, but felt convinced that a railway would not be slow in coming.

The road now used from Urumchi to the Russian border runs neither via Chuguchak to Sergiopol nor via Kuldja to Djarkent. Starting from Urumchi it passes Ussu, Sinerhtai and Horgos, a city on the border. From there it is six hours by motor car to Saraosek, which was said to be the terminal of a branch of the Turksib line. From Saraosek my informant had traveled by night train to Alma-ata on the Turksib line, which from there runs straight to Tashkent—and Moscow. It is two hours by motor car from Horgos to Sinerhtai, a long lake being passed on the way, possibly Sairam-nor. The spelling of the names given is uncertain, and my authority was not quite certain of the location of the branch line in relation to the Turksib line. But he did declare that the road he had followed from Urumchi to the Russian railway is located a short distance north of the road over Manas and Kuldja to Djarkent. As Horgos no doubt is identical with Chargos, mentioned on the maps and not far east-north-east of Djarkent, the road must cross the Boro-khoro mountains in the Talki pass, which is about 2,200 meters above sea level.

Even if certain details are still vague and we know nothing definite about the quantities of war material being transported from Alma-ata through Urumchi and over the Silk Road to the aid of China, we do have reliable information that the enormous transcontinental highway actually exists and is in use. Its existence as a reserve exit and entrance to and from the outside world should be as great a comfort to the Chinese as the knowledge that they cannot be hemmed in on all sides.

In my book, *The Silk Road*, published in the autumn of 1936, I said:

"There is nothing fantastic about the idea that the time need not be far off when it may be possible for an enthusiastic motorist to start out in his own car from Shanghai, follow the Silk Road to Kashgar, drive through western Asia to Istanbul, and then via Budapest, Vienna, and Berlin to Hamburg, Bremerhaven, Calais, or Boulogne...." Little did I dream when I wrote those lines that by the summer of 1939 it would be possible to go by motor car from Boulogne to Shanghai. The road crosses the one I had imagined, but the stretch between Turfan and Lanchow is the same in both cases and coincides with the old Silk Road.

The highly cultivated and well informed Chinese government official from Chungking who gave me this information also had a glowing interest in the parts of Central Asia that I had visited on my journeys. Above all he concentrated his attention on Eastern Turkistan and showered me with questions about its natural resources and production, its climate, precipitation, and fertility, the population, its density, its races, its mental and physical qualities, religion, intelligence, thriftiness, courage, vigor, whether the various races intermingled, what they thought and said about the Chinese, whether the latter were clever administrators or committed errors that could be remedied—and many other things.

But the most important question of all was whether rational farming, the exploitation of coal, iron, gold, and other metals, and the utilization of the oil supplies available at Urumchi and Manas, could enhance the present value of the country. Well, of course the 3.5 million Turks, Kirghiz, Mongols, Tadjiks, and others, plus the Chinese now inhabiting Eastern Turkistan, might be increased in number. As there is but little precipitation in the belt of oases surrounded by high mountains in Eastern Turkistan, the river water must be rationally utilized for irrigation purposes. At the beginning of this chapter I mentioned that I suggested to the Government that the water of the lower Tarim be used for irrigation purposes, which water now flows out into the desert to no use at all. The old kingdom of Lou-lan would then be transformed into a new, fertile Mesopotamia on a small scale.

My Chinese guest also inquired whether Tibet, which is four times as large as France, could not be cultivated and populated. In this case I could not inspire him with any hope, but the fact that Chinese enterprise also extends to these desolate and little accessible areas is evident from the fact that new roads are being built through the Tibetan border land.

The train of thought behind all this activity and behind all these questions is easy to conceive. It is correct and logical and expresses a natural force whose inexorable laws Japanese as well as Chinese must obey. We are here primarily concerned with the powerful and irresistible national movements which before our very eyes are causing an uproar all over East Asia, and whose drastic realization predicts not only what the Japanese call "a new order in East Asia" but also a gigantic removal of enormous masses of people from east to west.

The new diagonal road which runs straight through Asia is not only China's last exit over land, but also—when the war in its present aspect comes to an end and when a railway has also been built from western China to Urumchi and Kashgar—the great artery which will connect the mother country in the east with new colonial lands, the Hsi-yü of olden times, or "The Western Lands," bounded by Tsungling or Pamir. The day may thus dawn when the old Imperial Highway, the route of the precious silk to Rome, will acquire a far greater importance than it had two thousand years ago.

XXX

The War round Marshal Chiang

THE JAPANESE WAR IN CHINA HAS BEEN A TRIAL OF
strength between two great nations without alliances or pacts
with other countries. Like Japan, China has stood alone with
no other support from without than the arms and raw material imported.

Those revolutionizing events, the German-Russian non-
aggression pact of August 21, 1939, and the outbreak of a
new European war, will probably—unless those in power
come to their senses before it is too late—influence the destiny
of the whole world for generations to come, and not least
the development and consequences of the war in East Asia.

Before beginning to consider the probable influence of the
great dramatic events upon the relationship between China
and Japan, it may be desirable to cast a rapid retrospective
glance on the general political situation of the two fighting
nations from the time of the outbreak of the war, July 7,
1937, to August 21, 1939.

All this time, thanks to the Anti-Comintern Pact or the
Berlin—Rome—Tokyo triangle, Japan was receiving support
which certainly did not strengthen her military power or
influence her war with China, but still created a state of
mutual understanding.

We have followed step by step the reciprocity and rivalry
which ever since 1895 has prevailed between Russia and
Japan in Manchuria. Through Japan's conquest of "The
Three Northeastern Provinces" Russia was driven out of the
debated area and even had to relinquish the Chinese Eastern
Railway.

In many quarters it was thus believed that Russia would make use of the opportunity to invade Manchuria while Japan was busy with her war in China. When this did not happen, it was by some attributed to the fact that at that time a number of high officers were being removed in Russia, while others believed that Russia did not dare to strike for fear of Germany. Still others advanced a rather far-fetched explanation, namely, that Russia was unwilling to fight on the Chinese side because of the energy Chiang Kai-shek had displayed in fighting communism in the Middle Kingdom.

Japan had no reason to fear China. On the coast and in Vladivostok, Russia was her real enemy and rival. Thanks to Manchuria and to her occupation of Outer Mongolia without a war, Russia was in possession of an enormous glacis against an anticipated Japanese expansion. Japan on her part needed a reassuring glacis against the Russian power and consequently invaded and settled in Manchuria.

The frequent disturbances along the northern borders of Manchuria prove that the relationship between Russia and Japan has been strained throughout the East Asiatic war. The question has repeatedly arisen whether such skirmishes were the forerunners of a war between the two neighbors, or whether the local activity on either side has merely been intended to find out the preparedness and strength of the other party.

Through the Anti-Comintern Pact, Germany automatically became politically opposed to China, which did not prevent the sympathies of practically the entire German nation from resting with China. Of late years the German interests in China had had varying destinies. Toward the end of the Great War, China had also declared war upon Germany. But "the chief result of that war was that the English were allowed to annoy the Germans in China and that the German commerce there was destroyed" (Bernhard Karlgren). With outrageous cruelty the Germans were chased out, and regardless

of age or sex they were driven on board cattle ships, where
the wives of the missionaries, sometimes in a state of advanced
pregnancy, were forced to lie on crude bunks, and where
the unfortunates died in large numbers in the tropics. The
name of the British Minister in Peking, Sir John Jordan, is
intimately connected with the shameful treatment of white
men and women in an Asiatic country. The Chinese stood
aghast and questioning before such cruelty toward people
they honored and esteemed. During the horrors of the Great
War it was suggested in Christian Chinese congregations that
Chinese missionaries should be sent to Europe to preach Christianity!

Germany gave up her extraterritorial rights and other advantages in China, as Russia had done before her. On this
account and because of the treatment of the Germans at
Versailles, Chinese sympathy was aroused, and it did not take
long before German trade in the Chinese markets took the
lead ahead of that of the old treaty powers, particularly England. Finally Germany ranked as number three, coming after
Japan and the United States, in trade with the Middle Kingdom.

A Frenchman (Jean Escarra) wrote in 1938 about Germany's chances in China after the end of the East Asiatic war.
Having stated that the privileges of the white nations in
China after this war will never be the same as they have been
ever since 1842, regardless of who will be the victor, he says,
"There is one power, however, which, thanks to great diplomatic skill, will find it equally simple to take up negotiations
with the victor as with the vanquished. That power is Germany." He speaks of the Berlin-Rome-Tokyo triangle, and
brings to mind that in spite of this pact Germany has
been able to maintain her commercial position in China as it
was before the war. "And up to now she has retained in
China her first-class military mission, whose members have
co-operated intimately with the Chinese in their effective re-

sistance at Shanghai. Germany has exported large quantities of arms and ammunition to the Chinese Government. And finally she (Germany) has attempted at least twice to induce the warring nations to accept her porposals for mediation. . . . Herein lies the skill of German diplomacy." After the war, when the time comes to co-operate with the victor regarding the exploitation of the disputed provinces and the utilization of natural products, "it is certain that this co-operation will come from Germany, perhaps only from Germany."

He says of the peace terms: "And in the event of a Japanese victory it is probably only Germany that can obtain less rigorous terms for China."

In 1938 these reflections were undoubtedly quite correct. But after the signing of the German-Russian pact in Moscow the situation became radically different. This pact was an advantage for China, and hardly welcome to Japan. It strengthened Russia's position in the east. Russian pressure on Japanese possessions, first of all Manchuria, was thus increased, and since 1905 and 1931 Russia has had one or two bones to pick with the Land of the Rising Sun. It was almost possible to hear the Siberian snow creak under the paws of the Russian bear and the rustle of the wings of the Soviet eagle over the endless lands of Manchuria.

Prophecies and predictions are dangerous, particularly in such a gigantic and complicated game of chess as the one now being played on a board represented by the whole world, especially Europe and Asia. Let it then suffice that we suggest the possibility that Germany and Russia together may find it advantageous for the balance in the world, partly that China and Japan make an honorable peace as soon as possible, and partly that Japan be left in uncontested possession of all the land she owned before she began her last annexations in China. Great Britain possesses no conquests other than Gibraltar on the mainland of Europe; just as little is Japan in need of any great expansion in Asia. Just as England has spread her empire over foreign continents and islands, the rulers of her counterpart in the east are said to have far-reaching aspirations for both land and islands in the south and for the sovereignty of the endless seas where the islands of Nippon raise their volcanoes above the water deserts of the Pacific. Every true friend of Japan and every admirer of her brave, manly, and capable people would regret it if the Land of the Rising Sun, as a result of her failure in China, should be changed into the Land of the Setting Sun. For it is possible to like and respect a pleasant and diligent people, even if there is no sympathy left for the military party that has usurped the power over this people and has caused streams of blood and tears to flow over the yellow earth of China. Whatever happens in China, it is certain that the Japanese are and will be a strong and progressive nation.

The part played by Great Britain in East Asia ever since July, 1937, is unfathomable, illogical, and above all un-English. That Britain answered Japan's repeated insults and persecutions with nothing but diplomatic notes and protests instead of protecting her treaty rights with the means at the disposal of the greatest naval power in the world, cannot be explained in any other way but that the situation in the Mediterranean and Europe had paralyzed her power of action and bound her fleet to the home waters. Britain's power on the coast of China, founded on traditions more than a hundred years old, has been badly damaged by Japan's aggressive policy, and in East Asia Britain has lost face as never before. Japan would not have dared to treat Britons and British property as she has, had she not been very well informed regarding the tension in Europe. The statesmen of Britain had to make a terrible choice: either the home fleet had to be risked or Britain's possessions in East Asia had to look after themselves for the time being. In either case the Empire was in danger. The latter course was chosen; the fleet was kept at home and the Japanese were allowed to do what they liked.

Mr. Eden's declarations in the House of Commons in July, 1937, immediately after the outbreak of the war, aroused great delight in Japan, the Japanese interpreting them as a British acknowledgment that the Chinese and not the Japanese were responsible for the war. According to the Japanese press, Britain agreed that Japan was entitled to station as many troops as she liked anywhere in northern China, although the Boxer Protocol does not contain any clause to that effect. Mr. Eden declared that Japan had not intentionally provoked the situation and that he "sympathized with Japan's difficulties." In reply to a question put by a member of the House of Commons whether the British Government had called the attention of the Japanese Government to the fact that the former could not approve of any more provinces being severed from Chinese sovereignty, Mr. Eden gave an ambiguous and evasive answer, at any rate a reply that did not express strong disapproval of the division of China.

In the two years following the outbreak of the war, Mr. Eden had reason to reflect upon "the sympathy he felt with Japan's difficulties." The action in Shanghai, the air raids on British property, on the British Ambassador, and on British gunboats, and the unmistakable intention of the Japanese to put an end to Britain's dominating position in Shanghai and the Yangtse Valley, the insults at Kulangsu, the undressing affair at Tientsin, the agitation of the Chinese mob against Englishmen, and a number of other hostile actions, probably made it clear to Mr. Eden that Britain, not Japan, rightfully deserved sympathy in her difficulties. Concessions and international settlements fell rapidly in value, and the powerful people that was busy introducing the "New Order in East Asia" sneered at the "unequal treaties" and other injustices of the white peoples.

The Japanese attacks on Britain culminated in the blockade of Tientsin, the aim of which was to force Britain to acknowledge Japan's sovereignty in northern China, to close her trading firms in the face of a Japanese monopoly of the same kind as the one already established in Manchuria, to evacuate the concession, and to surrender the fifty million dollars in silver belonging to the Central Government of China and deposited with European banks in Tientsin, and which the Japanese intended to use for the stabilization of the currency introduced by the Federal Reserve Bank. Another of the Japanese demands was that they wanted delivered into their hands four Chinese patriots suspected of participation in the murder of a Chinese customs officer in Japanese service.

The Chinese Foreign Office did not conceal the disappointment felt by China's people because of the attitude of the British Government at the conferences in Tokyo, saying; "It is deeply regretted that the British Government has found it advisable to take to heart the so-called special requirements of the Japanese army in China. . . . It is also astonishing that the British Government has agreed to request the British authorities and British subjects in China to refrain from every action or move that might endamage the Japanese invading forces in their efforts to reach their goal. . . . It is hardly necessary to remind the British Government of the promises made, in accordance with the various resolutions of the League of Nations, not to do anything that might reduce China's power of resistance and thus increase her difficulties in the present conflict. Moreover, the British Government has promised to make all assistance to China as effective as possible.

"In spite of the uncertainty caused by the British-Japanese agreement, the Chinese Government trusts that, when dealing with the so-called local Tientsin questions, the British Government will assume an attitude in line with its legal and moral obligations toward China, and that it will display a firmness in its political attitude in keeping with the situation prevailing as a result of the Japanese attack."

The cancellation of the commercial treaty between the United States and Japan was met with the greatest satisfaction in China. It was looked upon as a proof that the United States desires to maintain its position and prestige in the Pacific. It was a step furthering the development of peace, right, justice, and order between the peoples.

Statements made by Japanese statesmen, officers, and newspapers, and the movements of the Japanese fleet in eastern Chinese waters, have clearly demonstrated to the world the real purpose of this war. Not long ago huge crowds of demonstrators in Peking demanded that all Englishmen should disappear from Asiatic ground. Originally a blood-drenched war with China, the Japanese action successively became an unrelenting attack on England and her possessions and interests in East Asia.

The South China Sea is one of the most remarkable of the peripheral seas on our planet. It is bounded on the northwest by the Asiatic mainland and on the southeast by an archipelago, one of whose islands is one of the largest in the world. The fauna and flora of the surrounding countries, their surging throngs of humans of different races, their wealth of valuable natural resources, their trade, and not least their political importance, indeed make the South China Sea remarkable, and to all this we must now add the part this wonderful world of countries and islands may play in a near future in the final contest between the great powers, the struggle for a fair distribution of the earth. Just as the Mediterranean separates Europe from Africa, so does the South China Sea separate Asia from Australia. There lie the Sunda Islands and the Philippines like a breakwater against the Pacific, like grotesque and eccentric ruins of collapsed columns once supporting a gigantic bridge between the two continents.

Near this border sea, the South China Sea, there are but two completely independent countries, the Chinese Republic and the Siamese monarchy, whose capital is Bangkok. The other countries and islands round the sea have been conquered by white peoples from Europe and America. We find French Indo-China, the British and Dutch possessions, the Portuguese town of Macao, and the Philippines, formerly Spanish but an American possession since 1898.

Since 1895, Formosa has been the southernmost outpost of the Japanese Empire[1]. During the present war the Japanese have occupied the large island of Hainan. Mr. Arita explained that this was done for military reasons, and that the island would be restored to China when such conditions no longer prevailed. In the hands of the Japanese, Hainan is certainly a menace to French Indo-China and Hong-Kong. The occupation of this island meant an enormous improvement of Japan's strategic position in the South China Sea. From there it would be possible for Japan to control French Indo-China, Hong-Kong, and the route from Hong-Kong to Singapore.

In its southeastern part, southwest of the island of Palawan, the South China Sea is filled with shoals, atolls, and coral reefs. Sea-quakes are not infrequent, and typhoons are common visitors, so that world trade avoids these hazardous waters and hugs the shores of the Asiatic mainland.

In this Godforsaken part of the sea, between Saigon on the coast of Cochin China and the northernmost point of Borneo, lies the small group of coral islands and atolls called the Spratly Islands, which name has but seldom been heard until recent times. When the typhoons do not tear like furies across these waters, heaving the breakers over the scraggy coral reefs and atoll rings, silence and solitude reign over the Spratly Islands, which since 1917 have been inhabited by but a few Japanese. Insignificant though they may be, they are large

[1] The Marshall Islands and the Caroline Islands, which are mandates, lie farther south, but outside the waters now discussed.

enough for wireless stations, fortifications, stores, and repair shops, and their lagoons afford landing places for hydroplanes and harbors for submarines. Any great power utilizing these islands for purposes of war will control the South China Sea, for that power will control all the main routes between Singapore and Hong Kong and the Singapore-Manila-Formosa sound. Fortified according to all the rules of modern technique, this group of islands might become of very much the same importance as Malta in the Mediterranean.

On March 31, 1939, Japan informed the French ambassador that the islands were occupied and had been made part of the General Government of Formosa. The situation was discussed at a cabinet meeting in Paris on April 1. It was stated that the islands had been occupied by the French Navy as early as April 4, 1930. A protest was sent to Tokyo. France suggested that the question should be solved by arbitration. But before any meeting had taken place Japan had occupied the islands, and England refused to listen to the French appeal for support.

This question was then drowned in the typhoon of greater problems that raged around the coasts of East Asia. An arrow with its tail at Formosa and pointing toward the Spratly Islands will indicate the direction of the Japanese expansion and the districts where the Japanese Empire will grow on the southern and southeastern coasts of Asia.

On September 3, 1939, England and France declared war on Germany. The old Buddha of Kamakura then smiled his kindest on the sons of Nippon, and the bronze seemed to sound a triumphal march. All Japan rejoiced as if they had won a great victory, and those looking farther ahead could see the Union Jack pulled down from every mast in East Asia and the flag of the Rising Sun flying over the waves, its red sun in the white field symbolizing the glowing cannon ball of the Japanese fleet triumphing over the collapsed rule of the whites in Asiatic waters.

The hazardous game the Japanese war party started when it commenced war with China, in 1937, had been successful beyond expectation. On many occasions things looked bad for Japan in the Middle Kingdom. Chiang Kai-shek's resistance had increased, and the task of crushing China had turned out far more difficult than expected. News of the German-Russian pact was received on the twenty-second of August. The country was half stunned by this blow which instantly threw overboard all hopes of a German-Japanese military alliance. But at the very moment when darkness had descended upon the islands of Nippon, the sun once more appeared, more radiant than ever. England and France had declared war upon Germany! Oh, Eternal Buddha, blessed be thy name! We Japanese and no others are now masters of Asia! England and France are bleeding in a fatal war with Germany and are bound with chains of iron to the coasts of Europe. They have thrown their Asiatic possessions to the winds and are unable to send a single gunboat to the defense of Shanghai, Hong Kong, or Indo-China. We need but go on board and follow the coasts in order to gather the fruits that have been ripening for a hundred years and to claim the harvests formerly reaped by white men. We Japanese have won an enormous victory without sacrificing one drop of blood or a single ship. The whites now have more important concerns. Instead of preserving their East Asiatic domains, they are committing harakiri.

Is anyone childish enough to believe that the Japanese out of sheer considerateness and chivalry will guard the British and French possessions like "watchdogs" while their rightful owners are busy elsewhere? No, the sons of Nippon are not so foolish as that! The Eternal One of Kamakura has given them the greatest opportunity they ever had. They will use it with skill and care and will make sure that the strokes of the death bell announcing the end of the supremacy of the whites in East Asia are just as solemn and regular as the hangman's drumming on the road to the place of execution in Peking. One shudders at the thought of the responsibility shouldered by the statesmen who have recklessly left the East Asiatic possessions to their fate. And this enormous change appears still more tragic when one considers how much more difficult Chiang Kai-shek's noble and brave fight becomes, how much heavier his burden, and how much smaller his chances when the help of arms and money previously received from the great powers becomes less or perhaps ceases entirely.

But allow me to say one thing—the war against Chiang Kai-shek is not to be settled on the battlefields; it is the invincible, almost enigmatic tenacity of the Chinese race which has weathered the storms of more than four thousand years that will decide the issue. The paralyzing events in Europe cannot make me alter a single line of my opinions as expressed on the foregoing pages of this book. Japan is headed for a period of resplendent greatness and will throw out the English from the Asiatic seas and coasts—but China will always be victorious on the continent.

What India thinks of the future was disclosed by Sir Brojendra Lal Mitter, the prominent lawyer, when he visited Stockholm. Among other things he said: "It is quite natural that all India is alarmed to see the advance of the Japanese, for the farther south and west they come, the more they approach our boundaries. To be sure, Burma was separated from India several years ago, but we have our defense in common. There are certainly no possibilities for Japanese air raids on us at present, but a further advance may expose Burma as well as the northeastern parts of India to such risks. Under the pressure of war, the Chinese, as you know, have built an important road from Burma to China, which also in times of peace may be of great importance, but along which enormous quantities of ammunition are now being transported. On the whole one must admire the enterprise the attack has aroused in China. Without this unparalleled provocation the Chinese would not have experienced such a quick and thorough regeneration. But Japanese activity does not stop with China. India is also worried by signs of a successful Japanese penetration into Siam. On the other hand the British Empire possesses unconquerable Singapore not far off. The Japanese policy is certainly not causing an acute crisis, but we are making preparations."

In the middle of January, 1902, I met Sir Binden Blood at Lahore. After service in the Boer war, he had just returned to his post in India. He said, "When we have taught the Indian princes and peoples to govern themselves without foreign assistance—then we have filled our mission and can return home." And he added, "The British Empire resembles a huge spider. The motherland, the British Isles, is the body; the lines of communication to the possessions beyond the seas are its legs. If someone stronger than we should come along equipped with a huge pair of scissors, it would be a simple thing for him to cut off the legs of the spider, leaving nothing but the body alone in the Atlantic."

> *Far-called our navies melt away;*
> *On dune and headland sinks the fire:*
> *Lo, all our pomp of yesterday*
> *Is one with Nineveh and Tyre:*
> *Judge of the Nations, spare us yet*
> *Lest we forget—lest we forget.*

It was the knowledge that this marvelous empire was in danger in a time of surging unrest throughout the world, that prompted England to declare war on Germany—not a desire to save Poland.

Anyone who has had a chance to see part of this enormous empire, and particularly the most exquisite gem in its crown,

India, cannot help admiring the genial and prudent manner, the consistency and strength, with which an Asiatic country of 365 million inhabitants has been governed by England for 170 years. Colonial history can present no other case of a European nation's solving such a gigantic civilizing problem in so brilliant a manner. And if the development of this imposing empire is followed from the time of Sir Francis Drake and Captain James Cook, it must be admitted that it has been built and shaped with unsurpassed foresight, skill, and confidence into a skeleton of steel embracing five continents, which has given the whole world stability and discipline, a blessing to all peoples and races, to all humanity.

It is easy to understand that this grandiose empire, where the sun never sets, is worth a war. The English are not risking their empire for the sake of eastern Europe. No, the empire itself is at stake, Pax Britannica; right or wrong, my country!

The war between the two East Asiatic powers is but part of the great gamble for power on the surface of the earth, the struggle between totalitarian states and democracies, between Germany and England, between countries who possess but little and others who possess much. Unless a world conference settles all wryness, injustice, and folly prevailing in the world, the unrest and continuous paroxysms shaking all humanity must be smothered in blood. It is futile to try to find the one or the ones responsible for the present war, for war is a natural force that cannot be resisted, and as long as man's actions are dictated by selfishness, avarice, and hate, war will always be unavoidable. Unless strong hands avert the catastrophe, it will become a feud that will leave Western civilization in shreds and Europe a pile of smoking ruins.

When studying the positions at the opening of the game, a few figures are always instructive and interesting. They follow as short aphorisms and speak for themselves.

The solid crust of the earth is 149 million square kilometers. Asia is 44 million square kilometers, Europe 10 million square kilometers, and Europe is really only a peninsula, cut up at random, which the mother continent, Asia, thrusts out toward the west. Asia is inhabited by 1,003 million people, more than half of mankind; Europe by 460 millions, or about as many as in China or in the British Empire. The density of the population in Europe is 46 individuals per square kilometer, in Asia as a whole 22, and in China 83.

Including Dominions, colonies, and protectorates, but excluding Egyptian Sudan and the League of Nation mandates, the British Empire covers 34,360,000 square kilometers, or nearly one fourth of the surface of the earth. The motherland itself has an area of 242,600 square kilometers and a population of 46 millions.

Germany with her 693,000 square kilometers and 85 million people has no overseas possessions.

Soviet Russia has an area of 21,236,000 square kilometers, China proper 5,840,000, and her tributary countries (Sinkiang and Tibet), 2,600,000.

When the German-Russian nonaggression pact became known to the world it aroused much joy in Chiang Kai-shek's capital, for the Chinese Government considered that China automatically should be party to the German-Russian alliance.

Germany has a surplus of industry and skill in all technical sciences, but lacks raw materials. Russia lacks industry and skilled technical knowledge, but possesses an inexhaustible wealth of raw material. The two countries thus complement each other, and the German power of organization would have endless fields of activity on Russian ground. Roads are already being built for the transportation of raw materials and food from Russia to Germany, and in the event of a long war Germany cannot be forced to her knees through a blockade, at least not so quickly as in the Great War.

In Japan the immediate result of the German-Russian pact

was the resignation of the Hiranuma cabinet, and the accession of a new government under General Abe. The result of the pact on Japan's treatment of the Englishmen in China was equally rapid: the persecutions ceased and the blockade of Hong Kong was raised. A little later, on September 5, the press announced that Molotov, the Russian Foreign Minister, and the Japanese Ambassador Togo had decided in Moscow to put a stop to the hostilities and the frequent frictions between Outer Mongolia and Manchuria. Unlike the German-Russian pact, this agreement was a disadvantage to China and an advantage to Japan. For Japan could remove some of her troops from the northern boundary of Manchuria and instead throw them into the war with China. It is not very probable that the artful Russian diplomats should have done Japan such a great favor for nothing. They can sleep peacefully in Vladivostok, and Japan is no longer Russia's enemy, which fact, considering the relations and tension between the two countries ever since 1895, is really most astonishing. But this state will probably not be of long duration; the two countries are too much in each other's way for that. But what did Russia get in return for the agreement? Is she giving Japan a free hand to continue her advance southward along the coast of the South China Sea? Perhaps Russia will try to persuade Japan to abandon her continued advance in the southern seas, for fear that she otherwise may become too powerful and too dangerous a neighbor on the Russian coast of the Pacific? But on the other hand, Japan's power would grow also if she were to become master of China. Germany at least is thus no doubt interested in a cessation of the war between Japan and China as soon as possible, and would like to see peace between the two countries on reasonable terms. It is equally important that China be rebuilt and be given time to recover from the devastating war. It is only when this has taken place that trade can be resumed on a large scale.

Japan has declared that the events in Europe in no way influence her policy vis-à-vis China. The war is to be continued until the goal is reached. I have expressed my personal opinion that the Chinese certainly may be defeated in the field, but that their country can never be brought under the yoke. A temporary paralyzation of China must absolutely be followed by a fatal repercussion. Professor J. G. Andersson has expressed the same opinion thus:

"If Chiang Kai-shek can hold out until the Japanese give up, China will be the leading power in the East by 1950. If the Japanese should now succeed in subduing the country, the Chinese will not recover the position due them on account of the wealth of their country and the qualities of their people until around the year 2000. China is such a continental unit, and in its peace-loving diligence the people is so sound, that it cannot in the long run remain enslaved. Once struck to the ground, it will rise after the devastation of the war."

The same sentiments were expressed by Professor Owen Lattimore of Johns Hopkins University and editor of *Pacific Affairs,* who has spent a great part of his life in China. At my request he gave me his opinion in writing on August 21st, 1939, during his visit to Stockholm. It read as follows: "It seems to me inevitable that China will win this war. Japan has by no means expended all its strength; but it has expended enough to show that the kind of strength that Japan possesses is not adequate for the conquest of China. Japan is today only a little better organized for a long war than it was two years ago; China is much better organized. The Japanese aim was a quick victory; this has been defeated. The Chinese counted on a long war; and their success has been greater than the world expected. Japan has produced no great general and no successful new military tactics. China has produced in Chiang Kai-shek, a leader who is beyond question a greater man than he was two years ago. China has also evolved a method of fighting which has already baffled the Japanese

Japanese Troops Scaling a Wall of the Kiangyin
Fort on the Yangtze in December, 1937.

Photograph by G. L. G. Samson-Pix

Salt Carriers Lay Down Their Loads and Rest Near Kunming. The Chunks Are Carefully Shaped to Fit a Man's Shoulders. On Each Can Be Seen the "Chop" or Seal of the Provincial Tax Bureau.

'enveloping' tactics, which is becoming steadily more effective, and which is capable of passing eventually to successful offensives against the Japanese. In a word—it is not Japan, but China, which stands for a 'new order in Asia.' A European war might make a longer time necessary, but would not change the result. The New China of Chiang Kai-shek will triumph as inevitably as did the New America of George Washington."

In his book, *Maktkampen i Fjärran Östern*, Professor Bernhard Karlgren, the well-known Sinologist, summarized the present war situation in the following words: "Generally speaking the Japanese campaign has been characterized by the fact that the Japanese forces have almost always been victorious in regular battles and in taking the Chinese fortified positions, this on account of the considerable Japanese superiority in war material, above all heavy artillery, tanks, and bombers. On the other hand, the Chinese soldiers have, physically and morally, been far better than anticipated by their enemies, and the tenacity and bravery of the Chinese have often been so great that they have almost counterbalanced the material superiority of the Japanese. Thanks to the latter, however, the invading armies have inexorably reached their strategic goals."

A clear and penetrating light is thrown upon Chiang Kai-shek's character and his attitude toward Japan in the message he delivered to the sons of Nippon on the second anniversary of the outbreak of the war. Having pointed out that the militarists are the enemies of the Japanese as well as the Chinese people, the Marshal declared that he knew more than well that he himself was the real target for the attacks of the Japanese militarists. He finds this quite natural, for when the militarists wish to wage war on the Chinese people, they must also want to attack its commander-in-chief.

"But I should like to make it clear to you (Japanese) that it is absolutely wrong to believe that by removing Chiang

Kai-shek, you can subdue China. It is true that I shall use my endeavors to the utmost to offer resistance to the invaders of China, but you must understand that the Chinese nation is united and that it possesses many other capable men. I simply represent the spirit and will of the armed forces of the Chinese people, as I carry out the imminent task of resistance and restoration. You must understand that the existence of a strong and independent China is an advantage to Japan, for only a China that is strong and progressive can be a true guarantee for peace in the East. Japan will be the first to derive benefits from this peace."

Finally Chiang Kai-shek emphasized in his message that the independence and existence of a new China are not undermined by Japan's armed attacks, and that it is the Japanese themselves who will ultimately suffer from the damage caused by their own attacks. "The armed Chinese forces and the civil population still look upon the Japanese as a peace-loving people, and consider them to be their good friends. They sincerely hope that also the Japanese will realize what are the interests of the two countries and that they will co-operate with the Chinese in offering common and energetic resistance to the militarists and thus express the desire that strength be built up on the grounds of justice."

In reply to all the bullets and bombs that have sought his life and all the notes demanding that he disappear before any peace be concluded, he has not a word of hate or ill will, but only conciliatory words directed to the people whose armies have ravaged his country and killed millions of his people.

There must be a solution and an end to this mad and hopeless war that is ravaging and impoverishing two great peoples, who, instead of devastating and damaging each other might join their forces and interests to a common end, producing a state of prosperity and happiness. Japan's industry is at the high level of our times but it has no raw materials. China possesses a surplus of raw materials but lacks industry. The conditions are the same as with Germany and Russia. If the two countries agreed upon a common peaceful program, they would complement each other, give each other help where needed, and together reap the harvest of their work. We who love and admire these two great and kindly peoples would be delighted to learn that Japan had offered China honorable and just peace terms, a peace that would be a blessing to the Far East.

In the middle of the surging sea that is roaring around him, Chiang Kai-shek stands firm, admirable—head and shoulders above all others.

Epilogue

HUMAN RECORDS FROM ALL AGES EVER SINCE THE ANCIENT past disclose that the interior of Asia has always been the scene of tremendous and revolutionizing national movements. In trying to study these, it is found that they recur at regular intervals as if driven like the waves of the sea by a natural force, and they have always been directed westward—in the direction of Europe.

Asia has seen the birth of the great religions, those of Buddha, Jehovah, Christ, and Mohammed, and the old wisdom which has found adepts also among Europeans. The cradle of the human race also stood in the heart of Asia, from where people have spread throughout the world and have during eons of time developed into different races in different zones and climates. The human waves that from time to time have swept like hurricanes over Europe likewise originated in East Asia.

Mongolia is the original birthplace of the great human waves. Hiung-nu, the Huns, that mighty nomad tribe, lived there, and at the end of the Chou dynasty (1155-255 B.C.) they sent their plundering hordes of horsemen to China. The Emperor Shih Hwang-ti of the Ch'in dynasty (255-209) built the Great Wall to protect his peaceful people of farmers against the invaders. The Huns then turned west and chased the Wu-sun and Yüe-chih peoples from their pastures in northwestern Kansu. The descendants of the Huns themselves being driven westward by their neighbors in the east, they again turned up in the Altai Mountains, now as Turks, while the bulk of them spread farther and farther westward.

More than two thousand years ago the Huns were China's most dangerous enemies. A century before the birth of Christ a Chinese chronicler described them as inhabiting the countries south of Mongolia, northern Chihli, Shansi, and Ordos. They possessed large herds of horses, oxen, and sheep. They were unsurpassed archers and horsemen and they shunned no dangers in war. Yearning for prey and plunder, they threw themselves over the Middle Kingdom, penetrating as far as the Great Wall which stood like a breakwater in their way.

From their humble origin the brave nomadic Huns created a great power, the domains of which included all Mongolia, the valleys of the Altai Mountains, and the wastes of Ordos and Sungaria. The Huns became the propelling power that started mighty migrations farther and farther westward to the Ili valley and Trans-Caspia. One of the peoples who had been forced to break up from their old pastures, the Saka, plunged into Bactria and Parthia, about 130 B.C., put an end to the Hellenistic power, and penetrated as far as India.

Through their daring activity the Huns deeply influenced China's history. Thanks to them the great Han Emperor, Wu-ti, was forced into foreign politics on a large scale, and his envoys and troops found their way as far as the countries east of the Caspian Sea. Cruel wars were fought in the Tarim basin between Chinese and Huns over Lou-lan and other kingdoms, which struggle after hundreds of years ended with the defeat of the Huns.

Defeated by the Chinese, the Huns directed their horses toward the Occident, in whose history they and their chieftains were to play an important part and later be extolled in such epics as the *Nibelungenlied*.

Between 370 and 380 A.D., a branch of the Hun tribes penetrated from the steppes north of the Caspian Sea into southern Russia, eastern Iran, and India. Having crushed the Alani of Iran, they laid the Ostrogoths under their knouts and chased the Visigoths to Transylvania and the Balkans.

In the year 447 Attila, the renowned king of the Huns, commenced his great campaign against Europe, invaded Greece, and got as far as the walls of Byzantium. For a time the Roman empire could buy its liberty with gold, and the Emperor Theodosius had to pay dearly for peace. In 451 Attila led his murdering, burning, and sacking hordes of horsemen against the Western Roman Empire, marched through southern Germany, which was forced into submission and alliance, and with 500,000 horsemen he advanced over the Rhine into Gaul where he was thoroughly beaten by the Roman general Aetius on the Catalaunian plains.

After his defeat Attila advanced on Rome but was persuaded by Pope Leo I to retreat. He then repaired to his headquarters at Pannonia in western Hungary, where he died in 453. When Attila was at the height of his power, he had conquered all peoples from the Volga to the Rhine, many Teutonic tribes, the Ostrogoths, Longobards, Franks, Allemands, and Burgundians. He swept like a scourge over them and over the Roman Empire, and no grass grew on the meadows trampled by his horses.

The product of Turkish, Mongolian, Finnic-Ugric, and perhaps also Iran elements, the brave horsemen of the Huns, after some five hundred years of ravaging in the east, had left their old homes in East Asia and invaded Europe, a veritable plague to Christendom. But like other Asiatic nomad peoples who have broken in upon our continent, the Huns failed in their attempt to found a lasting dominion on European ground. Only a people that for thousands of years has been rooted to the earth can create a dominion. Egyptians and Indians have lived under traditional conditions in the countries whose ground they have cultivated since time immemorial. The tilling of their own soil left no time for thoughts of conquest. This was true also of the Japanese until 1894 when they were corrupted by the knowledge they gained of the "civilization" of the white race.

More than any other people the Chinese are rooted to the good earth, where their characteristics have developed and where they have preserved their innermost soul for thousands of years. The tenacity and diligence of the peasant class is the foundation of the Chinese nation. The plow, not the sword, has enlarged and fortified the Middle Kingdom. The foreign conquerors that have subdued the Chinese in the field have been assimilated, absorbed and drowned in the Chinese sea of humans.

Only permanently domiciled peoples have a written history and can create an epic. Bedouins, Huns, and Mongols have not immortalized their deeds in annals.

Seven hundred and seventy years after the death of Attila and the fall of the Hunnic Empire, Europe was once more harassed by an Asiatic invasion of gigantic dimensions.

Temudjin, the son of Jessugai, was a shepherd who lived all his life in a felt yurt and who rode with his horses on the pastures of Mongolia. He had never seen a city and had vague ideas about ancient lands and high cultures. He could neither read nor write and had access to no literature that could supply him with knowledge of the world. But he was unsurpassed as a warrior, and like all Mongols he was one with his saddle.

While he was still a young man, he gathered Mongol chieftains from far and near under the nine-cleft banner. He subdivided his first army of 13,000 horsemen into 13 *gurans* or troops and trained each *guran* to carry out its operations as an individual unit, attack the flanks of the enemy, and by a rapid and sudden shock break through his center. At the beginning of the thirteenth century he had built up an army whose skill and strength were unsurpassed in the West.

Chinghiz Khan, the name he adopted as Great Khan, aroused horror, fear, and hatred in all Asiatic and European peoples.

Having conquered Asia, he turned westward. At the head

of 250,000 horsemen, each of whom brought three spare
horses, he rode down one civilization after the other, leaving
only waste land in the tracks of his horses. In the middle of
the winter one division of the army crossed the Pamir passes.
I know these passes from winter journeys; they are usually
blocked by snow. After this feat, which surpasses Hannibal's
and Napoleon's marches across the Alps, the hordes invaded
the flourishing land of Choresm and transformed it into a
deserted waste.

It is fifty years since I rode from Meschhed to Rhages, but
I have not forgotten the piles of ruins still remaining of the
cities ravaged by Chinghiz Khan's armies. They did it so thoroughly that the cities never could be rebuilt. No lives were
spared; unchecked war made its first appearance. The silence
was that of a graveyard where the Mongols had passed.

When Chinghiz Khan ended his days in 1227, he was ruler
of the greatest realm that has ever existed in the world,
covering more than 100 degrees of longitude between the
Pacific and the Mediterranean, between the Siberian taiga and
the Himalayas. All the peoples living in felt yurt and in the
saddle were his subjects, and they were rigorously disciplined.
He promised them the whole world, or at any rate as much
of it as was covered by the hoofs of the small Mongolian
horses—the still living descendants of the Sungarian wild
horse.

Chinghiz Khan left his enormous country to his sons, Dja-
gatai, Ogodai, and Tuli. Djudji, the eldest son of the conqueror, had died two years before his father, leaving his son
Batu, who became Khan of Kiptjak and conquered eastern
Europe and large parts of middle Europe. The son of Ogodai,
Kujuk Khan, resided in the capital Karakorum, and became
known in Europe through his relations with its royal houses.
Tuli's second son, Khubilai, the Emperor of China, became
renowned in the west through Marco Polo.

Between 1237 and 1241 Batu Khan's wild hordes swept

ravaging through Europe, through Russia from the Volga over Moscow to Novgorod, through Podolia, Bessarabia, Transylvania, Wallachia, Dobrudja, Bulgaria, Serbia, Siebenbürgen, Slavonia, northern Italy, and Hungary. One cavalry troop traveled like a plague from Volhynia over Lublin, Sandomir, and Krakow through Poland to Breslau and Liegnitz, while another took the road through Lithuania, Prussia, Pomerelia, and Pomerania.

The picture that Europe, filled with hatred and hostility and internally torn, then presented to a common, outside foe should not be forgotten by the white peoples of today, the present situation in the world in many respects resembling that prevailing in the thirteenth century. Now as well as then the law about the human waves rushing in from the east can become a reality.

The only one of the princes of that time who realized the terrible danger once more threatening Europe in the form of a new Mongolian invasion, was Frederick II, crowned German Emperor in Aachen in 1215, twice excommunicated by Gregorius IX, a crusader, at the height of the culture of his time, clear-sighted, intelligent, and well taught by Arabian and Jewish learned men at his court in Sicily.

All Russia was drenched in blood; Kiev, the holy city, was in ruins, Poland was crushed, Hungary ravaged, Mongol hordes were advancing to the Adriatic. At Liegnitz, near the boundary of Germany, the frontier guard of Europe succumbed to the endless hordes of horsemen from Asia. All too late it was realized that it was high time to try to meet the enormous danger with united forces; the princes applied frantically to each other for help, and the German clergy recommended fasts and preached crusades.

On July 3, 1240, the Emperor Frederick sent a letter to his brother-in-law, King Henry III of England, urging levies and co-operation between all Christian countries. This letter is a masterpiece, and, as Jarl Charpentier says, it might "well

have been dug out of oblivion at late as 1914, when hordes
from the east once more were threatening the heart of
Europe."

The letter begins: "Frederick, Emperor, etc., to the King
of England, greetings, etc."

He wishes to bring to the attention of the King a matter
that concerns the Roman Empire and all devout Christian
monarchies, and which is threatening all Christendom with
destruction. A barbarous people called Tartars is spreading
like cancer. It is the judgment of God upon His people to
redress and chastise them. Destruction and devastation of rich
lands, sparing neither sex, age, nor dignity, in the hope of
extirpating the rest of mankind; desiring to rule alone by
dint of their enormous numbers and their power. These
Tartars, the sons of Hell, are armed with bows, spears, and
arrows, and murder indiscriminately with blood-dripping
swords. Like the wrath of God or a stroke of lightning they
suddenly descended upon the lands, completely devastating
proud countries and killing their inhabitants. The sluggish
King of Hungary and his people did not believe in the danger,
although warned. The Tartars rushed in like a whirlwind and
surrounded them. The Hungarians, their prelates and knights,
were all butchered in a slaughter of unheard-of cruelty. The
King fled to Illyria. First the Hungarian Kingdom beyond
the Danube was laid waste, then the rest. Reports had been
received by the Emperor from his son Conrad, from the King
of Bohemia, and from the Dukes of Austria and Bavaria.

Their army operated along three lines, one through Poland,
the second through Bohemia, and the third through Hungary, all advancing on the Austrian boundary. "Fear and
horror, instilled by their fury, outrage and arouse all people;
necessity demands that we resist them when the danger
threatens at our doors; the general destruction of the whole
world and Christendom in particular calls for quick help and
relief."

The Emperor describes the Tartars (the Mongols). They are wild and valiant and obey the slightest order of their leader no matter how great the dangers. They are dressed in hides, have taken armor and swords from fallen enemies, and are attacking us with our own weapons. They take our horses and cross the rivers with the assistance of hides sewn together.

The Emperor counsels His Magnificence and other princes in numerous letters and warns them: "Peace and love should reign between rulers; discord, which so often has brought disaster upon Christendom, must be put aside, and a common agreement made to stop them. . . . Forewarned is forearmed, and the common foe must not be allowed to rejoice at the outbreak of strife among Christian princes, which would smooth his road."

He appeals to God against the Pope, whose hostile attitude toward him has become a scandal the world over. The Pope has fostered the rebels against the Emperor; he causes discord and encourages crusades against the Emperor instead of turning the weapons of the Church against the tyranny of Tartars and Saracens, "who attack and occupy the Holy Land while the rebels insult Us and conspire against Our honor and Our reputation."

The triumphant spirit of the barbarians is kindled and encouraged by the wrath of Kings and wrangling between countries, and their strength grows.

Finally the Emperor cries with persuasive eloquence:

"We now implore Your Majesty most cordially in view of our common danger and in the name of Jesus Christ our Lord to guard Yourself and Your country—which may be blessed by the Lord—and immediately with care and foresight earnestly arrange for quick assistance in the form of strong knights and other armed men and weapons; we beg this of You for the sake of the blood shed by Jesus Christ our Lord and on the strength of the kinship that unites us.

And let them prepare to fight with us, manfully and wisely, to the glory of the Lord of hosts for the salvation of Christendom, so that with joint efforts we may be victorious over the enemies now preparing to cross the German boundaries, which are like the gateways of Christendom. And may it please You not to overlook these matters indifferently or set them aside through delay. For if—which God forbid—they should enter the German lands without resistance, then others must take care that the storm does not appear at their doors with the speed of lightning. And we believe that this is the judgment of the Lord, the world being disunited in itself, and the love of many has turned tepid, who should preach the truth and uphold it, and their dangerous example infects the world, breeding usury and many other kinds of simony and avarice. May Your Magnificence therefore take good care, and while our common foes rage among the neighboring peoples make wise preparations to resist them, for they had left their land, spurning death, with the intention of conquering the whole Occident—which God forbid—and of destroying and annihilating the faith and holy name of Jesus Christ our Lord. And on account of the unexpected victories which by the grace of God so far have attended their banners, they have reached such a degree of madness that they believe that all the lands of the world have come into their hands, for them to compel and to subjugate Kings and Princes and make them into their slaves. But we place our faith in Jesus Christ our Lord, under whose banner we have hitherto been victorious, that once we have been liberated from our enemies, also they, who have poured out of their hellish abode, will see their pride quelled by the united armies of the Occident, and that these Tartars will be thrust back into Tartarus. Nor will they glory any more in having marched through so many countries, conquered so many peoples, committing so many outrages with impunity, when their own blind fate, yes, Satan himself, has brought them face to face with the victori-

ous eagles of Imperial Europe to their own destruction; when
Germany cheerfully and in fury takes the sword, France, the
mother and fostress of chivalry, bold and belligerous Spain,
wealthy England, powerful with all her men and a strong
fleet ... and every proud and renowned country in the west
will gladly send her select knighthood under the banner of
the vivifical cross, which is feared not only by rebellious men
but also by the hordes of Satan."

It would seem as if the King of England should have
listened to this cry of warning. But it died away unheeded.
The political situation in Europe at that time made a common
action against the Mongols impossible. The tension between
the Pontificate and the Empire had reached its climax and
neither would yield. They were sworn enemies. Seized with
dread and terror, the peoples of Europe awaited their fate.
The Tartars are coming, the Tartars are coming! Help us, oh,
merciful God!

Without meeting any real resistance and by dint of his
excellent inherited sense of organization and the irresistible
strength of his *gurans* or horsemen, Batu Khan, the grandson
of Chinghiz Khan, advanced through eastern Europe as far
as Liegnitz.

A few years later, in 1245, Pope Innocentius IV sent the
Franciscan friar John de Plano Carpini, later Archbishop of
Antivari, to Karakorum with a letter to the Great Khan of
the Mongolian empire, Kujuk Khan, the son of Ogodai, cousin
of Batu, and grandson of Chinghiz Khan. Plano Carpini had
seen how the Mongols had flooded eastern Europe, annihilated
all prosperity and civilization in Russia, Poland, Hungary,
and other countries, burned, ravaged, murdered, and left deserted wastes in their wake. Had not the death of the Great
Khan Ogodai in 1241 compelled the wild hordes to return to
their native land in order to elect a new leader, western and
northern Europe would have met with the same fate and

would have been ravaged in the same manner as the eastern parts of the continent.

After his return home about 1248, Plano Carpini wrote down his recollections and impressions in a work that he called *Historia Mongalorum quos nos Tartaros appellamus,* a brief but comprehensive and valuable description of the life and customs of the Mongols, and a detailed account of their army, organization, war policy, and tactics. Finally he outlined the plan that should be followed in order to meet the new invasion, of whose preparation he learned at the court of the Great Khan. It would be dangerous to be deluded by their ostensible inactivity. The Khan himself had said "that they soon intended to extend their conquests in Europe farther westward, preferably toward the Baltic." Plano Carpini suggested that the European rulers "reconstruct their armies entirely, introduce lighter arms and more rigid discipline, develop the reconnoitering system, and not allow any disorder in the field, try to select suitable battlefields, and see to it that the crops in the areas threatened by the invasion are destroyed beforehand, thus preventing the Mongols from finding fodder for their horses. As their armies consisted of cavalry only, that would be a blow where they were most vulnerable."

The wise Franciscan friar stressed that individually each land and country would be lost if assaulted by the Tartars, and that only by forming an alliance could the various European countries escape total destruction.

So, when the Great Khan Kujuk requested him to head a return embassy from Mongolia to the Pope, he declined the mission because "if they see how wars and battles are daily occurrences with us, their courage to attack us will grow still greater."

Like Carpini, the Franciscan friar William of Ruysbroeck, who accompanied Louis IX on his crusade to the Holy Land and from there in 1252 made a voyage to Mönke Khan, an elder brother of Khubilai Khan, realized what a danger the Mongols were to the Occident and its peoples. In his instructive description he does not conceal his hatred of these enemies of Christendom, their arrogance, and their conviction that they surpass all other peoples in strength. They cross-examined him about everything and were well familiar with conditions in Europe, the death of Frederick II and the crusade and defeat of Louis IX. Mönke Khan did not underestimate the power of the European princes, but he was quite convinced that the testament of Chinghiz Khan would be fulfilled, and that the Mongols would conquer the whole world if they kept together in strict unity. Speaking of this, Michael Prawdin says, "Never has such an extensive plan been made to unite the whole world into one single dominion and never was it so near its completion as this time."

Thus warlike waves have rolled from east to west during past centuries, from Asia to Europe—the mighty Persian armies that threatened to flood Greece before the time of Alexander, the Hunnic hordes that plundered and ravaged their way to the other side of the Rhine, the devastating Mongolian swarms under Chinghiz Khan and Batu Khan, Timur's march on Moscow, and the Turkish siege of Vienna in 1683, when Christendom was saved by John Sobieski. When Timur defeated the Sultan Bajasid at Angora in 1402, he gave Constantinople a respite of fifty years, and was greeted by the Christians as a liberator. But in 1453 the hour of destiny struck for Constantinople, and the Christian cross on Santa Sophia was exchanged for the crescent.

The peoples now mentioned are by no means the only ones who swept our continent in times of yore as waves of armed humans. The Scythians, Alans, Vandals, Saramatians, Magyars, Bulgarians, and other tribes, also left their homes in Asia and came on predatory expeditions to Europe, the two latter having settled in this continent. Asia has been an inexhaustible source of human material and an inspiration to migrations on a large scale.

Why have the riding nomads moved westward at certain intervals? We know very little about them. They had no written language and have left no documents. Thanks only to objects that they acquired through bartering with better known, domiciled peoples, has it been possible for science to obtain some scant information about their ways and wanderings. Just as surely as the centers of the hurricanes wander from the sea of the Antilles across the northern part of the Atlantic to northwestern Europe, so do the human storms follow certain fixed courses in the opposite direction across the largest continent in the world.

With regard to the Huns, a certain reciprocity between Europe and China seems to have exercised influence upon their movements. When China was strong and well armed, the Hunnic hordes were thrown westward toward Europe, then a *locus minoris resistentiae,* but when China was enfeebled by high living and wealth she was not able to offer resistance to the voracious horsemen and was a tempting prey for pillage.

Whatever the reason for the westward wanderings of the Asiatic peoples, we nevertheless find, upon studying them in the frame of centuries, that they recur with astonishing regularity, like the locust swarms in Palestine, the microbes of cholera and bubonic plague, and the eruptions of Stromboli or Old Faithful in Yellowstone Park.

In the same manner the human waves from Asia seem to obey a natural law which has lost none of its power to this day. The only difference from former days is that the more time goes on, the greater their extent and the more perfect their armament.

Living 380 years after the days when Nostradamus wrote his prophecies and predicted the outbreak of a racial war between Asia and Europe in 1982, we need not look to the

stars for information as to the future. And if heavenly kindness has granted a man the privilege of wandering for decades
through the deserts of Asia in the tracks of the vanished
millions, it is no wonder that he listens attentively to the
sound of the ever-humming loom of time. He cannot avoid
seeing the immense drama now being enacted throughout
practically the whole of Asia. He notices how three of the
greatest and mightiest peoples of the continent are obeying
the law of olden times, and, driven by invisible forces, are
beginning to move westward, always westward.

The Japanese islands have become too small for their population. By conquests, the surplus population is seeking homes
on the mainland and is thus moving westward.

The Chinese are driven from the occupied areas to the
provinces bounding on Tibet and the deserts. Part of the
Chinese people is thus being shifted westward. Thinking
Chinese are already discussing the problem of whether it will
be possible for the oases in Kansu and Sinkiang and the desert
around the lower course of the Tarim, which through irrigation has been changed into productive land, to receive millions of colonists and settlers. This move, too, is westward.

And if we take yet another step toward the setting sun,
to the enormous border land between Asia and Europe, the
land that during the late Mongol period was governed by the
Golden Horde, we see now how the great eagle, which at
the time of Charles XII wore the crown of Czar Peter, with
its right claw grasped part of the Baltic states and Finland
outside our very doors, thus once more strengthening its
position in the Baltic, while the left claw has grasped for
Bessarabia and supremacy in the Black Sea. Between these two
footholds the eagle sits staring westward, the sunset making
his eyes glow like fires.

If Europe but stood united, its peoples need never fear any
impending dangers. Plano Carpini, who made this statement
seven hundred years ago, was right. Just as the Emperor

Frederick II tried to win England's support for the defense of Europe against a common Asiatic foe, it would also now suffice for the safety of the continent if the European nations were on the same side in a fateful racial war. But if our continent is internally torn as at present, its future looks very dark indeed. If the idea expressed more than once by British statesmen that the Empire will fight for three years, or as long as it considers necessary for complete victory, should be carried into effect, then Europe has written her own death sentence and there is no hope for her future.

Index